FICTION WRITER'S WORKSHOP

JOSIP NOVAKOVICH

STORY PRESS
CINCINNATI, OHIO

 Published by Story Press, an imprint of F&W Publications, Inc., 1507 Dana Avenue, Cincinnati, Ohio 45207. (800) 289-0963. First edition.

Other fine Story Press Books are available from your local bookstore or direct from the publisher.

99 98 97 5 4

Library of Congress Cataloging-in-Publication Data

Novakovich, Josip
Fiction writer's workshop / by Josip Novakovich.
p. cm.
Includes index.
ISBN 1-884910-03-3
1. Fiction—Authorship. 2. Fiction—Technique. 3. Fiction—Technique—Problems, exercises, etc. 4. Creative writing.
I. Title.
PN3355.n68 1995
808.3—dc20 94-48107
CIP

Designed by Clare Finney

Dedicated to Joseph and Jeanette

ACKNOWLEDGMENTS

I am especially grateful to Jack Heffron for helping me with this book. I'd also like to thank Paul Mandelbaum, Lois Rosenthal, Robin Hemley, Mikhail Iossel, Matthew Sharp, Alan Davis, Richard Duggin, John Drury, Jim Heynen, John Cussen, Barbara Selfridge, Robert Shapard, Steve Yarbrough, Manette Ansay and my teachers at the University of Texas at Austin—Jim Magnuson, Peter LaSalle, Zulfikar Ghose. And I'm grateful to my son Joseph for not crawling on my keyboard while I was writing.

CONTENTS

INTRODUCTION

To be a good writer, you must have the paradoxical trait of being a gregarious loner. Marcel Proust claimed that he needed to leave his friends so he could truly be with them; while thinking and writing about his friends, he communicated with them far more thoroughly and excitingly than when he was with them at a party.

As a writer you need a strong sense of independence, of being and thinking on your own—so go ahead, work alone. I will give you a lot of advice, but you need not take it. Especially when you disagree, you will formulate your own principles. No matter what advice I suggest in this book, which is designed to be a fiction workshop you can attend on your own, you ought to write freely. *Ought* and *free* don't seem to fit together, and that's another paradox of writing: If you can incorporate several writing principles and yet retain and even advance your independence of writing, you've got it made.

Ultimately, write any way that gives you a sense of freedom. What a teacher and a fellow workshopper might discourage as a vice might, through practice, become a virtue.

So even before you continue with this book, with its writing assignments and its advice on writing fiction, you might let yourself write absolutely anything for a couple of weeks—a hundred pages, let us say—to see if some interesting patterns emerge. That is what I did at first. I avoided advice on how to write, and I wrote several hundred pages of drafts, filled with silly puns and opinions, arbitrary plots and memories. I avoided letting anybody cramp my style. However, I think that I avoided advice and workshops a little too long; some lessons that I learned on my own, I could have learned faster from some good advice. That's why I hope that the basic principles of writing fiction outlined here, with exercises for how to implement them, will help you become a more productive fiction writer.

HOW TO USE THIS BOOK

It's simple. The chapters first give you some basics of the elements of fiction. We cover how the elements work and how you can use them in your fiction. The discussions are not meant to be definitive, but orientational.

At the end of each chapter are a dozen or more exercises, some of them calling for brief sketches, a sentence or a paragraph long, some two or three pages long. Do the exercises with an open mind. Don't dismiss them as too simple or too complicated. There are all sorts of finger exercises to keep you in shape in writing, just as there are scales in music. So get into shape, and stay there. When you get ready to write, or you are between writing projects, you certainly can benefit from exercises, no matter how advanced a writer you are. Keep the channels between the brain and the fingertips open—let your neurotransmitters happily leap in the direction of the page.

As you do the exercises, concentrate on the task. Don't strive for prettiness, unless that's the assignment. Strive for clarity. Communicate your thoughts and images as directly as possible. Now and then, for a change of rhythm, you may shroud things in long sentences and rich language, but in general, there's nothing more effective than a succinct, straightforward way of putting things. If you aren't direct, on the other hand, don't worry. You will have time to go back and cross out the imprecise words and put in better ones, until you are satisfied. In drawing, some people use a lot of lines to get at the expression on a person's face; some use few or only one. No matter what, give us a world. Don't rely on adjectives of aesthetic judgment because these are abstractions. Instead of saying "ugly" or "wonderful," give us pictures to that effect. Show us what you mean, don't tell us what you want to mean.

The principle with exercises: You get out of them as much as you put in—a little more, actually. If you like an exercise, do it several times. A painter may sketch a face a dozen times, and each time is new. The French writer Raymond Queneau wrote *Exercises in Style* as ninety-nine variations of one simple event: In a bus, a man steps on another's toe. If you don't like something, still give it a try. Don't use your dislikes as obstacles. It's only too easy to find obstacles.

After each exercise, you may ask: How do I know whether I have done it correctly? In a workshop, your peers can tell you what you've missed. If you work alone, you must do it yourself. I'll simplify it for you and ask you questions to consider. Don't read these questions until you are finished with the exercise. Keep them in mind as you read over what you've done. Revise or rewrite your exercise until you get it right. There's a point at which you know that you've done your best, given the limited time you have.

So go back over what you've completed, not so much for what you've done wrong as for what you could do right, more right. Don't work on developing a self-critical—that is, self-inhibiting—consciousness; do work on developing a sense of where you can jump back in and draw one more line that'll give life to what you already have down or where you could delete a line that may obscure our view of a good line you've drawn.

How much time should you spend on each exercise? I'd say twenty to thirty minutes should be enough. If something stimulates you, of course, keep going, up to an hour. Beyond that, if an exercise has struck a strong chord in you, I'd say you are no longer doing an exercise but writing a story. Great. That'll be the fringe benefit to doing the exercises: You will examine many things, turn many stones and find your treasures. Still, discipline yourself to go back to the exercises and finish them outside of your story writing time.

If you spend five to six hours on exercises in each chapter, you could be through with this book in two months. It would be ideal to spend an hour a day, regularly, so that by the time you finish this book, you will have acquired the writing habit. This habit is the rare kind that is beneficial. It helps you sort out your impressions, memories, thoughts, fantasies, and that should be healthy. Something in the movement of fingers on the keyboard enhances thought. I may not be particularly thoughtful as I write, but much more than if I were simply staring out the window. Some philosophers walked to think more clearly; they belonged to the peripatetic school. Walking provided them with a good flow of blood and oxygen, and with a sensation of doing, moving, going. Fingers pull your thoughts forward. Fingers are in some ways an extension of your brain, with a lot of cortex associations at their trigger. Get them going!

You don't need to wait for inspiration to write. It's easier to be inspired while writing than while not writing, so you don't need to be inspired to sit down and begin. You don't need to be "in the mood." I think you will benefit if you don't worry about moods: One, you will get in the habit of writing under any circumstances; two, since writing reflects your mental state, you will have a diversity of moods in your piece. The diversity will make your writing more interesting. You are depressed? Fine, perhaps you can portray a depressed character. Elated? Don't waste the mood on celebration. Convey it onto the page. Many pieces suffer from moodlessness; perhaps the writers are willing to work only when they are calm.

Ultimately, talk about talent, inspiration, genius, is a distraction. Sit down and do it! Whenever you lack an idea, use some of the exercises in this book—they should keep you busy.

If you think that the business of fiction is an impossible one, John Gardner ought to encourage you. In *The Art of Fiction*, he says: "Most people I've known who wanted to become writers, knowing what it meant, did become writers. About all that is required is that the would-be writer understand clearly what it is that he wants to become and what he must do to become it." In *On Becoming a Novelist*, he claims that there are more failed businesspeople than failed artists. Yet in business schools, optimism prevails.

CHAPTER ONE

SOURCES OF FICTION

Many writers say that you can find a story anywhere. The greatest source of fiction is experience. The experience need not be yours—you may observe someone else's struggle and use it for your fiction. For example, Nikolai Gogol wrote his famous story, "Overcoat," from an anecdote he heard at a dinner party. A poor man had been saving up for years to buy a hunting rifle, and before he could go hunting, somebody stole it. Gogol, a better humorist than anyone else at the party, was the only one who did not laugh at this. He felt chilled and sorry for the man, went home and wrote a story from that sorrow about a clerk who saves for a long time to buy an overcoat. When he buys the overcoat, it gets stolen, and the man suffers, while everybody laughs and jeers at him.

Gogol transformed the original fact into fiction. Instead of a rifle, he uses a coat. Instead of hunting, he deals with office work. He had worked as a clerk, so he could bring realistic details to his story. The jeering and ridicule in the story may have been taken from the party attendees who laughed at the rifle man. Fiction writers can use their experiences, and the experiences of others, in their work. When transformed by the writer's imagination, even true details, like the ones that Gogol imported from his experience of clerkship, become fiction.

You do not need much for an impetus, the seed of a story. In his essay, "The Art of Fiction," Henry James described how an English woman wrote a novel about French Protestants. In Paris, as she ascended a staircase, she "passed an open door where, in the household of a *pasteur,* some of the young Protestants were seated at table round a finished meal. The glimpse made a picture; it lasted only a moment, but that moment was experience."

French novelist Claude Simon claimed that to collect materials for a novel, it's enough to take a walk around a city block. Come back, report what you saw, thought, felt, remembered and so on, and that should do! Okay, he may be exaggerating, but his point is clear: Your experience need not be grand to be useful as fiction material.

Simon's point affirms the principle: Write about what you know. On the other hand, some writers advise: Write about what you don't know because you will be free to imagine; knowledge will constrict you. James' method of writing from a glimpse—so that you don't know much about the people in particular but do know about their world (James' novelist knew a lot about French Protestantism)—should give you a perfect compromise: enough knowledge but also enough ignorance and darkness to guess and imagine.

Whether to write from knowledge or from a lack of it is not an either/or decision. I can't write about something that I don't know at all; and I can't write about something that I know absolutely, for what do I know? Socrates thought that the only thing he possibly knew was that he did not know anything. Last week while leaving for school, I remembered that I had left my car keys on the counter, but they weren't there. Yet I spent an hour looking for them; I found them on the window sill in another room. My memory was not knowledge; it was, in fact, *fiction.* Even if you write from memory, you will have enough elements of what you don't know, or aren't sure about, to avoid the constricting influence of knowledge.

I must say, however, that I have seen many people blindly follow an outline of an event in a story (they say, "But that's what happened!") even when some simple, made-up adjustment might lead to a better, more rounded story.

Your inclination may be not to work from a glimpse but from a chunk of your life, autobiographically, like Marcel Proust and Harold Brodkey, who have relied on direct experience for everything—plot, details, characters. Or your inclinations, like mine, may vary from story to story.

FICTION AND NONFICTION

How much one needs to know about what one writes varies from writer to writer and from story to story. As you write, let that be a constant assignment: Find out how much you need to know about the raw material from which you make a story. If you find out that you persevere in reconstructing events from memory as faithfully as possible, without following impulses to make up anything, or even to exaggerate and beautify or uglify details, you are a natural nonfiction writer. You might still call what you write fiction, if you like, though the term will then be the only fiction in your writing. If you can with a straight face tell people that what you write is fiction, you will often find yourself in a precarious position to explain how you made something up. I would then advise you to acknowledge that you write nonfiction, and to enjoy the apple of that tree of knowledge. There's no reason to consider fiction more glorious than nonfiction.

The reverse also can occur. You might want to become a nonfiction writer, and yet at every turn you distort things, exaggerate and embellish them, and even introduce characters, places and events that had nothing to do with the original material. In that case, you are a born fiction writer, which is much nicer than saying you are a born liar. Fiction is a lot like lying. You start from something real, but for some specific purpose (not to get caught, to trick, to get money or whatever) you change at least one key element of the account. Instead of admitting that you got a black eye in a bar when you were hitting on someone's girlfriend, you might say that you skied in Vermont and bumped into a sleeping bear's nuzzle in a curve. To defend your pride, you lie and tell a story. If you habitually lie, why not get the sinful impulse out of your system through writing fiction?

How you treat your original material determines the type of writer you are. It may still be too early to classify yourself. As you do the exercises throughout the book and afterward, pay close attention to what you are doing, and you will eventually decide what you are writing: fiction or nonfiction.

On the other hand, you may do both, as do many writers, including me. Sometimes an event, or an impression, intrigues me. I don't make a decision about what I'll do with it right away. I jot down notes, write a bit here and a bit there, and I see if I get an impulse to reshape the material, rearrange, make up. If I do, I know I am writing a piece of fiction, and I encourage myself to change things even further. However, if I find that I don't transform anything, that I think about the event and write down my thoughts, I know I am writing an essay. I like essays just as much as I like stories, so I don't feel disappointed. I am happy in either case that I have something to say (essay) or something to play with (fiction).

BLENDING FACT AND FICTION

There's always a mixture of fact and invention in writing fiction. (Are *fact* and *fict*(ion) so similar by accident? If these words were written in the old Hebrew style, which was written without vowels, they would both be *FCT*, and it would depend on the context how you would pronounce it!)

Here's what several writers say about how they mix two kinds of FCT. My purpose in showing you this is twofold: to demonstrate that most fiction incorporates a lot of fact, and to give you models for making your own fiction.

Tobias Wolff says this about the source of his short story "Firefly": "What impelled me to write it in the first place is its emotional core—that sense, hardly unique to me, of being outside the circle of light, a feeling so pernicious that even when you are where you want to be you shy away from the joy of it and begin to fear banishment and loss."

Wolff uses his emotional experience as the core for a story that is fictional in other respects—a good way to blend fact and invention.

Joanna Scott offers this comment about her story "Concerning Mold Upon the Skin, Etc.": "I intended to refer, plainly or indirectly, to the history of medicine in each of my stories. So I went looking for fifteenth- and sixteenth-century scientists in such quirky and unreliable books as Howard Haggard's *Devils, Drugs, and Doctors*. . . . Leeuwenhoek's fierce secrecy caught my attention. . . . About the character of the daughter: as a fiction writer, I'm interested in the vast silences of history, and like many women, Marie floats silently in the background of her father's biography. So she became the center of the narrative, the presence that enabled me to reshape history into fiction."

Scott combines information from history books with her thematic interest, silent experiences of women, to imagine how Marie lives. History books and biographies are major sources of fiction. Once you get something intriguing from a history book, why not play with it and see where it leads you? The history need not be tremendously old—it could be close to current affairs.

Pulitzer prize-winning author Robert Olen Butler says this about writing his story, "A Scent From the Mountain": "I finally began to hear the voice of this tale when I found an occasion—the traditional, formal leave-taking with their friends and family that the Vietnamese often make at the end of their lives—and when I found a first sentence, spoken in the voice of a man nearly one hundred years old, 'Ho Chi Minh came to me again last night, his hands covered with confectioners' sugar.' After that, it was simply a matter of letting the old man speak."

Pay attention to how Butler relies on hearing a character's voice to carry him through writing. This ability to tune into a person's voice and to adopt it for writing fiction works for many writers.

Robin Hemley (author of *The Last Studebaker* and *All You Can Eat*) says he works from dreams. One impression from a dream is enough to inspire a story. For example, he awoke with an image of a man digging a hole in his ex-wife's yard. He wondered why one would do something so bizarre, and in trying to answer the question he wrote a story about a man and a woman whose baby dies, who divorce, and now the man, haunted by guilt and love, digs in the yard. When I asked Hemley over the phone what other sources of fiction he used, and while he tried to describe something complex, his wife shouted, "He gets his best stories from me!" So, pay attention to dreams and spouses.

Mark Richard, author of *Fishboy*, explained that he got a whole story out of this first sentence, "At night, stray dogs come up underneath our house to lick our leaking pipes." He said, "I knew everything I needed was in that sentence. . . . So I sat down one night after staring in the sand all day thinking: At night, etc., etc. And it all came down at once like I was just the radio. . . ."

Many writers claim that all they need is a good sentence with tension in it, and the story simply unfolds from that. I can't say that I am that lucky. Here's how I arrived at the starting points for some of my stories. Perhaps this could work similarly for you, and if not, you'll at least see where I come from when I talk about fiction.

One. My brother-in-law and his father competed in building huge homes, working so hard that they both developed heart problems. At first I thought I would write a story about their competition, which could have made an interesting essay, but as I looked at their big granite homes, the thought that they were building their tombs crossed my mind. Out of this metaphor, I wrote a story about a man building a sophisticated tomb. For the character I drew upon quite a few Croatian *Gastarbeiter* ("guest workers") in Germany, and came up with a composite character. Because of all kinds of superstitions in Croat villages, it was easy for me to believe in the plausibility of such a story. It's mostly made up, but obviously, some of it is not.

I built this story from a metaphor. Rather than sprinkle the prose with metaphors, try to make your whole story a metaphor—and a prolonged metaphor, of course, makes an allegory.

Two. While living in New York City I could not afford a computer, so I got a job where I would be able to do my writing after hours—word processing for Smith Barney investment bank. I worked on the fiftieth floor, and every day I mused on the sensation of suddenly feeling much heavier as the express elevator decelerated on the way down. Once I saw a woman in advanced pregnancy wince during the deceleration, and later I wrote about a woman jumping out of an airplane and giving birth to a boy when the parachute opens. The impulse for the story came from a strong sensation.

Three. A friend once called to tell me he was in love with his psychiatrist and she forbade him to visit her. He joined a Buddhist group but could not stop thinking about her. I made up a character who desperately seeks to seduce his psychiatrist—and I pursued the conflict further, to his getting arrested and thrown into jail, and then explaining to his wife what happened. You can get ideas for stories from talking to people, especially once you hear of a clear conflict. If you pursue the conflict to its logical conclusion in your fiction, you are bound to have a developed story.

Four. A friend told me how he could not forgive his father for being a German soldier, a volunteer, during World War II, so that he refused to talk to him even when he was dying. My friend's being so adamantly principled struck me as no better than his father's participating in the siege of Stalingrad to defend Lutheranism from communism. So I wrote a story about him and his father. As I knew nothing else of the dynamic between the two, or of post-war Germany, I made up most of the details, so it ended as a piece of fiction, though it began as a narrative essay.

I got the seed of this story in a conversation with a friend. What made that seed grow into fiction was my curiosity and my lack of knowledge about the two people involved. Whenever something intrigues you about the people you know, you may be better off using your fascination as the energy for a new story rather than for daydreaming and gossip. Many stories benefit from both impulses—to daydream and gossip.

THE ORAL TRADITION

When groping through my memory, imagination and books for something that would trigger a story, I hoped I could rely on the oral tradition, a big deal among the people of my native region. I was in fact so desperate to find material for stories that I used even that feeling as the material for a story. You will see what happens in my quest for fiction in these condensed excerpts from my story "The Burning Shoe":

Nenad told me about Prince Marko, who sucked his mother's breasts for seven years, and for seven more ate nothing but honey. Marko could squeeze water out of a log dried for nine years. His horse could jump the length of nine lances and the height of three. Marko slew Musa Kesejiya, in whose breast, beneath three rib cages, were three hearts—the first working, the second dancing, and the third nesting a sleeping snake. When the snake awoke, the dead Musa leaped over the barren land.

So twenty years later, remembering Nenad's telling me this, I thought that instead of going through a writing workshop in the States, I would simply listen to Nenad for a couple of days and nights and find the formula for triggering a wellspring of storytelling from our common ground. I rushed to Weeping Willow, the village in Croatia where he now lived. Where once horses ploughed the fields along a dirt road, tractors oozed green oil in puddles along a paved highway. A cracked wooden shoe hung from a pole on Nenad's house to advertise his trade, clog-making.

After we shook hands and he found out what I was doing these days, sure enough, he talked so much that I couldn't squeeze in a word, except I did interrupt him: "Nenad, where did you learn how to tell tales? At the hearth, on your grandfather's knee?"

"I went to the library," he said, "read them, and told them to you right after it, while the stories were still fresh in my memory."

A myth fell apart right before my ears.

"Of course," he said, "I added a thing here and there."

"But I believed that you were an epic storyteller!"

"After every story you said, 'More!' So what could I do? I went to the library on lunch breaks."

"Still, who taught you how to tell stories? Grandmothers?"

"No. Why are you so stuck on this? It's easy to tell a story, what's the big deal? You start right here and lead the listener far away, or start far away and get us here."

"Easy to say. Do it!"

"So you are holding this beer mug. All right, start with it. A long time ago there was a beer mug, and it lived in a tavern, in an unhappy family of twenty-three beer mugs. Many a dry lip . . . and off we go, see!"

"But how would you go on?"

In reply he laughed and tapped me on the shoulder so I did not know whether he could go on, or whether he was teasing me, or whether my stubborn simplicity amused him. "You want a refill?" he said.

I still insisted that he tell me a story, and I would not let him give me a ride home until he did so, just as—though it's not worthy of such an archaic comparison—Jacob held fast to the Angel of God until obtaining a blessing.

"All right, I'll tell you something like a story as we drive." He motioned me toward his Fiat clone, a Yugo, and as we opened the car doors, he said, "See that tall house? That's where my childhood home, made of baked clay, used to be. At the beginning of the war, the Germans barged in there, seized my father from the dinner table and shot him to death against the barn.

"A couple of years later a dozen Germans walked into our yard. I hid in bed and shivered under a goose-down cover. A pair of boots stamped over the floor boards toward me, louder and louder. The cover was pulled off and a huge soldier loomed over me. An *Agkh* broke out of my throat. The German lowered his hand, I thought, to strangle me. He placed his cold palm on my forehead. Then he poured a glass of water from a bucket in the kitchen, put some white pills into the water, crushed them with a spoon, and pressed my lips with the edge of the glass against my teeth. The liquid was shudderingly bitter. I thought I would keel over and die. It was no poison, but aspirin.

"And he took a paper sack out of his leather bag and out of it a honey cake. He gave it to me. He looked sternly at my mouth as I chewed. When I finished, he handed

> me another, and I chewed slowly. After I swallowed the last of it, my eyes shifted toward the paper sack.
>
> "The German raised his forefinger and shook it and said, *Nein*! He then walked out into the yard, shouted to the soldiers, and they all marched away, raising a screen of dust. Eh, my brother, you can't imagine how I felt. First he—for me it was the same German—kills my father and then gives me the sweetest cakes I've ever had—before or after."

The story goes on. Another day I visit the storyteller, he refuses to tell me stories because he's had nightmares triggered by the honey cakes and my visit. But here's another moment when he does tell a story:

> Nenad's tabby jumped, grabbed the rim of his cap, and tried to pull it out of his hands. Nenad scratched the cat on the head and said, "My dear kitty."
>
> He patted her more tenderly than I had ever seen a man his age do, and he relaxed and talked: "One night the Germans entered the village and were about to round up thirty people to kill because the partisans had killed three German soldiers. But the Germans now first axed some chickens to cook quietly on an apple orchard hill where nobody from the rest of the village could see them. There were some black cats there, and no black cats ever came to our end of the village. So when I saw a black cat running down the road with a bloody rooster's head in its mouth, I screamed, "The Germans are coming!"
>
> "We ran into the woods and listened to the shotguns. The Germans killed ten, but most of the people in the village were saved—by the black cat!" He picked up his tabby, which looked like a camouflaged paratrooper.

The story goes on, but the main point here for me is that what I thought was the oral tradition turned out to be bookish stuff, a dead end. However, in the story just as I give up, the man tells me a story from his own experience. The storyteller told his story with almost traditional oral-style repetition, in a Croatian dialect, but I rewrote the story from memory, in a different rhythm, without much repetition. My retelling this makes it a tradition, that is, a transmission of stories from one generation to another, from the World War II generation to mine, the current Balkan wars generation. The transmission is both oral and scriptoral.

Is "The Burning Shoe" fiction or nonfiction about fiction? It is both. Most materials I got directly from my experience and my conversation with a man I knew from my childhood. The cat tale and several others within the story, which I can't reproduce here for the lack of space, I got elsewhere, but put them all into the mouth of the storyteller. Some details and jokes I made up, but most of the material comes from my eyes and ears.

Still, the report works as a piece of fiction. The editors who published the story never asked me, "Is this true?" What concerned them was whether the piece worked as fiction. The honey cake story follows a classical bell curve (rising action-climax-resolution) of a piece of fiction, so even if it comes from the storyteller's experience (and I can't verify that) without my changing it much, that story does have the shape of fiction. So does the frame story, my quest for the oral tradition. The setting and my motives are established in the beginning—I want stories to learn how to write. The first lead turns out false—first turning point. The second lead (story about the beer mug) also turns out to be a pipe dream—second turning point. My desire to hear a story yields one just as I am giving up, on the way out. That's climax, getting the real thing, the cake story. The story continues, with a falling action, more anecdotes (the cat story), and this resolution, in the form of an epiphany:

> As I walked to the train station, the leaves in the woods—the tongues of the wind—murmured. The stones on the shoulder of the road crunched beneath my feet and told me how Jesus was tempted in the desert to make bread out of stones and instead how he later made wine out of the water. The stones retold me how the vicious armies and the good people had passed. And I thought, If the stones can tell the stories, I can too.

I was not thinking this as I left the storyteller for the second time, so the resolution is fictional. I made up most of the dialogue and the descriptions, such as the blue Bosnian mountains appearing as workers' shirts on the line. I changed all the names.

But the story is mostly autobiographical. Notice that in analyzing the story I freely use *I* for *I*. I don't say, "the first-person narrator," which I would use if this were a piece of nonautobiographical fiction cast in a first-person point of view. (More on the persona business in chapter five.)

My quest for the oral tradition disabused me of mythical notions of some kind of *Odyssey* coming down to me through a peasant. I had bad luck in my quest: An old man, whom my brother, a doctor, had met on his rounds in a Slavonian village, died just several days before my coming to talk to him, and an old woman who also could tell great stories was ill when I visited her. There were several other peasants I could get in touch with, but now these peasants, some of whom are Serbs and some Croats, for years won't say a word and won't trust anybody because of the recent war. So that avenue is closed to me.

But not other things that people talk about. It's healthy to listen to how people talk and what they say, because some of the best storytellers are not writers. Communication with the audience to them is the most important experience in telling a story, and because of that, they talk rather than write. Those of us who prefer to write and are somewhat awkward speakers should certainly emulate the liveliness of an original communicator, on the page, if possible. Perhaps you can hound some of these good talkers.

I believe my experience in researching and writing "The Burning Shoe" could be useful to you. You may look for your special source—where you spent your childhood, where you heard old railway workers talk—Appalachia, Harlem, wherever. By all means, do that. You may be more successful in your search of a direct source than I have been. But while you are looking for one thing, be open to recognizing another that might be just as good or even better. Looking for old folk tales, I recognized a new tale. I wish I followed this paradigm more often myself, but I'll be happy if you do.

FURTHER SOURCES OF FICTION

You can get stories from almost anywhere. William Faulkner described this quest for materials: "An artist is completely amoral in that he will rob, borrow, beg, or steal from anybody and everybody to get the work done."

Rob the Cradle

Draw on your childhood mercilessly. Leo Tolstoy was only twenty-two when he wrote the trilogy that made him a writer, *Childhood, Boyhood, Youth.* Charles Dickens based several of his long novels on his childhood.

Willa Cather wrote, "Most of the basic material a writer works with is acquired before the age of fifteen." Recently I talked to Deborah Joy Corey (author of the novel *Losing Eddie*), who told me that she was writing her third book, still about her childhood. She was almost embarrassed about not outgrowing it, but I think she's lucky. Of course, drawing on your childhood doesn't mean that you write straight memoir; transform the material, use it to build other characters, write in the third person, if necessary, or in the first, if you like. Write the way Mark Twain wrote *Huckleberry Finn,* using his childhood experiences but creating a persona certainly different from himself, with a different voice. Or write autobiographical fiction. But don't neglect this primary source of fiction.

Rob the Grave

Look into the lives of your ancestors and tell their stories. Maxine Hong Kingston (author of *The Woman Warrior*) has successfully done this in her autobiographical fiction. Knowing little about how her ancestors lived in China and the States, she filled the gaps in her knowledge through flights of imagination and through the power of the word. She described believably and poetically the agonies of her great-grandfather in building the railways. You can invoke and summon the ghosts of your ancestors, for they live on, somewhere in you. Throw words at them, your memories of them, as bait, and they might come out. At least a version of them will appear: yours. They will not be the same great-grandfathers as in "real life," for you don't know that much about their real lives—of necessity, they will come out as fictions, apparitions, illusions.

Rob From Books

Learn from the works of other writers. I don't mean that you should plagiarize, but you can write variations on themes. It's easy to imagine that there is something derivative and secondary in this method, something offensive to the concept of originality. But even the very idea of a story is something we take on as a tradition. It's just as silly to claim to be a nontraditional story writer as it is to claim that you are independent if you still live in your mother's house. So, working in a tradition is a form of gratitude to your literary ancestry. And a form of inheritance. If you stand to inherit a fortune, you may be foolish to renounce your parents and grandparents. Look at some historical precedents. Homer composed *The Odyssey* and *The Iliad* out of battle reports; Virgil patterned *The Aeneid* on Homer's work and, in a way, continued it; Dante wrote *The Inferno,* based on Odysseus' trip to the underworld and on incidents from *The Aeneid;* and hundreds of works take from Dante. And James Joyce, in *Ulysses,* went back to *The Odyssey,* making the trip home a psychological experience of trying to understand how the mind works with words.

Here's another literary lineage. In *Notes From Underground,* Fyodor Dostoyevski writes, "Only if I could become an insect!" Franz Kafka takes this line and makes "The Metamorphosis" out of it: "As Gregor Samsa awoke that morning from uneasy dreams, he found himself transformed in his bed into a gigantic insect."

In reaction to Kafka's opening line, Gabriel Garcia Márquez says: "When I read the line I thought to myself that I didn't know anyone was allowed to write things like that. If I had known, I would have started writing a long time ago." Márquez wrote his story "A Very Old Man With Enormous Wings," strewing the angel's wings with parasites and insects.

Once, while trying to finish a biblical story, I wrote a tale. I wanted to write a variation of Jacob's exile. It intrigued me that while in love with Rachel, he mistook Leah for her at the wedding. For a while I kept too close to the original. Then I reversed the genders: A woman cannot tell the difference between two brothers; a man usurps his brother's place in her bed. It struck me that nowadays—in our merciless age of electricity and information—this sounded highly unrealistic, so as a challenge I set the story in modern day Salt Lake City.

Whenever you don't get your impetus to write a story from real life, look into books, for this is your medium. When something startles you in your reading, take off from there. Either try a variation on a theme, or venture ahead into something new.

EXERCISES

1. One page. According to Henry James, a writer wrote a novel from a glimpse of a seminary students' dinner party. Write a scene of a story from a glimpse you have had of a group of people—in a café, zoo, train or anywhere. Sketch the characters in their setting and let them interact. Do you find that you know too little? Can you make up enough—or import from other experiences—to fill the empty canvas?

Objective: To find out if you can make much out of little. If you can, great. If you can't now, don't worry, you might later, or you'll have to get your stories from other materials.

Check: Can you visualize these people further? Can you begin to hear at least one person speak? If not, go back and find a way of talking that might fit one of the people in the group, and carry on from there.

2. Three paragraphs. When you go out to a restaurant or a bar, jot down your observations in a notebook. In one paragraph, describe a loner's looks and behavior. In another, a couple's looks and interaction. In the third paragraph, describe how a waiter or a bartender communicates with the customers. Some

of these observations will come in handy, sometimes to augment a scene, if not to make an entire story. (You could do a similar exercise, jotting down your observations of people in a grocery story or at a street corner.)

Objective: To gear up your observations of the world around you toward writing.

Check: Have you found something intriguing that raises questions that beg to be answered? For example, I once saw outside the Ritz Hotel in New York a woman in a fancy fur coat digging with her bare hands through a trash can for soda cans. What the hell was she doing? Was she poor but just looked rich? Was she rich and in the habit of hoarding so much that she could not let a five-cent can rest in peace? Did she throw an incriminating love letter into the garbage and then only pretend that she was doing something else in case she was followed by a private detective? See, a story easily begins to suggest itself and to offer several directions of development from one intriguing glimpse. True, I don't see something that intrigues me like this every day, but a couple of times every month is enough to write a new story every month. The main goal is to find something to wonder about, and that wonder should generate the story.

3. Two to three pages. Write down your first three memories. Can you make a story out of any of them? Try. Even if you aren't sure what you remember exactly, keep going. Imagine that you remember more than you do. Expand and rewrite in the third person and forget it's you. This could be precious material for you. Renowned psychiatrist Alfred Adler thought that first memories reveal the psychological leitmotif of your life.

Objective: To begin to write stories that deeply matter to you.

Check: Have you been playful about this? Kids play, and even when they don't, they have a certain charming way of thinking. Have you hooked your imagination into childhood logic? If your drafts sound grave and heavily psychological, go back and lighten them up by inserting funny insights.

4. Two to three pages. Write down the first dreams you remember. Don't mention that they are dreams.

Objective: Similar to Exercise 3. Remember that in dreams you can't be held accountable for making everything plausible. Strange things happen, and not everything is explained. Don't punctuate, just drift words and images together into a dreamlike stream of consciousness. You can't remember all the details of your early dreams—maybe you can?—but don't let that deter you from writing at least two pages. If you manage to get into a primitive dreamlike state of mind, you'll create strange connections and images. This approach could be productive for helping you develop unique moments in stories.

Check: Read what you've written. Do you have something bizarre? If not, distort things. For example, bring in wolves to create an expressionistic painting, because that's what dreams do. They express your hidden fears. And fears should mobilize you into a fight-or-flight alertness; use that energy for flights of fancy.

5. Recall a physical or verbal fight, and construct it as one scene.

Objective: To see that some kinds of stories come pretty easily, as this one will. When I use it in class, my students' pens keep moving even after the class is over. Struggle, war, quarrel, or any kind of conflict is an energetic source of stories.

Check: Is the writing dynamic? Are the words appropriately quick and strong? Cross out excess adjectives and adverbs and long Latinate words; use short ones.

6. Two to three pages. Think about an incident that you avoid remembering—or can't clearly remember—and write about it. Write about a moment of terror you experienced, or about a defeat that hurts your pride. You can choose a terrible incident that, though crucial to you, you could not witness. For example, when my father was dying, I came to his bedside late, when he was probably unconscious, bloody foam on his lips. My brother witnessed all the stages of my father's death and heard his last words, yet it was I who wrote a story of the death—probably because I missed it. For years I could not write about it, but when the event was sufficiently removed from me, it easily became a

story, with hundreds of made-up details.

Objective: To help you deal with what matters. Even if you are afraid to think about something—or *especially* if you are—muster the courage to plunge right into the middle of your frightful memory. You will come up with something that matters to you, and if you evoke it clearly, it should matter to the reader, too.

Check: Don't. Keep going for a long while before you look back. This should be an uncensored outpouring. Save it, and revise months later.

7. (From writer-teacher Jim Magnuson) Two to three pages. Write "My mother never . . ." at the top of a page, then complete the sentence and keep going. Read what you've written only after you are finished with the draft.

As you write, begin to fictionalize. Construct scenes. Take out sentimentality (statements like "My mother is my truest friend"), and forget it's your mother. Take yourself out, too.

Objective: To probe your background beyond the usual limits. No harm—it'll be fiction. If you think of what your mother does, you may not write fiction; but if you write what she doesn't do (what your mother never did) and imagine her doing it, you create an interesting match of character and action.

Check: You should find something surprising and outrageous in what you've written. If you don't, perhaps you did not loosen up enough. Try again, with a variant: "My father never. . . ."

8. Read Bible stories. Can you make variations? Can you finish the story of Cain? The story of Jacob and Esau? Joseph and Potiphar's wife? In Midrashim—that is, the Hebrew tradition of interpreting biblical stories through filling in the gaps—one basically expands a given story. Can you do that?

Objective: To learn how to play with variations on a theme. Don't ever say, "It's been done." If it's worth doing once, it's worth doing twice.

Check: Did you run out of the story too quickly? Make people talk, eat, wash, and do a whole series of ordinary things, until they become real people to you. Linger on details. You needn't stick to the original. If the story sounds too stiff and formal, like an old translation, go back and rewrite it in simple and dynamic language. If the ancient times don't do anything for you, nor you for them, transfer the action to present-day America.

9. One to two pages. Do some historical events intrigue you? Do you keep wondering how things really happened, outside of the glory of patriotic propaganda? Can you find a figure that was only mentioned, like Marie in Joanna Scott's example on pages 8-9? Now, describe the historical event as seen by that briefly mentioned person, and make the person play an important role.

Objective: To use history to create fiction. After all, the history we get is reconstructed from letters, hearsay, newspapers, archaeology and so on—sounds like writing fiction from multiple sources!

Check: Same as in Exercise 8.

10. Two pages. Take one intense emotion you've experienced—envy, fear, greed, lust—and give it to a fictional character. Make sure the character is not you, but the emotion should be yours. Create a scene employing the fictional character and the emotion. Involve another person as an antagonist or a co-protagonist.

Objective: To get a good start—and a core—for a story.

Check: Review what you've done after you've written a couple of pages. Is the character radically different from you? Her way of talking should be different from yours, as should her way of walking, drinking and so on. But the basic emotional conflict should be yours.

11. Two to three pages. Imagine some event that could have happened to you but did not—something that you wanted or feared. First, make up the basic outline of the event, and then incorporate true details. Put your teapot and cats into the story; they won't sue you. Your knowledge of these details will help you convince your reader of the truthfulness of the story's main event. Don't spend much time on introducing this event or on drawing conclusions. Just give us the scene with your desire (or

fear) acted out. Keep yourself as the main protagonist.

Objective: Desire and fear are the most productive dynamos of fiction and imagination. Around the desire (or fear) you can easily integrate the character, conflict, setting—all the basic elements of fiction easily fall into place once you have a character with a strong motive.

Check: Have you given us a clear enough picture, so we, as readers, can identify with the desire? Or have you given us a terrifying enough picture so we understand your character's fear? If not, go back and add convincing details—show us the threat, the needle, the gun, the blind alley.

12. Two to three pages. As soon as you wake up tomorrow morning, jot down what you remember from your dream. Keep a dream journal for three or four days. Then choose the one dream that puzzles you most and write a brief story—or a story sketch—out of it. Ask: How could a thing like that happen? And then make it happen, no matter how unrealistic and absurd. Use a deadpan approach. Don't worry about being caught saying something unbelievable. Make it believable by introducing real details, as in Exercise 11.

Objective: To get your stories from wherever you can. Why not get them from your freshly revealed subconsciousness?

Check: Are the dream's images and events beginning to make sense? Some connections, no matter how wild, should take place. If not, analyze the words to see which images recur and connect to others. Try to bring logic to the connections, some kind of cause and effect, or conflict, or desire that needs to be realized but is obstructed.

CHAPTER TWO

SETTING

When and where does your story take place? Give us that place. Setting means a certain place at a certain time, a stage. You might even start your fiction by showing us the stage briefly. For example, Grand Central Station during the morning rush hour on the first day of winter in 1988. You might give us the details of the train station (the flipping of destination letters on the blackboard, slushy water on the tiles, crackling loudspeakers with Long Island nasality) and the people (the jacketed commuter crowd, a gaunt police officer with a startled dog). What startled the dog? We are ready to visualize the action now that we have the stage and something to look for on it.

PLACE FOR A PLACE

Do you need real places for your fiction? The strongest novels I can think of—*War and Peace*, *David Copperfield* and others—are set in real cities or during real wars. Setting has these days fallen out of fashion at the expense of character and action. Perhaps this trend has to do with our not being a society of walkers. Big writers used to be big walkers. Almost every day, Honoré de Balzac spent hours strolling the streets of Paris; Charles Dickens, the streets of London; Fyodor Dostoyevski, the streets of St. Petersburg. Their cities speak out from them.

There is a common argument against detailed descriptions of setting: They can be outright dull. In their eagerness for excitement, readers often skip the passages that deal with establishing the setting. I certainly do—it took me years to return to Thomas Hardy's *The Return of the Native* because the first ten pages of the novel are spent mostly in describing landscape, and no matter how fine the descriptions, I suspect that even the English readers of the leisure class skipped those pages.

Many writers avoid laying out the setting because they fear boring their readers, but the lack of a vivid setting may in turn cause boredom. Without a strong sense of place, it's hard to achieve suspense and excitement—which depend on the reader's sensation of being right there, where the action takes place. When descriptions of places drag, the problem usually lies not in the setting, but in presenting the setting too slowly. Make your descriptions dynamic and quick; give bits of setting concurrently with characters and action. Take cues from drama: It would be a peculiar play in which all the props were displayed for half an hour before the actors walked on stage. Stage managers give you only the pieces necessary for a scene with actors already present. So as you write, though you may have sketched out all the jails, creeks, and mules, don't show them all first, before the characters. And when you show the setting, be selective, giving only a few details that'll evoke a place. If the chosen details are vivid, the reader will piece together the whole picture from her imagination. Leave her that pleasure.

I've mentioned vividness (a result of using setting correctly) as a necessity for excitement. Fiction, in many ways, is similar to painting. Henry James certainly thought so. In "The Art of Fiction," he wrote: "The analogy between the art of the painter and the art of the novelist is, so far as I am able to see, complete. Their inspiration is the same, their process (allowing for the different quality of the vehicle) is the same, their success is the same. They may learn from each other, they may explain and sustain each other." Medieval paintings had no landscape for background, and the characters they portrayed expressed little emotion—no laughter. By the end of the Middle Ages, exuberant life appeared in the foreground and landscapes and cityscapes in the background. Coincidence? I don't think so. So, give your characters—children of your imagination—a lot of rich ground to move on, to play out their drama. A child with sand on a beach has a chance to be more active and creative than a child without sand.

These days, many writers—certainly not all—withdraw their gazes from city architecture and country life, and as they do, their fictional worlds diminish. The exterior and the interior go together. A destitute vision of what's around us can't result in a wealth of inner substance. Writing that deals only with ego—*Did my father abuse me?*—to my mind attains the humorless bleakness of a medieval painting, in which only the questions of sin (abuse) and pardon (recovery) matter. A character, let's say a sculptor, is interesting by virtue of what he does to the stones around him. If we never see the sculptor tackle the stones and other materials, his being a sculptor is merely an abstract trait. Whatever happens psychologically can be expressed in the environment: Mark Twain's humor in *Huckleberry Finn* would not work without the Mississippi setting.

Of the journalist's six questions—*who, what, when, where, how* and *why* (a good piece of fiction strives to substantiate as much as a good piece of journalism does)—setting answers two—*where* and *when*—and therefore is extremely important.

Real or Imagined Setting

Before beginning to write a piece of fiction, decide whether you want to use a real place for your setting or an imagined one. The advantage of anchoring your writing in a real place—entirely or partially—is that you will be rooted, you will draw new inspiration (and some old ghosts) out of the houses and streets. Each town, street, house has its own history; if you walk around a street, talk to its residents, read about it in old newspapers, you might unearth all kinds of interesting facts that'll compete to enter your fiction. In portraying a place accurately, don't fear a lawsuit, which could happen only if the locations give unmistakable leads to real people. So, import your characters from other places and mask them so that not even their fathers would recognize them, or better yet, make them up.

Notice how proud people are if their town has been used as

a setting for a movie. The same is true of a successful book that uses an authentic setting. However, if you fear lawyers, you can always change the name and the looks of the town and its streets, and lie in a disclaimer on the front page that any resemblance to real places is purely accidental. I think, though, that if you have a talent for lying, you are better off transforming the places you know in your fiction than making such disclaimers.

SETTING AS THE GROUNDWORK OF FICTION

For me, setting has been the primary source of fiction. Once I left Croatia, I began to set most of my stories there. That caught me by surprise because I had been terribly eager to get to the States. My stories gained resonance from my knowledge of Croatian towns far more than from American settings, which took time to reach my imagination. People ask me if my work is autobiographical. "No, it's topographical," I say, and though people stare at me blankly, I do mean it. I write about places.

The importance of the setting could be expressed in this formula: Setting = Character = Plot. Out of a place, a character is formed; out of a character's motives, plot may follow. This may sound like a psychological theory that the milieu is everything, that a character is a product of her environment. On the other hand, to disregard the importance of setting and to rely on a character's innate nature may sound too much like determinism. If the genes or something else in a character take care of everything, why bother playing out the drama in the environment and on a novelistic stage? Without places and actions influencing the character, you can't have much link between events. For a novelist, the theory favoring environmental importance can usually function better than the theory disregarding its importance.

A compromise, giving weight to both nature and nurture, works best. This approach could be expressed as Setting + Character = Plot. Out of a character's relationship with the setting, or out of the character's conflict with the setting, you get the plot (or at least a part of the plot, or a dynamic backdrop for your plot). The character, of course, has some independent inner core, some traits that can't be explained merely by environmental influences.

Let me illustrate this formula in practice. In my story, "Rust," a setting and character in conflict with each other generate the plot:

> If you walk through the green and chirpy tranquility of the park around the castle at Nizograd, Yugoslavia, past the Roman Baths, you will come upon this monument: two dark, bronze partisans stuck on a pedestal uncomfortably high, back to back, one perpetually about to throw a hand grenade, another shoving his rifle into the air and shouting a metallic silence, his shirt ripped open. Their noses are sharp, lips thin, cheekbones high, hands large and knotty. . . . The monument was done by Marko Kovachevich, a sculptor educated at the Moscow Art Academy who was a Communist before the war and one of the first partisans.

The sculptor's work, as a part of the place, introduces to us the man and, later, his home completes the picture.

> His house was a grand sight—the redness of its bricks cried against the forest in the background. Its massiveness cast a long shadow over the backyard, prostrate and vanishing in the darkness of the woods. What was in the shadow attracted even more attention, so much so that the bright house would sink into a shadow of your mind, while the darkened objects in the backyard would begin to glow—planks of wood with bent nails sticking out, bike chains, rusty train wheels, tin cans, cats, buckets, winding telephones, a greater disarray than Berlin on May 2, 1945. The backyard seemed to be a witness to the collapse of an empire. Marko seemed entrenched in a war of sorts, with chaos gaining the upper hand.

By casting the shadows of World War II in a story set in the seventies, I build the plot. Marko, as a World War II guerrilla fighter, continues his fight, now against his former comrades, against the town and against himself: because he does not know how to live in peace. Instead of working as a sculptor, he makes tombstones, to bury communists. Just as his iron-strength rusts, and he collapses, without ever conforming (since he got stuck in the past), so does Yugoslavia collapse, for the second time (since she got stuck in the World War II mentality, which gutted any kind of progress). The setting is as much a character as Marko is. I wrote this story in the eighties—before Yugoslavia collapsed. I don't mean that there was anything prophetic in the story. The setting gave me nearly everything—the seed for a grand character and for the intuition about Yugoslavia's doom.

Even if the setting and the character together do not give you the plot, your story should appear as though the formula worked so that the place, the people, and the action are integrated. If you import a plot from a newspaper (or wherever) and apply it to places and people you know, you must transform the places and the people so that the plot—what happens—would be completely believable. Your characters should have sufficient motives to act the way they do, and these motives should be tied to the environment. To give a simple example, don't organize a water polo game on a baseball field; or if you insist, you must first make a swimming pool in that field. It's simpler to find a swimming pool elsewhere.

SETTING AS ANTAGONIST

In a wide range of stories—westerns, journey stories, nature adventure stories, detective stories, war stories, prison stories, Gothic romance and most successful nongenre stories—setting provides the groundwork for the action. For example, Guy de Maupassant set many of his stories in the aftermath of the Franco-Prussian War. In his story "Ball of Fat," he describes Rouen before the arrival of the Prussian troops:

> A profound calm, a frightful, silent expectancy had spread over the city. Many of the heavy citizens, emasculated by commerce, anxiously awaited the conquerors, trembling lest their roasting spits or kitchen knives be

> considered arms. . . . Shops were closed, the streets dumb.

When the Prussians come:

> A strange, intolerable atmosphere like a penetrating odor, the odor of invasion . . . filled the dwellings and the public places, changed the taste of the food. . . .

Since a character can be shown better in defeat than in victory, Maupassant uses the setting to unmask people. A prostitute is brave and generous—she shares her last food with a group of rich travelers and lets herself be raped by a Prussian officer in order to set the travelers free. When it becomes their turn to share their food, they refuse, despising her on "moral" grounds.

The man-against-nature story (in which a character struggles, usually for survival, against a natural element) depends entirely on setting. (See further discussion of this kind of story in chapter four.) For example, in "To Build a Fire" by Jack London, a man encounters a powerful antagonist, the cold, while he hikes in the Yukon territory in the middle of winter.

> As he turned to go on, he spat speculatively. There was a sharp explosive crackle that startled him. He spat again. And again, in the air, before it could fall to the snow, the spittle crackled. He knew that at fifty below spittle crackled on the snow, but this spittle had crackled in the air. Undoubtedly it was colder than fifty below.

London describes how creeks freeze through to the bottom, except for springs under the snow which "hid pools of water":

> Sometimes a skin of ice half an inch thick covered them, and in turn was covered by snow. . . . There were alternate layers of water and ice skin, so that when one broke through he kept on breaking through for a while . . . wetting himself to the waist.

In subzero temperatures, being wet means freezing to death, unless you build a fire. The man falls into a spring and builds a fire, but a wind buries it in snow, and he freezes to death. After reading this story, you will remember the crackling of spittle in the cold much better than the man. (This detail, by the way, turns out to be false—I've spat in windchill of minus eighty in North Dakota, and nothing crackled. But for me, London's description still crackles.) The setting is the main character of the story, as grand and unforgiving as God in the Book of Genesis.

Setting can sometimes generate the plot directly. For example, Nikolai Gogol based his novel *Dead Souls* on nineteenth century rural Russia, where a population census was conducted once every five years. If the last census was in 1830, and a serf died in 1831, the serf's death would be registered in 1835. Gogol's plot: A schemer travels around the country buying up dead serfs—relieving the landowners of the tax on them—to appear rich so he can mortgage his fictitious property and raise cash to buy real property. The schemer relies on the distance between the villages so that he won't get caught as a swindler.

The setting need not be exotic, nor do you need it only if you write a long story or a novel. Even a short piece of fiction benefits from a strong sense of place. Jim Heynen, the author of the story collection *The One-Room Schoolhouse*, sets his stories on an Iowa farm. I suppose if you don't live in Iowa, the setting may strike you as exotic, but if you do, it will not. The same applies to any place. Heynen's trust in the place created a genre: midwestern farm tale. Here's an excerpt from one, "Dead Possum":

> The boy whose job was to check the level of the big cattle drinking tank found a dead possum floating in it. . . . The dead possum had a big red apple wedged in its wide-open mouth. It looked like somebody with a big mouth who had been bobbing for apples.
>
> The boy wanted to yell for the others to come see, but knew they wouldn't believe him or, even if they did, wouldn't be in the mood. One of them would probably say something like, A dead possum with an apple in its mouth? Why don't you ask him to share?

Isn't this something? he said to the cows. Isn't this something?

Some nodded, then stepped past him to drink.

Heynen does not even have a distinct character here, just "the boys," which gives us more of a setting of boyhood than a single boy as a character. The place—populated with animals, vegetables, and farm boys—makes the story. Heynen gives you the place—no more than necessary—as the story moves along. This way, there's no risk that the reader will say, "When does this description end? I hope soon."

He offers you two viewpoints taken by the boys. Some treat the dead possum as quite familiar—and one boy treats it as something truly extraordinary. The group of boys, feeling jaded, familiarize even strange things, but the boy who checks the water level "defamiliarizes" them, finds something exotic in the potentially drab place on a dreary day. As a writer you should attain the skill for defamiliarizing your immediate surroundings, like the boy.

Every place is exotic to those who are far away from it. Write about the places exotic to you, but it's cheaper (no air fare), and usually more effective, to find the exotic in the familiar. The trick is to treasure your impressions of the places you know well. When you neglect a place, you impoverish yourself.

Heynen is right to give us a young boy as the bearer of the freshest vision. I took my eight-month-old son to the zoo to see the elephants. He found a bee circling around us far more intriguing than a dancing elephant. Instead of gibbons leaping in trees, he noticed fish in the water. It struck me that his perspective had a tremendous advantage over mine: He saw the world while I saw the zoo.

By noticing with a fresh eye the fall of a common apple, Newton revolutionized science. He did not need a pineapple.

But you need not limit yourself to the places you know. If you write science fiction, you do not run away from the obligation to give us a setting. Without creating a thorough setting—imaginary science and technology, fashion, architecture, cuisine, drugs—you don't make a good science fiction story. So devise ideas and images that will be unfamiliar to the reader, but make them appear familiar.

And for historical fiction, you can't have experienced every place and time. So you research to make sure that your characters in 1920 don't watch television and that your characters in Philadelphia of 1840 have the option to ride trains or at least listen to the whistles.

SETTING FOR SPECIAL EFFECTS

Many stories spring out of strong settings, but even those that don't use setting. In movies, music and landscape shots often appear as a backdrop for the action, especially to augment suspense, romance, and sometimes simply to dazzle you. The quality of photography—the selection of details, the angles of light and shadow—engage you most. In writing, we can achieve similar effects with words describing landscapes and cityscapes. So consider the following auxiliary uses of setting.

Setting as Quality of Vision

In a dialogue scene, delicate imagery and metaphors may seem unnatural to your reader, so break away from the drama occasionally to give bits of the stage—the clanking of spoons on china. Here's your chance to show your skill and speed, to build your reader's confidence in your narrative vision. If your words render a setting keenly, the reader might be inclined to accept the psychological insights implied in the action and dialogue. With sharply observed bits of the world, you convince. A touch of extraordinary landscaping here and there may be enough to draw us into the story and to keep us in it.

In *The Easter Parade* Richard Yates grabs our attention in a printing room scene by engaging our perception:

> Workmen hurried everywhere, all wearing crisp little squared-off hats made of intricately folded newspaper.
>
> "Why do they wear those paper hats, Daddy?" Emily asked.

> "Well, they'd probably tell you it's to keep the ink out of their hair, but I think they just wear 'em to look jaunty."
>
> "What does *jaunty* mean?"

Shortly after the dialogue, Yates gives us this description:

> They watched the curved, freshly cast metal page plates slide in on conveyor rollers to be clamped into place on the cylinders; then after a ringing of bells they watched the presses roll. The steel floor shuddered under their feet, which tickled, and the noise was so overwhelming that they couldn't talk: they could only look at each other and smile, and Emily covered her ears with her hands. White streaks of newsprint ran in every direction through the machines, and finished newspapers came riding out in neat, overlapped abundance.

There's a lot of dialogue before and after this moment; the narrative pause effectively grounds the scene. Yates makes us feel that we are there in the pressroom, with the ringing bells, shuddering floor, tickling feet. Although the novel is not about the newspaper business, but about two girls growing up unhappily, this scene establishes a strong backdrop. The daughters are impressed by their father, and they are ready to believe anything he tells them. Reading scenes like this, I believe, too, for I am there, I see. I see the father's work place. If I didn't, his working for a newspaper would not mean much.

Here's an example of the quality of vision in Michael Ondaatje's novel, *The English Patient*. In the scene, a Bedouin healer treats a wounded man:

> He crouched by the burned man. He made a skin cup with the soles of his feet and leaned back to pluck, without even looking, certain bottles. With the uncorking of each tiny bottle the perfumes fell out. There was an odour of the sea. The smell of rust. Indigo. Ink. River-mud arrow-wood formaldehyde paraffin ether. The tide of airs

> chaotic. There were screams of camels in the distance as they picked up the scents. He began to rub green-black paste onto the rib cage.

Ondaatje engages your senses. "The smell of rust": You smell and see. "Screams of camels": You hear and see. ". . . to rub green-black paste onto the rib cage": You see and feel. The texture of the sensations is so rich that you experience the scene before you can doubt it. This healer's handling his tools in his desert creates and sustains a scene—with substantiated characters in a setting. By substantiated I mean that we see the healer at work with his substances. Ondaatje does not merely tell, he shows.

Mood and Atmosphere

You can set the tone of a scene with your handling of the setting. This is especially important in horror stories, romance, and other "mood" genres.

Here's a mood-setter from a Gothic classic, Emily Brontë's *Wuthering Heights*:

> One may guess the power of the north wind, blowing over the edge, by the excessive slant of a few stunted firs at the end of the house; and by a range of gaunt thorns all stretching their limbs one way, as if craving alms of the sun. . . . The narrow windows are deeply set in the wall, and the corners defended with large jutting stones. . . .

The narrator completes the image of the house's exterior with the following description:

> A quantity of grotesque carving lavished over the front, and especially about the principal door, above which, among a wilderness of crumbling griffins, and shameless little boys, I detected the date "1500."

Then she gives us the interior:

> Above the chimney were sundry villainous old guns, and a couple of horse-pistols, and, by way of ornament, three gaudily painted canisters disposed along its ledge. The floor was smooth, white stone: the chairs, high-backed, primitive structures, painted green: one or two heavy black ones lurking in the shade. In an arch, under the dresser, reposed a huge, liver-colored bitch pointer surrounded by a swarm of squealing puppies; and other dogs haunted other recesses.

The barren landscape, with stunted trees, thorns, and lack of sunshine, create a threatening mood. The interior of the old house, with its darkness, intensifies the sensation of threat. The smooth white stone adds coldness. Although the mere mention of all these details would create a threatening enough mood, the narrator does not stop there. She slants the verbs to distort the picture, to make it spooky. Chairs *lurk* in the shade. Dogs *haunt* recesses. Even the adjectives are slanted: *villainous* guns. She could have described pretty much the same thing with different verbs, "Chairs repose in the shade, and dogs roam in the recesses," and she would have relaxed the mood. She guides the reader with verbs, adjectives, and adverbs toward a single mood.

However, you don't always need to use a long description to be effective. For example, German writer Günter Grass, in his novel *Dog Years*, gives us a startling detail to establish a surreal atmosphere:

> . . . where the dike burst in '55 near Kokotzko, not far from the Mennonite cemetery—weeks later the coffins were still hanging in the trees—he, on foot . . .

This is the middle of a half-page-long sentence, and the humble placement of the image of coffins hanging in trees only sharpens its effect, to augment the theme of postwar Germany, where war deaths hover in the air. Grass does not need to point with slanted verbs and modifiers at this grotesque image. It does its own work—but isn't subtle, since it is a loud image. Grass' technique is not superior to Brontë's technique. They achieve different effects. Brontë's narrator, passionately involved in the story, explicitly works on the mood, which anticipates disaster. Grass' narrator, ironically detached, works his way out of a catastrophe, without needing to embellish it. Both methods are effective. When you choose a narrator emotionally involved in a drama, you might choose Brontë's method; when you want distance, choose Grass' cooler, more matter-of-fact method.

Foreshadowing

You can use setting to steer the reader's expectations. Mood is a big part of foreshadowing. In the preceding example, Brontë foreshadows something frightening. The mention of villainous guns raises the suspicion that someone will be murdered. Darkness, griffins and haunting dogs forecast something on the verge of the supernatural. Later, she delivers on most of her promises.

In Stephen Crane's "The Blue Hotel," a Swede believes that Nebraska is the wild West, and that he will be killed there. He provokes a fight, wins it, goes to another bar to brag about it, and there he is killed. As we follow him, we encounter these images:

> In front of the saloon an indomitable red light was burning, and the snowflakes were made blood-colour as they flew through the circumscribed territory of the lamp's shining.

The snowy night and the red flakes obviously foreshadow the bloodshed. In your writing, you may strive for a bit more subtlety, but it's probably best to be somewhat obvious. If your foreshadowing is too subtle, there won't be any shadows to see.

Setting as Alpha and Omega

In a screenplay, before every take you must indicate whether you are inside or outside, and the time of day. As a fiction writer, you may find these "establishing shots" tiresome, but you are not exempt from the obligation to establish where you are and what time of day the drama takes place. Of course, now and then it becomes boring to say, "in the evening." So you may try twilights, dusks, noons, teatimes, and some other times, but eventually, even these will run dry. So be it. You still need to write, "in the morning," just as in dialogue you must rely on one simple word, *said*. If you don't tell when your action takes place, it might appear to happen in some generic time or always, as a repeated action. Unless you want that effect, indicate the days and nights.

For an example of how to open a piece of fiction with a setting and orient us as to the time the action takes place, take a look at Dickens' brief opening of *Our Mutual Friend*:

> In these times of ours, though concerning the exact year there is no need to be precise, a boat of dirty and disreputable appearance, with two figures in it, floated on the Thames between Southwark Bridge, which is of iron, and London Bridge, which is of stone, as an autumn evening was closing in.

The beginning draws us into a scene. We have a stage. At first we do not see the characters and the boat clearly, but enough is established for us to begin seeing and wondering.

In introducing the setting, it's important that you orient us, make it clear where we should be imaginatively. Here's how Guy de Maupassant opens "Mademoiselle Fifi." He places us in an interior, with a vantage point toward the exterior:

> The Major Graf von Farlsberg was reading . . . with his booted feet on the beautiful marble fireplace, where his spurs had made two holes, which grew deeper every day, during the three months that he had been in the chateau of Urville.
>
> A cup of coffee was steaming on a round marquetry table, stained with liqueurs, charred by cigars and hacked by the penknife of the victorious officer. . . . After throw-

> ing three or four enormous pieces of green wood on to the fire—for these gentlemen were gradually cutting down the park in order to keep themselves warm—he went to the window. The rain was descending in torrents, a regular Normandy rain, which . . . formed a kind of wall with oblique stripes.

Although de Maupassant does not tell us directly that it's daytime, he makes it clear: He tells us several paragraphs later that the cup of coffee is Major's sixth cup since that morning and that the officer looked over the flooded park (which he could not see at night).

Both of these openings set up moods and expectations—first for some murky action; second, for whimsical deeds to kill the boredom of a rainy day.

You can also close a story with the impressions of a place, which, in cinematic terminology, can create a perfect fade-out. This is how James Joyce closes his "The Dead" after the main character realizes that without having passionately lived, he would fade away and die:

> A few light taps upon the pane made him turn to the window. It had begun to snow again. He watched sleepily the flakes, silver and dark, falling obliquely against the lamplight. Yes, the newspapers were right: snow was general all over Ireland. It was falling on every part of the dark central plain, on the treeless hills, falling softly upon the Bogg of Allen and, farther westward, softly falling into the dark mutinous Shannon waves. It was falling, too, upon every part of the lonely churchyard on the hill where Michael Furey lay buried. It lay thickly drifted on the crooked crosses and headstones, on the spears of the little gate, on the barren thorns. His soul swooned slowly as he heard the snow falling faintly through the universe and faintly falling, like the descent of their last end, upon all the living and the dead.

What's more to say after this? If the story ended with a

philosophical statement, the impact would be smaller. In this way you'll carry the images for days after you've read the story.

Setting as a Character Portrait

It's hard to describe a person's face in a fresh and telling way. After all, in how many ways can you describe eyes and a nose, if you don't rely on metaphors? Not many. However, by describing a person through how he arranges his surroundings, you have quite a few options.

In *Dead Souls*, Nikolai Gogol uses objects in a living room to portray a character:

> A lemon completely dried up, and no larger than a broken walnut-wood knob from an arm-chair; a wine glass covered with a letter, and containing some sort of liquid and three flies; . . . a toothpick, which was quite yellow, and with which the owner had probably cleansed his teeth prior to the arrival of the French in Moscow. . . . From the middle of the ceiling hung a chandelier enveloped in a linen bag, to which the accumulated dust gave the aspect of a silkworm's cocoon with the worm in it. . . . It would have been impossible to affirm that a living being inhabited the apartment, had not an ancient, threadbare nightcap, which lay upon the table, borne witness to the fact.

The setting of the room gives us the character, a hoarder. This portrayal is augmented by other details:

> For all of his domestic servants . . . Pliushkin had but a single pair of boots, which was always to be found in the vestibule. Anyone who was summoned into the master's presence generally ran across the yard barefooted; but on entering the vestibule he pulled on the boots, and, thus arrayed, made his appearance in the room. . . . If anyone had glanced out of the window in the autumn, and especially when the first morning frosts were setting

> in, he could have seen all the house-serfs taking such leaps as are hardly made on the stage by the most accomplished dancers.

How's that for describing a stingy character? Certainly better than a pile of adjectives. To adhere to the principle "show, don't tell," present people by what's around them.

EXERCISES

1. First (two pages), describe the town you grew up in—the streets, shops, schools, churches, rivers, bridges, rails. Don't mention your emotions; don't be sentimental.

Then (half a page), indicate a place in the above sketch where something happened. Map out the event with special attention to the physical details of the setting. It need not be a big event—your shattering a window or seeing a teacher you had a crush on kiss a cop will do. Naguib Mahfouz, the Egyptian Nobel prize winner, wrote a novel, *Midaq Alley*, describing life on a little street in Cairo.

Objective: To remind you of your treasures. If you have a strong sense of place, it'll be easy for you to write a lot. Let the bricks speak.

Check: Have you described the childhood places vividly? Do you mention enough details to construct a visual impression? Do you engage other senses, not only sight? Read your descriptions slowly. Are you there? If you haven't mentioned enough real details, perhaps you aren't there. Try it again—until you mention the concrete objects you see. You can revise the exercise, deleting and inserting words, until you feel that you've brought us into your town.

2. Two pages. Make a one-page list of all the objects you remember from your childhood home. Don't use any particular order or many adjectives. Don't censor yourself—something seemingly unimportant may evoke strong impressions.

Read your list and circle the objects that evoke the strongest feelings and memories of events. What are these events? Do you see a story lurking there? Now write one page and describe one of these events. Rely on topography. Where exactly did it happen? What objects were involved?

Objective: To let your home begin to write stories for you. Memory is your best source of settings.

Check: Same as for Exercise 1. Now go over the details and cross out the ones that don't evoke strong impressions. It's good to bring out many details and then select the ones that work best; select a few, condense. Your reader will appreciate this economy.

Make sure that you haven't used sentimental vocabulary. It's fine to be sentimental, but *mentioning* the sentiments won't give them to the reader. Connecting the details with the events might. For instance, "I walk down the yellow marble stairs where my grandfather slid one winter and broke his hip. That was the last step he took; he died shortly after the injury. In the space beneath the staircase I find my old dog's house, with his shaggy hairs caught in the rough edges of the wood planks, although the dog is long gone." If you don't dwell on the emotional significance of the grandfather and the dog, but move on, you avoid sentimentality. If the grandfather is important, you can show that in a scene, an interaction with the man so we can experience him and your loss of him. We won't miss an abstraction about the man.

3. Two pages. Describe with care the most ordinary items you can think of. Look at them as though they were strange and unusual. Conversely, describe extraordinary things—meteors, rockets and so on—in familiar language as just another stone or a piece of rolled sheet metal.

Objective: To learn how to control your distance from the objects you describe. If you are too close, you may not see the shape; if you are too far, you may not see the details. Get into the habit of shifting the focus away from what would be your automatic focus, and you will see items in a fresh way. Practice the art of creating surprising details. Skip something obviously important and use something apparently unimportant.

Check: Do the ordinary objects sound fascinating? Do the extraordinary objects sound ordinary but interesting? If not, go back and in the first half of the exercise give us the details that amaze, and in the second, details that make us take a good look. Everything you observe with interest should sound interesting.

4. Three one-page descriptions. Describe three places you have been. Don't worry about pretty words; mention the important and some unimportant details you remember.

Objective: Sooner or later you'll need these places in your stories. It's good to have them handy, so you don't have to make up everything at once. You need a hospital? Pull it out of your files. You do it anyway—your brain has the files, and as a writer, you'll facilitate your job if you let your papers or your computer share them. Externalize your materials. Of course, when fitting these descriptions into a piece of fiction, you'll need to tailor them for desired effects—mood, atmosphere, foreshadowing—so you'll need to pick and choose your details.

Check: Have you been specific enough? Instead of a bird, let it be a pigeon; instead of a tree, a cedar. Have you externalized enough? Instead of a place being enjoyable (which is your internal reaction to it), mention, for example, the murmur of champagne.

5. Two pages. Describe places where you have worked—a hospital ward, a law firm, an army barracks, a fish cannery, a restaurant, an oil rig and so on. Describe how the people handle their tools and machines. If you are at a loss, take a look at Richard Yates' example on page 34, and try to describe a workplace, similarly engaging our senses.

Objective: To concentrate on the details and energy of a workplace. Workplaces make perfect story setups because they make it easy for you to integrate the place and the character. People shape the place, the places shape the people. Remember the importance of linking place and character for plot development (or for a plot backdrop).

Check: Would we know we were in a chocolate factory—or wherever you choose—without your telling us? If you stated,

"This is a chocolate factory," delete the sentence, and see whether the place still is clear. It should be, if you've let us feel, hear, smell and taste the work. If you haven't, go back and mention the sounds, smells, sights, and feel of the place.

6. One page. Describe a train ride—the rhythm of the rails clicking, the sound booming back from a close wall, the sensation of motion when a parallel train moves and yours doesn't, the sticky beer stains on the floor, the smell of new towns and so on. (Or if you prefer, describe a different kind of ride—on a boat or in a car, for example.)

Objective: To show the experience of travel. Journey is one of the basic story forms. Maybe you carry a story that the setting of travel will give birth to. Try it. (For example, a friend of mine wrote a dozen postcards from Germany to the States, and when she got back was surprised that nobody got them. She had mistaken a clean German garbage bin for a mailbox.)

Check: Have you shown us the train? Go back over the description and delete adjectives—*beautiful, menacing*—that tell us what you'd like to show us. Have you described the corridors, signs (in what languages?), lights?

7. One page. Describe the setting of a Man-against-Nature story. Use a mountain you've climbed, or a river you've rafted, or a sea you've sailed. Describe the flora, fauna, weather, but not yourself (become subjective later). Give us what you saw, as precisely and objectively as you can. Show the nature, the danger.

Objective: To learn how to landscape dramatically, truthfully.

Check: Did we get a sense of danger from your description? Delete adjectives (like *terrifying*) and change metaphors into realistic pictures. (Instead of "Each wave was a dragon frothing at the mouth," let it be something like "The tall wave crests burst into foam above us.") If after the psychological projection—emotional adjectives and metaphors—are taken out of the picture, we still get the sense of terror, you've done a great job. Later—if you choose to go on with the story—you can switch into metaphoric and hallucinatory vision of the terror.

8. One page. Write a story opening set indoors and include the occupants of the rooms. What time of day is it? What's the weather like? (For an example, read the excerpt from "Mademoiselle Fifi" on page 39.) Then write the last page for the same story. Close with an impression given by the environment, which should correspond to the mood you want the story to express.

Objective: To learn how to visualize a stage for a story. Once you are mentally in the place, you'll be able to envision the action and move forward. The same is true with ending the action.

Check: Can we see what you are talking about? I don't mean every eyelash in the onion soup and every cigarette stub on the bathroom tile floor—you don't need to count lashes and stubs, but do mention them.

9. Two pages. Write one page preceding the death of a car salesman from his point of view. Describe street traffic, weather, pedestrians or birds in such a way that we begin to feel the gloom and resignation of the man about to die.

Then write one page preceding the birth of a daughter, using the same street as above, to create a sensation of hope, anxiety and joy from the perspective of the car salesman.

Set up the mood for both events through the choice of details. Don't be too obvious about what you are doing, but don't be too subtle either. (But if this inhibits you, make a parody of foreshadowing—be either too obvious or too subtle!)

Objective: To realize the expressive potential of objects and places.

Check: Do your images accumulate to create an atmosphere of gloom and resignation in the first half of the exercise and of anticipation in the second? Do you achieve a gradual increase in intensity? If not, reorder the images to create the progression.

10. One page. Describe a setting for a horror story. You might pattern it after Emily Brontë's example on page 36. Use the same lack of narrative distance as she does—let your narrator show us an ominous atmosphere through choice details, and let her tell us about it also, through slanted verbs and adjectives, just as

Brontë does. The balance should be in favor of the details. (If horror does not appeal to you, try to achieve another mood.)

Objective: To practice using setting for a strong mood, using all your means, showing and telling.

Check: Did you evoke the mood? Although it's all right if some of your imagery turns out to be stock horror stuff (howling winds), make sure that at least some of your images are original, new, something that you haven't seen before. (For example, Brontë uses this fresh, memorable image, "range of gaunt thorns all stretching their limbs one way, as if craving alms of the sun.")

11. Two pages. Recall your favorite bridge—surely you have one! Describe it in one page from the perspective of a woman who has received a letter offering her a great job.

Then, in one more page, describe the same bridge from the perspective of the same woman, who has just found out that her boyfriend committed suicide. In both instances, don't mention emotions, plans, regrets. Leave the expression of the emotions to your selection of details—the bridge's stones, the vegetation on the river banks, the water, the river traffic.

Objective: Same as in Exercise 9. Work like an expressionist painter. Don't worry about being realistic and precise with detail. Paint in broad strokes—slant and twist—to make the commotion of the soul looking at the bridge as visible as the bridge itself.

Check: If, in the first part, you express cheer, do you give us a flock of swallows fluttering over cherry trees on the banks of the river? In the second part, do you show a grimace on an ancient face with blank stones for eyes? Or something similar?

12. One page. Make a character visible through her surroundings. If she loves plants and cats and hates people, her house might assume certain traits. Sketch the house, listing the sights, smells, sounds. (See page 41 for how Gogol does it.)

Objective: To learn the power of setting as a means for character portraits. Bits of environment are your tubes of paint.

Check: Read the sketch. Do you give us precise details? Rather than "The place smelled stuffy," do you show the stuffiness? Rather than "plants," list the names of plants.

CHAPTER THREE

CHARACTER

Most people read fiction not so much for plot as for company. In a good piece of fiction you can meet someone and get to know her in depth, or you can meet yourself, in disguise, and imaginatively live out and understand your passions. The writer William Sloan thinks it boils down to this: "Tell me about me. I want to be more alive. Give me me."

If character matters so much to the reader, it matters even more to the writer. Once you create convincing characters, everything else should easily follow. F. Scott Fitzgerald said, "Character is plot, plot is character." But, as fiction writer and teacher Peter LaSalle has noted, out of character, plot easily grows, but out of plot, a character does not necessarily follow. To show what makes a character, you must come to a crucial choice that almost breaks and then makes the character. The make-or-break decision gives you plot. Think of Saul on the way to Damascus: While persecuting Christians, he is blinded by a vision; after that, he changes, becomes St. Paul, the greatest proselyte. Something stays the same, however; he is equally zealous, before and after. No matter what you think of the story of Paul's conversion, keep it in mind as a paradigm for making a character.

Of course, not all characters undergo a crucial change. With some characters, their unchangeability and constancy makes a story. In "Rust," my story about the sculptor-turned-tombstone-maker, everything (the country, family, town) changes, except the character. Even his body collapses, but his spirit stays bellicose and steadfast. Here he is, at work:

> He refused to answer any more of my questions. His hands—with thick cracked skin and purple nails from hammer misses—picked up a hammer. Veins twisted around his stringy tendons so that his tendons looked like the emblem for medicine. He hit the broadened head of the chisel, bluish steel cutting into gray stone, dust flying up in a sneezing cloud. With his gray hair and blue stubbly cheeks he blended into the grain of the stone—a stone with a pair of horned eyebrows. Chiseling into the stone, he wrestled with time, to mark and catch it. But time evaded him like a canny boxer. Letting him cut into rocks, the bones of the earth, Time would let him exhaust himself.
>
> Seven years later I saw him. His face was sunken. His body had grown weaker. Time had chiseled into his face so steadily that you could tell how many years had passed just by looking at the grooves cutting across his forehead. But the stubbornness in his eyes had grown stronger. They were larger, and although ringed with milky-gray cataracts, glaringly fierce.

Whether or not there's a change in you, character is not the part of you that conforms, but rather, that sticks out. So a caricaturist seeks out oddities in a face; big jaws, slanted foreheads, strong creases. The part of the character that does not conform builds a conflict, and the conflict makes the story. Find something conflicting in a character, some trait sticking out of the plane, creating dimension and complexity. Make the conflict all-consuming, so that your character fights for life. Stanley Elkin, author of *The Dick Gibson Show*, emphasized the need for struggle this way: "I would never write about someone who is not at the end of his rope."

Think of the basic character conflicts in successful stories. "The Necklace" by Guy de Maupassant: Mme. Loisel, unreconciled to her lower-class standing, strives to appear upper class, at all costs. Out of that internal conflict ensues the tragedy of her working most of her adult life to pay for a fake necklace.

"The Girls in Their Summer Dresses" by Irwin Shaw: Though

married and in love with his wife, a young man is still attracted to other women.

In Henry James' "The Beast in the Jungle": John Marcher waits for some extraordinary passion to take hold of him; he dreams of it so much that he does not notice he is in love with May Bertram, who is at his side all along. Only when she dies, of neglect, does he realize it.

In "The Blue Hotel" by Stephen Crane: The Swede, visiting a small town in rural Nebraska, imagines that he is in the wild West and consequently sets himself against a bar of ordinary people whom he imagines as gamblers and murderers.

In all these stories, characters suffer from a conflicting flaw. Aristotle called these character flaws *hamartia*—usually interpreted as "tragic flaw" (most often hubris or arrogance) when we talk about tragedies. Sometimes, however, a flaw may not lead to disaster, but to a struggle with a subsequent enlightenment. (St. Paul's zeal, for example, leads him to an epiphany.)

A flaw could result also from an excessive virtue. Look at the opening of *Michael Kohlhaas* by the early nineteenth-century German writer Heinrich von Kleist:

> Michael Kohlhaas . . . owned a farm on which he quietly earned a living by his trade; his children were brought up in the fear of God to be industrious and honest; there was not one of his neighbors who had not benefited from his goodness and fair-mindedness—the world would have had every reason to bless his memory, if he had not carried one virtue to excess. But his sense of justice turned him into a robber and a murderer.

Since his horses were abused at a border crossing between two principalities, and he could not get a just compensation in courts, Kohlhaas takes justice into his hands and burns down the castle where the horses suffered. In addition, he burns the city of Dresden, which protected the offenders. His sense of justice provokes a war. His uncompromising virtue may amount to vice—certainly it's a flaw, the plot-generating flaw.

ROUND AND FLAT CHARACTERS

Most of the characters in the above examples could be called round characters because they have three dimensions, like a ball. These characters are complex, possessing conflicting traits. Mme. Loisel is both frivolous and responsible. The Swede is paranoid yet insightful. John Marcher is sensitive yet callous. In writing, you must not oversimplify—that is, create flat characters. (It's all right to have flat characters as part of a setting but not as part of an interactive community, the cast of your story.)

Flat characters have few traits, all of them predictable, none creating genuine conflicts. Flat characters often boil down to stereotypes: fat, doughnut-eating cop; forgetful professor; lecherous truck driver; jovial fatso; shifty-eyed thief; anorexic model. Using these prefab characters can give your prose a semblance of humor and quickness, but your story featuring them will have about as much chance of winning a contest as a prefab apartment in a competition of architects. Even more damaging, you will sound like a bigot. As a writer you ought to aspire toward understanding the varieties of human experiences, and bigotry simply means shutting out and insulting a segment of population (and their experiences) by reducing them to flat types.

But can you have a character without types? What would literature be without gamblers and misers? The answer, I believe, is simple: Draw portraits of misers, but not as misers—as people who happen to be miserly. And if while you draw misers as people you feel that you fail to make characters but do make people, all the better. Ernest Hemingway said, "When writing a novel a writer should create living people; people, not characters. A *character* is a caricature." So, give us people. ("Give me me.") Let the miser in me come to life—and blush—reading your story.

SOURCES OF CHARACTERS

Where do you find fictional people?

You can completely make them up, using psychology textbooks, astrology charts, mythology, the Bible or, simply, your imagination. This is the *ideal method*—ideal in the sense that you work from a purely intellectual creation, an idea about a character whom you have not observed and who is not you. Although by using this method you don't draw from people you know to make your characters, you must speak of real passions, and each character must appear like a real person. *Real person* is a bit of a contradiction in terms because *persona*, the Latin root for *person*, means "mask." We usually take a mask to be the "unreal," phony part of a person. But wearing a mask at a carnival can help you live out your true passions that otherwise, due to social pressures, you keep in check. Fiction is a carnival. So give us real passions with good masks, and everybody will be fair game! Make up character masks, release dramatic conflicts beneath them, and you will create startling people, such as you would like, or fear, to meet.

The mother of all methods—though not necessarily the one you should use most—is the *autobiographical method*, for it is through your own experience that you grasp what it is to be a person. Because of this, you are bound, at least to some extent, to project yourself into the fictional characters you render by any other method. Many writers project themselves into all the characters they portray. This is, metaphorically speaking, the fission approach: an atom may be split into several, during which an enormous amount of energy is released. Fyodor Dostoyevski split his personality into many fictional ones, all of them as temperamental as he. Mel Brooks, the comedy writer and movie director, thinks this is the primary way to write: "Every human being has hundreds of separate people living under his skin. The talent of a writer is his ability to give them their separate names, identities, personalities, and have them relate to other characters living with him."

In the *biographical method*, you use people you have observed (or researched) as the starting points for your fictional character. This seems to be the most popular method. Despite legal limitations on the biographical method, don't shut down this basic source of fictional characters. Hemingway said that if he explained the process of turning a real-life character into a fictional one, it would be a handbook for libel lawyers. The notion that writers work this way will keep some people quiet around you lest you broadcast their secrets. For a long while it irritated me that my older brother would not believe that I was becoming a writer; and now that he does, he irritates me even more because he does not tell me anything about himself. To find out about him, I talk to our middle brother, and as soon as my older brother finds out that that's how it works, he probably won't talk to him either.

Most fictional characters are directly or at least indirectly drawn from life. E.M. Forster, author of *A Passage to India*, said: "We all like to pretend we don't use real people, but one does actually. I used some of my family. . . . This puts me among the large body of authors who are not really novelists, and who have to get on as best they can." (By the way, most novelists are not really novelists, and they must get on as best they can. Nobody is born with this stuff, and hardly anybody becomes quite secure in the craft. I think that's comforting: Novelists are regular people, like you and me.)

Using the biographical method, writers often compose their characters from the traits of several people. To express it with another term from nuclear physics, this is the fusion approach: You fuse character traits the way you fuse atoms. Lillian Hellman, author of *Pentimento*, supports this view of making fictional characters: "I don't think you start with a person. I think you start with parts of many people. Drama has to do with conflict in people, with denials." She looks for conflicts in real people and gives these conflicts to her fictional characters, whose traits she gets from other people.

The fourth way to create fictional characters is the *mixed method*. Writers frequently combine the biographical and the ideal methods since there's a limit to relying on direct knowledge of characters. In part, this stems from our inability to know people in depth. Somerset Maugham, author of *Of Human Bondage*, said: "People are hard to know. It is a slow business to induce them to tell you the particular thing about themselves that can be of use to you." Unless you are a psychiatrist or a priest, you probably will not find out the deep problems of the people around you. That does not mean you can't use some aspects of the people you know. But soon you must fill in the gaps, and let's hope that then you will create a character independent from the real-life model. You may use ideas and imagination, or it may happen spontaneously, as it apparently did to Graham Greene, author of *The Human Factor*, who said: "One gets started and then, suddenly, one cannot remember what toothpaste they use. . . . The moment comes when a character does or says something you hadn't thought about. At that moment he's alive and you leave it to him." If your character begins to do something different from what the real-life precedent would do, encourage this change, and forget about the real-life model. Soon you should have someone answering to the necessities of your plot and conflicts, not to the memory of the person you started with.

The ideal to strive for is a character who will come to life seemingly on his own. It will no longer be the person from life outside the novel that served as a starting point, but a fictional one, who not only is there to be written about, but who, in an optimal case, writes for you. Erskine Caldwell expressed this blessed autonomy of fictional characters: "I have no influence over them. I'm only an observer, recording. The story is always being told by the characters themselves."

Not all writers give their characters autonomy and allow them to dictate what to write down. John Cheever said: "The legend that characters run away from their authors—taking up drugs, having sex operations, and becoming president—implies that the writer is a fool with no knowledge or mastery of his craft. This is absurd." Of course, Cheever believed in his method and distrusted the methods of other authors. I think it's silly when a writer assumes that his method is the method for all writers. However, it is good to learn what approaches exist, to try them all, and to see which works best for you.

But one principle about constructing characters can be stated unequivocally. Whether your characters attain autonomy or not, whether they come from you or from Greek myths, the more you get to know them, the better you will work with them. To work with a character, you might need to sketch it in several ways. You could start with this questionnaire (or make one up for yourself): Name? Age? Place of birth? Residence? Occupation? Appearance? Dress? Strengths? Weakness? Obsessions? Ambition? Work habits? Hobbies? Illness? Family? Parents? Kids? Siblings? Friends? Pets? Politics? Tics? Diet? Drugs? Favorite kinds of coffee, cigarettes, alcohol? Erotic history? Favorite books, movies, music? Desires? Fears? Most traumatic event? Most wonderful experience? The major struggle, past and present?

If you give quick, spontaneous answers, you might surprise yourself with the character that emerges. Don't worry if this works like a Rorschach blot, if it reveals something about you. You might do it in a silly way, have fun, and still get an idea for a character. And you might do it quite thoughtfully, in relation to your plot, if you've chosen one. (Let's say, your plot involves a son who gambles away his patrimony, until he becomes a father, and then works so hard to leave his son with a patrimony that he can't spend any time with him, and his son disowns him. You must devise character traits that would make this plausible.) If you don't have a plot yet, some of the answers to these questions, particularly the last one—the character's major struggle—might give you ideas.

Once you know almost enough—you hardly ever know enough—about the character, test her out. Portray her.

PORTRAYING A CHARACTER

The way you present a character is at least as important as where you get the character. Fleshing out your characters in various ways may take up most of the story. So if you learn how to make your characters act on a stage, in your setting, you'll certainly be able to write stories. In this section you'll find a variety of ways to portray a character.

Summary

You can tell us outright what your fictional characters are like and what they do. If you answered the questionnaire at the end of the previous section, you have a rough character summary. Link the character traits that strike you as the most important ones, and you'll have a complete character summary. Here's a classic summary from *Don Quixote* by Miguel de Cervantes:

> This gentleman, in the times when he had nothing to do—as was the case for most of the year—gave himself up to the reading of books of knight errantry; which he loved and enjoyed so much that he almost entirely forgot his hunting, and even the care of his estate. . . .
>
> He so buried himself in his books that he spent the nights reading from twilight till daybreak and the days from dawn till dark; and so from little sleep and much reading, his brain dried up and he lost his wits.

Cervantes goes on with the summary for several pages, but I think this excerpt gives you an idea of how summary works. We find out Don Quixote's work and leisure habits, hobbies and passions, and the consequences of pursuing these—his obsession with books results in his illness, madness.

The advantage of this method is its simplicity and readability: The writer quickly focuses on the main character's conflict and supplies the background we need to know. You clearly set up expectations for what follows if you use this method in or near the beginning of your story. Unless you botch the summary, your reader will easily understand what the main character traits and conflicts are about.

The disadvantage to this method is that you are bound to tell rather than show what your character is like—this method makes it hard to see and hear the character. While the summary goes on, no dramatic action, no dialogue, takes place. We are waiting. Still, the character summary is often worth risking; after you orient the reader clearly and quickly, you will not need to stall the dramatic action (in order to supply the background) once it begins to take place.

Here's another example of how summary works, from *The Sun Also Rises* by Ernest Hemingway. See how quickly we learn the character's main concerns:

> Robert Cohn was once middleweight boxing champion of Princeton. Do not think that I am very much impressed by that as a boxing title, but it meant a lot to Cohn. He cared nothing for boxing, in fact he disliked

> it, but he learned it painfully and thoroughly to counteract the feeling of inferiority and shyness he had felt on being treated as a Jew at Princeton. There was a certain inner comfort in knowing he could knock down anybody who was snooty to him, although, being very shy and a thoroughly nice boy, he never fought except in the gym.

This is the opening of the novel. There's no scene for us to visualize, but we receive the basic outline of the character's psychology and motivation. Later, we'll hear the character speak, see him act, but for now, we have some guiding ideas about him (and the novel), which will help us understand what follows.

If this approach strikes you as too much "telling," try to show all the information in a dramatic scene, and you'll realize that you'll need at least several pages to do it. Since the action Hemingway is concerned with is not in the past but in the dramatic present (which will follow), to go back into the past dramatically would dissipate the novel's focus. The summary gives us the relevant aspects of the past, so we can stick with the dramatic present. While it's not the most graceful method, it's certainly useful.

Repeated Action or Habit

This is the most common notion of character—the expectation of how a person will behave in a given situation, based on the observation that she has behaved like that many times, that she has the habit. This may be an effective way of describing a person when you don't have the time to go into the scenes to show us how she behaves. Here's an example from "Where Are You Going, Where Have You Been?" by Joyce Carol Oates:

> She was fifteen and she had a quick, nervous giggling habit of craning her neck to glance into mirrors or checking other people's faces to make sure her own was all right.

Now we know that in many situations the girl behaves this way. It would take an awful lot of time to show this habit dramatically. If the sole point of the scenes were to show her habit, the scenes would be a strain on the reader. Describing it in a summary will save you time. That's the advantage. The disadvantage is that doing this will delay your entry into your main dramatic scenes, where the story takes place.

Self-Portrait

The writer may let the character introduce himself to us. Again, this usually will be a summary of the basic concerns, at least in the beginning. Notice that a self-portrait can be achieved indirectly, as Hemingway's narrator does in the example of character summary from *The Sun Also Rises*. The narrator says, "Do not think that I am very much impressed by that as a boxing title, but it meant a lot to Cohn." In this sentence we notice a certain sense of superiority, perhaps arrogance, on the part of the narrator. When he characterizes Robert Cohn as "very shy and a thoroughly nice boy," we hear the narrator's voice. Who would speak of a twenty-year-old as a "thoroughly nice boy"? We begin to surmise inferences about the narrator. The narrator's summary gives us an explicit portrait of Robert Cohn and an implied and indirect self-portrait. Good economy.

Here's a direct self-portrait by the narrator of *Notes From Underground* by Fyodor Dostoyevski:

> I am a sick man. . . . I am a spiteful man. I am an ugly man. I believe my liver is diseased. However, I know nothing at all about my disease, and do not know for certain what ails me. I don't consult a doctor for it, and never have, though I have a respect for medicine and doctors. Besides, I am extremely superstitious, sufficiently so to respect medicine, anyway (I am well-educated enough not to be superstitious, but I am superstitious). No, I refuse to consult a doctor from spite. . . . My liver is bad, well—let it get worse!

Here, the advantage over the third-person summary is that the way sentences are put together, the way of thought, is our picture of the character just as much as the content of the thoughts. The Underground Man thinks in paradoxes, spitefully, in intentional self-contradictions. He certainly prepares us for the humorous and self-destructive acts to follow, so the disadvantages of this method, that it is not dramatic and that it does not create pictures, are not significant.

Appearance

Image is not everything, but it does account for a lot. Through how a person looks, you may try to infer what the person is like—but appearances may be deceptive. Still, to suggest the person's character, you may select and interpret details, to guide the reader's expectations.

George Eliot uses this approach in the following paragraph from *Middlemarch*:

> Miss Brooke had that kind of beauty which seems to be thrown into relief by poor dress. Her hand and wrist were so finely formed that she could wear sleeves not less bare of style than those in which the blessed Virgin appeared to Italian painters; and her profile as well as her stature and bearing seemed to gain the more dignity from her plain garments, which by the side of provincial fashion gave her the impressiveness of a fine quotation from the Bible—or from one of our elder poets—in a paragraph of today's newspaper.

Eliot draws a portrait of a Victorian lady who drives the modesty of her dress to such an extreme that we are alerted by it. Immediately after this, Eliot gives us an inkling of how to interpret the appearance. "She was usually spoken of as being remarkably clever, but with the addition that her sister Celia had more common sense." Miss Brooke is so ascetic that she creates problems for herself; she imprisons herself in a sterile marriage to a priestly scholar. Her appearance points in the direction of the key conflict of the novel.

Eliot's description works like a painting, in which the surface details suggest character and mood. Sometimes the appearance of a character can indeed attain the quality of a good drawing, a cameo, as in the following example from "Patriotism," by the Japanese writer Yukio Mishima:

> For the beauty of the bride in her white over-robe no comparisons were adequate. In the eyes, round beneath soft brows, the slender, finely shaped nose, and in the full lips, there was both sensuousness and refinement. One hand, emerging shyly from a sleeve of the over-robe, held a fan, and the tips of the fingers, clustering delicately, were like the bud of a moonflower.

Notice how in the two above examples, the authors draw the hands more successfully than the faces. While hands are often more difficult than faces to render in paintings, in writing it's the reverse, because writing can capture motion and activity better than painting can. Hands can do more than faces can – unless we are mimes, and even with mimes, hands are at least as active as faces. In describing faces, it's easy to resort to smiles and frowns, and difficult to strike a fresh image. With hands, you can play with a large array of possibilities.

You can characterize someone even by his feet or his walk, as does Thomas Hardy in *The Mayor of Casterbridge*:

> His measured, springless walk was the walk of the skilled countryman as distinct from the desultory shamble of the general labourer; while in the turn and plant of each foot there was, further, a dogged and cynical indifference personal to himself.

No matter how you describe a character's appearance, your reader must be able to see it. If you rely on an adjective and give us little besides, you will probably fail to make us visualize anything. In his novel *The Citadel*, British author A.J. Cronin makes this mistake and gives us an example of what not to do:

> Late one October afternoon in the year 1921, a shabby young man gazed with fixed intensity through the window of a third-class compartment in the almost empty train labouring up the Penowell valley from Swansea.

This is the opening line from the novel. It accomplishes a lot in terms of setting, but the adjective *shabby* adds nothing. Judging from our being in a third-class compartment, we would get the notion of shabbiness anyhow, and *shabby* does not in any way give us the look of the man. *The Citadel* is an excellent novel, and it's good to see that not everything needs to be perfect for a novel to succeed. If you don't want to describe appearance, perhaps you can get away with it—but then don't pretend that you are depicting. Scratch out the *shabby*.

Scene

In a scene you set your character in motion. Especially if she's speaking, you can show us the character in action, without needing to summarize and generalize, although you may supplement the scene with a summary.

Christopher Isherwood in "Sally Bowls" draws a character portrait in a scene with dialogue:

> "Am I terribly late, Fritz darling?"
>
> "Only half or an hour, I suppose," Fritz drawled beaming with proprietary pleasure. "May I introduce Mr. Isherwood—Miss Bowls? Mr. Isherwood is commonly known as Chris."
>
> "I'm not," I said. "Fritz is about the only person who's ever called me Chris in my life."
>
> Sally laughed. She was dressed in black silk, with a small cape over her shoulders and a little cap like a page-boy's stuck jauntily on one side of her head:
>
> "Do you mind if I use your telephone, sweet?"
>
> "Sure. Go right ahead." Fritz caught my eye. "Come into the other room, Chris."
>
> "For heaven's sake, don't leave me alone with this

> man!" she exclaimed. "Or he'll seduce me down the telephone. He's most terribly passionate."
>
> As she dialed the number, I noticed that her fingernails were painted emerald green, a colour unfortunately chosen, for it called attention to her hands, which were much stained by cigarette-smoking and as dirty as a little girl's.

Here we meet the character through her voice, appearance, action, as though in a theater, and certainly, she is theatrical. She says, "He's most terribly passionate." This string of three adjectives is a kind of sophisticated excess that achieves a theatrical sound, as though we were listening to an ironic actor. Isherwood guides us to interpret the details, to see the little girl behind the sophisticated guise. The hands are as dirty as a little girl's. Emerald green for fingernail paint seems gaudy and excessive; in her attempt to appear sophisticated, she fails, but achieves a charm, especially through her flirtatious talk: "He'll seduce me down the telephone."

The advantage of introducing a character in a scene is that we hear the character's voice and diction, and we see the person. So when the narrator analyzes this character, he does not do it abstractly, but in conjunction with what we have seen and experienced. The scene combines appearance, action and dialogue; it's a highly versatile approach. The drawback is that you can't supply the background easily without stalling the scene.

Sometimes you can introduce a character through action, so we begin to see her without needing much dialogue, as does Bobbie Ann Mason in "Shiloh":

> Leroy Moffitt's wife, Norma Jean, is working on her pectorals. She lifts three-pound dumbbells to warm up, then progresses to a twenty-pound barbell. Standing with her legs apart, she reminds Leroy of Wonder Woman.
>
> "I'd give anything if I could just get these muscles to where they're real hard," says Norma Jean. "Feel this arm. It's not as hard as the other one."

The advantage of this method is that the reader is immediately with you, visualizing, experiencing a scene. You can show and suggest what you could have told us about—such as that Norma Jean is a fitness nut, a bodybuilder, a self-obsessed person. The scene implies all this information without completely committing such a blatant interpretation, so it's less judgmental than a summary to this effect would be. (This is most lifelike. We watch how people behave, we never see abstract qualities such as self-obsession—we merely see the signs, symptoms, which we interpret.) The author leaves the opportunity of judgment to the reader. Whenever you can, show character traits acted out in scenes. If you are interested in directly judging your characters, of course, rely on summaries and interpretations. (Judgment does have its virtues—it's abstract, possibly philosophical.)

The disadvantage to the scenic characterization method is that it's awkward to construct scenes that are outside of the main time frame of the story, unless you do flashbacks and memories. There's a limit to how many flashbacks you can handle without destroying the flow of the story. And there's a limit to how many things you can *show*, anyhow. Thus, although scenes are probably the most attractive method of characterization, you probably need to resort to summaries of relevant character deeds and inclinations outside of the story's time frame.

Combining Techniques

Most developed character descriptions combine two or more approaches. During the course of a novel, we see a character in the ways the author chooses for us. That, too, is lifelike—you hardly ever experience all the aspects of a friend right away. It takes time—different situations, communications, perceptions, and thoughts.

In Flannery O'Connor's "The Artificial Nigger," we see three approaches: habit, summary and appearance.

> The alarm on the clock did not work but he was not dependent on any mechanical means to awaken him. Sixty years had not dulled his responses; his physical re-

> actions, like his moral ones, were guided by his will and strong character, and these could be seen plainly in his features. He had a long tube-like face with a long rounded open jaw and a long depressed nose. His eyes were alert but quiet, and in the miraculous moonlight they had a look of composure and of ancient wisdom as if they belonged to one of the great guides of men.

"Strong character" is an abstract summary. "A long tube-like face" is a caricature, appearance. "He was not dependent on any mechanical means to awaken him" is a habit summary. These traits give us a quick synopsis of this man, which lead us into a scene, where we observe him in action.

> Mr. Head went to the stove and brought the meat to the table in the skillet. "It's no hurry," he said. "You'll get there soon enough and it's no guarantee you'll like it when you do neither."

Now we hear him talk. Later we'll see him talk and act at greater length, each time getting to know him better. O'Connor's approach is incremental.

Here's a portrait of a paranoid schizophrenic, drawn by summary of habits, appearance and psychology. In "Ward VI," Anton Chekhov portrays the character so gently that he undermines our trust in the diagnosis of madness; later in the story we begin to perceive Russian psychiatry as mad, so that the character is quite justified in feeling persecuted.

> Ivan Dmitrich Gromov . . . is always in a state of agitation and excitement, always under the strain of some vague undefined expectation. The slightest rustle in the entry or shout in the yard is enough to make him raise his head and listen: are they coming for him? Is it him they are looking for?
>
> I like his broad pale face with its high cheekbones. . . . His grimaces are queer and morbid, but the fine lines drawn on his face by deep and genuine suffering denote

> sensibility and culture, and there is a warm lucid gleam in his eyes. I like the man himself, always courteous, obliging, and extremely considerate in his treatment of everyone except Nikita. When anyone drops a button or a spoon, he leaps from his bed and picks it up.

I think this is an excellent pattern not only combining summary and scene, but also sympathy. Chekhov treats a type, a paranoid schizophrenic, with enough sympathy that the type no longer threatens to reduce the human qualities and complexities of Ivan's character. Ivan has become a person for us.

Gustave Flaubert portrays Madame Bovary in a succession of different approaches. Each time we meet her, we see a different aspect of her, in a new light, and in a new approach:

> [Brief Silent Scene] She made no comment. But as she sewed she pricked her fingers and then put them into her mouth to suck them. . . .
>
> [Silent Scene, Habit, Appearance] As the room was chilly, she shivered a little while eating. This caused her full lips to part slightly. She had a habit of biting them when she wasn't talking. . . .
>
> [Psychological Summary] Accustomed to the calm life, she turned away from it toward excitement. She loved the sea only for its storms, and greenery only when it was scattered among ruins. She needed to derive immediate gratification from things and rejected as useless everything that did not supply this satisfaction. Her temperament was more sentimental than artistic. She sought emotions and not landscapes.

And later, of course, Flaubert stages Madame Bovary, just as Isherwood does Sally Bowls.

I recommend this pattern of multiple approaches particularly for your main characters in a novel. If your character is complex enough, you might try all the approaches you can think of to understand who you are creating. Your readers will probably get involved, too, trying to understand with you. The trick is to be genuinely curious about the people populating your fiction.

EXERCISES

1. One page. Describe a remarkable person you admire—a teacher, minister, carpenter, doctor. What makes the person unique? Avoid sentimental statements (e.g., "I know Mother will always be there for me"). Can you make us see her? Hear her?

Objective: To create heroes from people you admire. Admiration for others is a writer's best friend (unlike self-admiration). As you admire a person, you naturally select traits and details that present the person in a heroic light. So you already know how to make heroes! With this capability, you are ready to become a fiction writer.

Check: Have you given us the person? If not, go back and show us your character struggling with a problem.

2. One page. Look in a mirror and describe who you see. If you have a scar, tell us briefly how you got it. If your nose is broken, recall how it happened. If you're wearing lipstick, tell us how you selected the color. Don't get carried away and begin to tell us stories—not yet. Come back to your face, mention other details, and describe them objectively.

Objective: To learn how to use bits of appearance as triggers for storytelling. Beginnings of stories are etched into many faces. The word *character* stems from the Greek word for a chiseled cut, an etching, a groove.

Check: Did you give us enough detail that we could begin to draw your portrait? We don't need to complete it on the page—let it be open enough for imagination to play—but we do need to have something we can visualize.

3. One page. Describe somebody's character by the shape, posture and gait of his body. Don't describe his head and don't tell

us that the character is lazy or happy. Show these traits through body language.

Objective: To learn how to look at evidence of character in the whole body, not just the face. The body expresses the mind. Take a look at Thomas Hardy's example on page 60. See how he builds meaning out of the man's walk. Perhaps he pushes the meaning his way—he knows what he wants us to see in the walk. Similarly, in Flaubert's example, Madame Bovary's sucking her thumb is obviously sensual. Don't be afraid to do likewise. Namely, be slightly subjective; interpret for us what we see; show us, even tell us, what psychology the body expresses.

Check: Do we see enough of the body's shape and motion? For a nervous patient in a hospital, did you mention his feet wrapped around a chair's leg like the emblem of medicine?

4. Five half-page exercises. Describe somebody's hands so that we get the idea that she is (a) nervous, (b) artistic, (c) rich (or poor) and (d) ill. Describe your hands at work. Review the examples from *Middlemarch*, "Patriotism" and "Rust" in this chapter.

Objective: To broaden the range of physical details you use when describing characters. Since what you can accomplish by describing noses and eyes may be too much strain on these organs, it's good to let the whole body do the work of developing the character. Just think of the skills you have in your fingers. Pay attention to appearance and motion.

Check: Are the hands expressing impulses? Can we see all you say? Rather than saying that the hands are nervous (graceful, sensual, determined and so on—adjectives that can rarely be visualized), do you give us a picture of a forefinger digging its bitten nail into the side of the thumb? (It's all right to say that hands are nervous, but show it too.)

5. Eight half-page exercises. Draw—in words—portraits of four striking people. First look into various faces to see whether any geometric shape, likeness of an animal, or other dominant trait emerges as an abstraction of the face. You can do this anywhere—on a train, in a bank line, in a bar, but don't blame me if you get a black eye in the process. Choose the most telling

lines. Is there one dominant word—*le mot juste*—that could bring the lines together? Try to achieve the efficiency of a caricature artist who draws a likeness of Brezhnev by sketching his overgrown eyebrows in several strokes and Mick Jagger by outlining his big lips.

Then portray four people by summarizing their behavior succinctly.

Objective: To learn how to select the most telling details, and how to compress behavior into a succinct summary.

Check: Have you singled out one trait in each sketch? (For example, if you've seen Senator Bob Dole on television, you've probably noticed how much he blinks—according to my study, at least fifty times per minute on the average. So you could caricature him as a blinker.) If you have five or six traits, cross out all but one.

6. Two to three pages. Create a character without relying on anybody you have known or seen. You might consult an astrological chart. (For example: The Sun in Aries is supposed to be egocentric, impulsive, solitary. Make the rising Sun be in Capricorn—ambitious, exhibitionistic, methodical. Do you see any conflict arising from combining the two signs?) Place this person in a social context, let's say, a cocktail party, and have him exchange several lines with the hostess. Let Sally Bowels from Isherwood's example on page 61 be the hostess.

Objective: To learn how to work from an idea, rather than from a real-life precedent, in making up a character.

Check: Have we gotten a sense of what this person is like? If not, insert a telling detail—such as in Exercise 5—and then place your fictional person in a social context with dialogue (like Sally Bowels).

7. Two to three pages. Write a comic scene in which a virtuous person struggles with one secret passion and resists the temptation. For example, make a kleptomaniac minister steal a pocket watch from a needy and sick parishioner—and then return it during the prayer for her.

Objective: To learn how to go straight for the conflict as the core of a fictional character.

Check: Did you you create an engaging scene? You might go back and concentrate on the minister's hands and words.

8. Two to three pages. Is there something in your past you are ashamed of? Make up a character different from you and let him deal with the conflict at the root of your shame. No doubt, you'll have a lot of energy behind this exercise; it should be easy to write as long as you forget that you are the starting point. Dostoyevski's *Notes From Underground* is a classic story done using this technique.

After you are finished, think of something in your past you are proud of. Make this a starting point for a character different from you, and write two to three more pages describing this character's triumph.

Objective: To learn how to create characters who are different from yourself, using the "fission method."

Check: Is your character alive? If not, let him move, speak, act. And let's see what he looks like. Besides giving us the general trait of the person, make the person concrete for us. Concentrate on several minute details—for instance, two red hairs sticking out of a mole, a quivering nostril, the sound of a snapping jaw, the smell of Dove soap.

9. Two pages. "Man is his desire," said Aristotle. Make a character desire something, and make the desire his driving force. Then through a scene or a summary create reasons why he can't have what he wants, ever. Let him try to get it at all costs anyway.

Objective: To draw a character around a flaw—an overwhelming desire—because that's the recipe for plot. Show the character persevering beyond reasonable limits.

Check: Have we gotten the sensation of desire? Make the object of desire desirable in our eyes—make us see from the character's perspective.

10. Two pages. "Man is his fear," to paraphrase Aristotle. Make a character fear something, and arrange her life as an

elaborate defense mechanism. You might show the house the character lives in, the clothes she wears, the car she drives, the animals she keeps, all centered around this leitmotif. For an example on how to use setting to portray character, go back to the previous chapter and look at Gogol's miser.

Objective: To learn how to select details around a psychological theme.

Check: Did you give enough details around the character to exhibit her fright? If she's scared of bullets, let her wear a bulletproof vest in the middle of a heat wave.

11. Present the character from Exercise 1 in four ways, half a page each. First make a summary of what the character is like; then show him through his looks, through a speech in a scene, and through combining several methods.

Objective: To learn how to present the same person in different ways because that's what you might need to do in a story.

Check: Does the character appear consistent in each description? Review on page 65 how Flaubert shows Madame Bovary as sense-oriented in each example.

12. One page. Portray a personality type, giving us the person with all her complexities. Use a mixed approach—a summary, a habit portrayal, and a brief scene.

Objective: To learn how to make a round character where it's easy to slip into stereotyping. Don't feel superior to your characters—if you despise them, your reader will be tempted to do likewise with your prose. "Nothing human is alien to me," said an ancient thinker. Whatever human beings do comes from something that you share with them—so try to step into the character's role imaginatively. Experience with the characters to understand them.

Check: Have you sympathized with your fictional character? Look at how Chekhov describes Ivan Gromov, the paranoid schizophrenic, earlier in this chapter. Chekhov's narrator even says, "I like him." If in your exercise you ridicule a type, or in any way sound aloof, rewrite it, using "I like him," and showing what you find likeable in the person.

CHAPTER FOUR

PLOT

Plot is the plan — the design — of your story. Or, to put it less architecturally and more organically: Plot is the nervous system of your story. In the same way that nerves connect your brain and muscles so you can move and live, plot interconnects and moves the elements of your story.

Of the journalist's six questions, plot answers as many as three: *what, how* and *why*. Plot is the key event of your story and the logic between the event and the supporting events, which serve to illuminate it. Plot establishes the causes and the consequences. Here is an example of a basic plot taken from "The Death of Ivan Ilych" by Leo Tolstoy: "Ivan Ilych's life had been most simple and most ordinary and therefore most terrible." The connection between the daily routine and terror, ultimately, death, organizes the story.

To establish this connection, Tolstoy relied on a traditional philosophy based on causes and effects. A plotted story usually depends on the connection between causes and effects (or at least a correlation among events) and on basic values to be treasured, such as life and love. Fyodor Dostoyevski could not have written his novel *Crime and Punishment* if his premise had been that human life is worthless, because what difference would it have made if Raskolnikov killed an old woman and got punished? Along these lines, playwright Harold Hayes says: "The essence of drama is that man cannot walk away from the consequences of his deeds."

Some modern and post-modern writers — accepting Werner

Karl Heisenberg's Principle of Uncertainty and doubting the theories of causality and of the linearity of time—have been incapable (or unwilling) to think up plots. Many writers work around plots—doing "experimental" fiction—because, supposedly, in our nuclear society it's not easy to find coherent logic in the events around us. However, the premise of meaninglessness should not warrant experiments, since the idea of experiment is based on the logic of cause and effect (or at least, of correlation between phenomena), trial and error, and learning from these meaningfully. Why experiment otherwise? So we need not look to philosophy to defend us against our basic obligation to organize our fiction coherently. Sure, it would be nice to say: Philosophers have dispensed with the dubious notions of causality and meaning; hence I can simply pile words on the page randomly, and that'll be high art. This might be an enjoyable way to write, but not to read. Since writing is an act of communicating—or at least a simulation of communication—we do need to make our words and events link coherently.

Plot clearly depends on basic values. What do your characters treasure most? Put it at stake. Let them fight for it. Let them fight for life, love, money, jobs. If your characters care about nothing, the actions around them might become random. Without passion, forget about plot. Even Albert Camus' *The Stranger*—in which a man is sentenced to death not so much because he committed murder as because he did not cry at his mother's funeral—would not work if it did not rely on a framework of expected passion, against which the character's indifference draws meaning.

I am not saying that you must believe in meanings of life and in moral values, but your characters, some of them, must. Fiction is like a medieval passion play. If you take away the prospect of crucifixion, the passion, then the play is gone. And passion is why most people read novels. Could romance survive without it? How about horror? Crime? Murder mystery? No murder mystery will work without a motive, the motive usually being some kind of passion.

To summarize (at the risk of oversimplifying): Plot depends on passions—on how characters struggle to fulfill them.

ORIGINS AND TYPES OF PLOT

Since we need not wait for the new experiments and findings in literature to write well-plotted stories, let's look into the tradition of plot. The concept of plot comes to us from Aristotle's analysis of drama, particularly tragedy: "The perfect plot . . . must have a single, and not (as some tell us) a double issue; the change in the hero's fortunes must be not from misery to happiness, but on the contrary from happiness to misery; and the cause of it must lie not in any depravity, but in some great error on his part; the man himself being either such as we have described, or better, not worse, than that."

So much for happy endings! Much serious fiction involves tragedy. Leo Tolstoy's *Anna Karenina* opens with "All happy families are alike, but each unhappy family is unhappy in its own way," and ends with Anna's suicide. Why should one write such depressing stuff? I think it's the nature of thought to deal with problems, with something amiss that can be—and may not be—straightened out and solved. If there are no problems, there is no thought. A mathematician without problems is idle, and so is a writer. Since most plots evolve largely from the main character's motivation, it's most efficient to place the problem in the main character, to give her the error that she must struggle to solve.

From Aristotle's idea of a person's flaw being the most efficient agent of plot (see chapter three), you see how tightly character and plot are intertwined. A person's flaw brings about problems and conflicts. Karenina's falling in love outside her tedious marriage as an uncontrollable error brings her in conflict with her husband, children and herself—enough problems ensue to fill seven hundred pages. Working from character is perhaps the most prevalent way of evolving a plot, as it is for Norman Mailer, who says: "Generally, I don't even have a plot. What happens is that my characters engage in an action, and out of that action little bits of plot sometimes adhere to the narrative." Mailer gives his characters problems. Without a character flaw, the character can hardly be rounded and interesting, in the sense that there's nothing to worry about and solve when we deal with him. A perfect character is a dead equation, as far as fiction is concerned.

Of course, having serious problems does not mean that all will end unhappily. If the outcome were so predictable, suspense would be lost. We need not share Aristotle's Balkan predilection for tragedy. Happy endings after a serious (or a silly) struggle are possible but certainly should not be the rule—especially not in the realistic novels that span a lifetime. Life ends in death; so unhappy endings are a natural tendency in much realistic fiction. (In most fiction written from fantastic, religious and stoical premises, there's not much tendency toward unhappy endings.)

But realistic fiction that deals with families (rather than only individuals) may naturally tend toward a happy ending. Life may end in the death of one person but it goes on in the birth of many: So perhaps the most comprehensive paradigm of true-to-life plot could be that of Jacob and his family. When he dies, he dies happily because eleven sturdy sons with grandsons are at his side.

How you solve your character's problems and errors, of course, should conform to no formula, except, I'd say, don't make it predictable. Make the struggle genuine and fair, with equal chances for failure and success. Although your world view (and your characters' world views) will largely shape the tenor of your fiction, do respect this necessary principle of the uncertainty of outcome.

Character Conflict Plots

There are several basic plots that are based on character conflict. The conflict most often takes place between a *protagonist* (the character we sympathize with and root for) and an *antagonist* (the protagonist's opponent). These are the plots:

Man Against Man (we should perhaps say Person
Against Person, but it would sound odd, since
this old list is famous in this shape)
Man Against Self
Man Against Nature
Man Against Society
Man Against Machine

Man Against God
God Against Everybody

Most fiction falls into these categories of "against"—that is, they are based on conflict. There are exceptions: for example, Ivan Turgenev's *Sketches From a Hunter's Album*—but the "sketches" can be seen as essays on hunting in the country. Even so, they are Man against Nature (at least the hunted grouse would probably think so). If this seems depressing, try putting *for* in place of *against*, and you will see that by implication there still will be an *against*. Man for Man could take place in the midst of a war, in which case Man would be against Society, the foreign and perhaps even the domestic army. Man for Nature might turn out to be Man against Machine and Man against Corporate Society.

You don't need much to make up a plot. Work from a conflict. The conflict suggests escalation of struggle into a climax—so follow the potential for a story that the conflict suggests. Once you know what happens in your story, you can organize the rest. If you have a clear conflict between two or preferably three or more characters, everything else will follow—even the beginning! You introduce the fight—and to make it intelligible, you introduce the fighters and the ring. Conflict may take the shape of a quarrel, a fight or a war—depending on the magnitude of action and reaction. A quarrel that precipitates a divorce may be more important to the protagonists than the Vietnam War taking place at the same time. Most strong conflicts—from the protagonists' point of view—resemble war. War is a useful metaphor for analyzing action in a story. In a war there usually is a contested territory—the Golan Heights, Nagorno-Karabakh, Sarajevo Airport. If you can manage to clearly define the contested territory in a story, you will have a powerful focus, out of which the story may flow with surprising ease. For example, conservative parents battle their liberal and impoverished daughter who wants an abortion. Clearly, the battle is localized on the uterus of the young woman, and to write the story, we must put the family together and let them fight. In terms of the simple chart of Man against Man and so on, this plot would become Woman against Society, Woman against Woman (Daughter against Mother), and in the long run, perhaps at the crisis point, it would boil down to Self against Self, if the woman gets to choose. No matter what other forms a conflict assumes, in most fiction the conflict will entail Self against Self, since the motivation that moves the struggle is usually internal, a part of the character's psyche.

Lest you think that plots are a grim business, I'd like to point out that the word origin for protagonist and antagonist comes from the Greek *agonia*, meaning "competitive play." So no matter what agony of plot you go through, remember, it's just a game.

Nonconfrontational Plots

If you still don't like any kind of *agonia*, no matter how playful, there are ways of writing nonconfrontational plots. One model is the ultrarealist (and sometimes surrealist) *slice of life*. Your plot is governed by the details and chores of a day—or an hour—of a character's life. You show what it's like to wake up in the character's apartment, walk down a street outside it, visit a bakery, drive to work and chat with colleagues. All that traditionally is the periphery of the story—the realistic details—becomes the center of the story; and the various confrontations and conflicts become the periphery. "Yeah, sure, I am going to jail in a month, but that's just a vague idea of something in the future, which at the moment recedes in the steam of coffee." If you understand your world like this, that the details around you are more important than the "events," this may be the type of plot—antiplot, really—for you to play with. In a story like this, scrupulous attention to setting is an absolute must.

Another model for a nonconfrontational story centers around *revelation* or *epiphany*. The story comes to a moment in which the protagonist has a personal insight. James Joyce used this theological concept for his stories. Consider, for example, the ending of his story "The Dead" (see chapter two). After learning that his wife has loved someone more deeply than he has loved anybody and while staring into the falling snow, Gabriel experiences an epiphany about his mortality. (There are confrontations in the story, but they pale once the epiphany takes place.) All the story's events accumulate toward this moment, literally, like snow, through which he now sees himself as though for the first time. (In the old paradigm of conflicts, the story sets out to be Man against Woman, but the man realizes that the conflict is deeper than that, and for a moment the drama centers around Self against Self, until he realizes that even this does not suffice. The epiphany about mortality transcends conflicts.)

Revelation could take place within a struggle, but revelation may be more important than the struggle. Here's a moment of such a revelation from Mary Gaitskill's "The Girl on the Plane." A man and a woman talk. The woman confesses her alcoholism. He's attracted to her and thinks he will reveal nothing about himself, will be casual. But this is what happens:

> "And about that relationship," he went on. "That wasn't your loss. It was his." He had meant these words to sound light and playfully gallant, but they had the awful intensity of a maudlin personal confession. He reached out to gently pat her hand to reassure her that he wasn't a nut, but instead he grabbed it and held it. "If you want to talk about mistakes—shit, I raped somebody. Somebody I liked."
>
> Their gazes met in a conflagration of reaction. She was so close he could smell her sweating, but at the speed of light she was falling away, deep into herself where he couldn't follow.

The man had participated in a gang rape, and though he saw himself as an onlooker rather than a participant, this revelation emerges and startles him. It also shuts down the communication with the woman next to him. It could be seen as a Man against Woman story, or a Man against Self—there are elements of both—but mostly it's a story of epiphany, of revelation about oneself. The man has met himself, his past, in a new way.

Epiphany should not be confused with a trick ending. For example, if you write a story in which a young woman looks forward to getting together with a man, giving this the appearance of a date, and then, in the last line of the story, it turns out that the man is Dad—and that's the whole point—you are not making an epiphany. The main character knew it all along, and the writer chose to hide this information to surprise us later. Now, this may be charming, but it's cheap. The character must come upon some genuine discovery.

Journey, as a form of nonconfrontational plot, may combine well with epiphany. For example, Dante's *Divine Comedy* is set up as a series of journeys that lead to insights about heaven, purgatory and hell. And a current example: Diane Johnson in "Great Barrier Reef" sets a man and a woman, who think they may be in love, on a journey to the Reef off the coast of Australia. The woman sulks throughout the journey, resentful that she is not enjoying herself, that she is stuck in a group of fat and aging Australians. When she arrives at the Reef, she undergoes something close to a vision.

> He was as dazzled as if we had walked on stars, and, indeed, the sun shining on the tentacles, wet petals, filling the spongy holes, made things sparkle like a strange underfoot galaxy. He appeared as a long, sandy-haired, handsome stranger, separate, unknowable. I, losing myself once more in the patterns and colors, thought of nothing, was myself as formless and uncaring as the coral, all my unruly, bad-natured passions leaching harmlessly into the sea, leaving a warm sensation of blankness and ease. . . . For me, the equivalent of J.'s happiness was this sense of being cured of a poisoned spirit.

Seeing the man as distant, she realizes that they will never marry, but at the same time, the beauty of the setting calms her and gives her something that's much more essential to her than marriage—a sense of herself as a part of nature rather than apart from nature. Afterward she behaves spontaneously and has fun.

Diane Johnson, who took the same trip as her protagonist, says about the story: "It seems to me that the Great Barrier Reef was a good metaphor for the condition of every traveler, barred from understanding the mind and customs of other peoples and places by the ideas and emotions she brings with her."

Journey gives you a natural motion for your story, for your plot. Setting here may be even more essential than the characters, and it certainly gives you chances to paint and reveal to us something verging on the transcendental, as you expand the psychological limits beyond the personal.

One of the oldest types of story, the story of *creation*, need not be confrontational. In forming a sculpture or composing a symphony or inventing a light bulb nothing needs to be an enemy. That's not to say there is no challenge, but it's the challenge of knowledge and skill, not of defeating someone, except one's own lack of faith.

Combination Plots

Many stories combine elements of nonconfrontational and confrontational plot. *Situational story* or *story of predicament* almost always does—in Franz Kafka's "The Metamorphosis," for example: "As Gregor Samsa awoke one morning from uneasy dreams he found himself transformed in his bed into a gigantic insect." Something strange has happened; this is not primarily a struggle of Man against Himself or Society, though it may become that later on. The story evolves mostly as a puzzle. Aristotle said, "Wonder is the beginning of philosophy." He could have equally well said, "Wonder is the beginning of story." How do you reconcile this, a man in an insect's body? Clearly you must straighten out something here, and the stranger the predicament, the more you must do. You must give us realistic details, to begin with, so we'll accept the strangeness. The difference between how things are and how they ought to be gives you the potential, the voltage, for the energy of your story.

Here's another predicament, from Peter Taylor's "The Old Forest":

> I was already formally engaged, as we used to say, to the girl I was going to marry. But still I sometimes went out on the town with girls of a different sort. And during the very week before the date set for the wedding, in

> December, I was in an automobile accident at a time when one of those girls was with me. It was a calamitous thing to have happen—not the accident itself, which caused no serious injury to anyone, but the accident plus the presence of that girl.

When you read this, you wonder how this guy got into the soup he's in and even more, how he'll get out of it. Out of this predicament, Taylor raises many questions—the story becomes a study of Southern morals and manners. The straightening out of the initial distortion drives the story forward. Eventually some conflicts are established, but at first what's important is the wonder; and in the end, the insights and epiphanies matter more than the conflicts.

TIME SEQUENCE AND PLOT

For structuring and plotting a piece of fiction, timing is one of the most important elements. Fiction, like music, is a temporal art. How the time passes during the reading of the novel shapes the fictional experience. A symphony classically opens with allegro, a fast movement. Andante or adagio, a slow movement (usually lyrical and thoughtful) follows, before two fast movements of varying speeds. Likewise, from the start, a piece of fiction should move quickly, and when it decelerates, it should become lyrical and thoughtful, as do many novels in quiet moments. A slow movement without lyricism and thought is untenable, as is a quick movement without an orchestrated rush of action. Vary your narrative speed, especially in long pieces. As you reach the climax you can linger on details (and render a confrontational dialogue, if the plot warrants it)—that is, develop scenes and achieve the dramatic slow-motion effect, amid the otherwise quickly paced evolution of drama. Each story may follow its own pattern of fast and slow movements; I don't want to push any bell curves of excitement, but your story does need to reach a crescendo sooner or later. (Development of climax scenes is covered further in chapter six.)

How your story is organized depends on the sequence of

events. In most cases it's best to handle time sequences in the simplest way possible. The clearest way to deal with time is to follow an action from beginning to end. Many eighteenth- and nineteenth-century biographical novels open with the birth of a character and end in his death, and many contemporary biographical novels cover a good chunk of a character's life. (Short stories rarely can cover so much time successfully—a development taking place from a couple of minutes to a year or two seems to be the usual span of the short story.) Likewise, you can start a story with the beginning of a conflict and end with its resolution. Since this structure is often too slow, writers frequently jump into the middle of the story's conflict and work from there, forward, occasionally supplying—as briefly and unobtrusively as possible—the necessary background information, without stalling the forward movement of time. (Which means, if you need to go back in time, it's usually best to summarize a past action and move on, rather than to dramatize the past action as a developed flashback and get stuck in the past for pages.)

However, you might open at the end of an action (to show the reader what the purpose of the narrative will be), and then trace the beginnings of the event in your second chapter. This is how "The Death of Ivan Ilych" works. We are introduced to the dead man in the first chapter. In the following chapters we start with his family background, his youth, and trace his biography efficiently, toward his mishap and disease and dying. Other than the lead, the story evolves in a linear fashion, from A to Y—from the earliest event up to the death, which precedes the wake (Z). We could delineate the chronology as Z, A-Y. The Z in the beginning gives us a reason to find out the rest. This is realistic—if you've been to funerals, you immediately recognize this as a paradigm of a death story. How did he die? When? What kind of man was he?

Murder mysteries, too, have justifiably nonlinear time sequences. We start with the discovery of a body—for example, a corpse in a phone booth in a lobby of a Wall Street law firm. As the investigation moves forward, timewise, with the new events, we also move backward, timewise, learning about the dead character's life and getting clues as to who the murderer is. We reconstruct the events leading to the murder from A to Y (Z is the premise for the investigation).

Much good fiction, however, attains the quality of "one-thing-led-to-another-and-before-you-knew-it. . . ." This seeming inevitability, one thing leading to another, can be best attained in a clean time sequence. The thing that leads to another should precede that other. This is basic for achieving urgency and suspense. Suspense depends on the question, "What will happen next?" There are exceptions, of course, such as finding out a surprising fact about the past, but this revelation works best within a steady stream of investigation moving forward.

Setting events in a straightforward time sequence may appear old-fashioned, but it can be a sophisticated discipline. When you don't want to commit yourself to knowing causes and consequences, you might still establish correlations between events—temporal and spatial sequences of what happens in your story—as though you were conducting a scientific study, where without stating that A causes B, it's enough to establish that A correlates with B. For example, instead of saying that the sun causes warmth in a stone, we can say: "The sun shone on a stone, and then the stone became warm," as does British philosopher David Hume. Here the two events—sun shining and stone becoming warm—are put into a temporal rather than a causal sequence. This method of making clear temporal relations lets the reader draw inferences and conclusions for herself. Whenever you can, out of consideration for your reader, use clean time sequences; they are easiest to follow and they speak for themselves.

HOW TO GENERATE PLOTS

The solutions for generating plots will partly overlap with what we covered in previous chapters. The primary generators of plots are character and setting—but sometimes a strange situation can give you that initial impetus. Learn from Franz Kafka's "The Metamorphosis" and Peter Taylor's "The Old Forest" (see page 79) about how to create plots from predicaments. Make up a strange situation and ask, "Why and how is it possible?"

If the idea of plot still intimidates you, and if you don't come up with plots before beginning to write your novel, don't be nervous. You can still write novels. In a *Paris Review* interview, Nelson Algren said, "I've always figured the only way I could finish a book and get a plot was just to keep making it longer and longer until something happens . . . you know, until it finds its own plot . . . because you can't outline and then fit the thing into it. I suppose it's a slow way of working."

You are lucky if you can spontaneously outline plots, but if you can't, get them somewhere. Steal them. Shakespeare stole them from Plutarch's *Lives*. Dostoyevski plundered newspapers.

You can find plots anywhere. Here's an example: I got a plot from a Baptist tract, in which self-abuse was likened to a hawk who flies high, gradually loses altitude, and crashes. When you find the body, you see a weasel's canines lodged in the hawk's breast. Instead of losing altitude, a boy who practices self-abuse loses good posture and grows blind. To make this fable feasible, I imagined myself as a boy with a pet hawk. After I read a book about hawks, the story—that is, the related details—came out easily. Trying to imagine how a hawk limited to an attic would feel, I chose freedom as the central theme of the story. I think that theme helped me bring the basic plot outline to life, because then I could generate and organize details to express the theme. Here's an example from the story:

> Yahbo flew the length of the attic and smashed into the glass window. He fell to the floor, stood up, flew back to the opposite end of the attic, vanishing in darkness under red roof tiles; and, in a couple of minutes, he flew again, pointing his body straight to pass through the space between wood laths. He crashed down again, to the sandy floor. Slowly he stood up and hopped to the window ledge, flapping his wings, scraping them against the raw bricks of the wall. Bewildered, he stood precariously on the ledge, his beak open and uttering no sound. A white film drew over his eyes and slowly peeled back into his head, his hazel eyes widening and glowing with wrath. Perhaps he could not understand what kind of air it was which did not let you out but showed you the wonders

> of your emerald homeland. He faced east like a Muslim facing toward Mecca, or like a Jew toward Jerusalem; for him the glass was an invisible wall of wailing.

The idea of freedom gave me the basic motivation. The hawk wants to fly home. But he has an obstacle. I made the boy's experience the same: frustrated longing for freedom. With the theme and the motivation, I brought many details together in a unified story.

You can create a plot by using a trick. Art Corriveau used an interesting trick to write his story "With Mirrors" (in *Story* magazine, Fall 1993). At night he tranfers odd fragments written during the day into a shoebox. One night these fragments led to a story: "I decided to draft a story from the first three slips of paper I pulled from the box. Slip number one: . . . 'Montreal is a weird place; write a story set there.' Slip number two was from last summer in Boston: 'What's up with the blond guy outside Park Plaza? Nods whenever you pass by. Is he a hustler or just friendly?' Slip number three: . . . 'Write about a room in a magician's house where you disappear when you walk into it.' "

He says the story was easy to write from this setup. The story opens as follows:

> When Zastrow says he can't pay me this time but he'll teach me a few tricks instead, I tell him sorry but I left the farm too many years ago. I tell him he'd better try one of the boys a little farther up the block.

Note that his first card gives setting (actually, only mentions it); second, character; third, bits of setting, character and plot. We have a question here: "What does this character want?" To answer it, Corriveau unleashes a magician, whom he makes gay, so that the basic motivating force of the story—want—could propel the action. The magician wants sex but can offer magic rather than money; the blond hustler wants money, and would prefer to be with women, but can't get out of his economic bondage; he "disappears" in the magician's room.

Some people use this trick of cards quite systematically. They keep one pile of cards with brief character sketches, another with brief setting sketches, and a third with brief action sketches. They draw a card from each pile, put them together, and see if a story begins to suggest itself—then repeat this process until the cards seem right. Thus you make connections among different possibilities for setting, character and action. How you connect these elements will make your plot. That's how imagination works: You create many permutations and select the most effective ones. This card method, even if you don't employ it physically, could liberate your imagination. Use the method's logic. Make many random connections until you can make sense of one of them. In this way you avoid the most obvious connection—the right person at the right place at the right time doing the right thing. Many plots work best with at least one "wrong" element: the right person at the right place at the wrong time. And you can make permutations even out of this, making a "wrong" choice in any of the four places. This "wrong" might turn out to be right for the energy of your story as you try to fit it in.

Another way to find plots is to parody existing ones. Your plot becomes a variation on a theme, a completely legitimate way to compose music and certainly to write stories. For an example of a western parody, here's a segment from Stephen Crane's "The Bride Comes to Yellow Sky":

> Potter was about to raise a finger to point the first appearance of the new home when, as they circled the corner, they came face to face with a man in a maroon-colored shirt who was feverishly pushing cartridges into a large revolver. Upon the instant the man dropped this revolver to the ground, and, like lightning, whipped another from its holster. The second weapon was aimed at the bridegroom's chest. . . .
>
> The two men faced each other at a distance of three paces. He of the revolver smiled with a new and quiet ferocity. "Tried to sneak up on me," he said. "Tried to sneak up on me! . . . The time has come for me to settle with you, and I'm goin' to do it my own way and loaf along with no interferin'. So if you don't want a gun bent

> on you, just mind what I tell you."
>
> Potter looked at his enemy. "I ain't got a gun on me, Scratchy," he said. "Honest, I ain't. . . . You know I fight when it comes to fighting, Scratchy Wilson, but I ain't got a gun on me. You'll have to do all the shootin' yourself."
>
> His enemy's face went livid. He stepped forward and lashed his weapon to and fro before Potter's chest. "Don't you tell me you ain't got no gun on you, you whelp. Don't tell me no lie like that. There ain't a man in Texas ever seen you without no gun. Don't take me for no kid." His eyes blazed with light, and his throat worked like a pump.
>
> "I ain't takin' you for no kid," answered Potter. His heels had not moved an inch backward. "I'm takin' you for a—fool. I tell you I ain't got a gun, and I ain't. If you're goin' to shoot me up, you better begin now. You'll never get a chance like this again."
>
> So much enforced reasoning had told on Wilson's rage. He was calmer. "If you ain't got a gun, why ain't you got a gun?" he sneered. "Been to Sunday-school?"
>
> "I ain't got a gun because I've just come from San Anton' with my wife. I'm married," said Potter.
>
> "Married!" said Scratchy, not at all comprehending.
>
> "Yes, married. I'm married," said Potter distinctly.
>
> "Married?" said Scratchy. Seemingly for the first time he saw the drooping drowning woman at the other man's side. "No!" he said. He was like a creature allowed a glimpse of another world. He moved a pace backward, and his arm with the revolver dropped to his side. . . .

Crane clearly parodies the conventions of westerns—the sheriff and his antagonist, tough talk, gun drawing and so on. Though the story is comic, Crane manages to make it serious too by introducing a complication. The sheriff has gotten married. You can parody any type of genre story, and throw in a new element. While you have fun playing with the genre, poking a bit of fun at it, you might still make it a serious story as Crane does. The marriage "deconstructs" the stereotypical western situation. Stripped of the predictable model, Scratchy is at a loss, out of genre, and you can sympathize with him.

Almost anything is worth trying out in constructing a plot. A friend of mine is writing a series of stories based on television commercials. Some things will work, others won't. Experiment. Sketch many preliminary drafts for your fiction, and use the ones that promise to work. Only a few ideas need to work to keep you busy for a year or longer. One way of testing whether an idea for a story (or a novel) will work is to begin with a big moment—a crisis scene—and decide whether or not your characters can carry on a good fight and an engaging conversation.

PLOT AS GUIDE FOR THE FINAL DRAFT

For some writers, the notion of plot is more important in revising a story than in drafting it. Plot demands that all the parts of your story are coherent in relation to the main event. This is the "Chekhov's gun" principle: If you display a gun in the first act, you better use it before the curtain falls. (Of course, sometimes you may use a gun for atmospheric purposes such as when you portray a police station or a western town. But if you continually display a gun, it must figure in a key event; otherwise, it will count as a loose end—and loose ends do not advance the action.)

So go through your story and make sure that whatever objects you display prominently serve their purpose. Let these objects appear again, to connect the earlier scene with the later ones, or use your guns in an action. The same holds true for characters: If you introduce one in the beginning, presumably she'll reappear later and play a role. You may use characters as a part of the setting and for no other purpose, especially in travel stories, but that can lead to a loose structure. Novels have more room for such luxurious usage of objects and characters, but even there it's healthy to put your players to the best use.

NOVEL PLOT VS. SHORT STORY PLOT

There's no strict border between the short story and the novel, though it's safe to say that a manuscript longer than two hundred double-spaced pages is a novel. A manuscript shorter than fifty pages is a short story. Whatever falls in between could be called a *novella*, although many people prefer to call a manuscript between fifty and a hundred pages a *novelette*.

Novel comes from Italian for "the news." Novella, "little news." Novelette, "tiny news." I think it's useful to keep in mind the etymology of these words. When you write a novel, inform us, tell us as though reporting the news. Offer big news, with many complexities, witnesses, participants. For a novelette, perhaps gossip is a good enough model.

Story comes from the Greek word for "history" (*'istoria*), meaning both story and investigation, and later from French *histoire*, an account of an event. These words might remind us that a short story is best told as an event thoroughly investigated and accounted for. The short story invites concentration on a singular event and its background; a novel disperses attention to a series of events, in the way, for example, that war reporting does, when it searches for an overarching coherence. (There are many exceptions, so it's not crucial that you follow this plan.)

The magnitude and number of events can determine the length and therefore the category of your story. A short story can be constructed around a moment of revelation, around a singular event, around one character. For novels we usually need several events and several characters, and frequently several turning points and revelations.

Still, there is no simple rule here. Some short stories have plots that could be used in novels. Thomas Mann wrote a short story, "Felix Krull"—which outlined the life of a man—and then made a novel out of it. This is a biographical plot—it follows a good part of a man's life starting from childhood. That Mann chose to span a long time helped him to make a long piece of writing. On the other hand, James Joyce's long novel *Ulysses* simulates a man's perceptions during a single day. Joyce stretches the story through his investigation of how the mind works—he covers free associations, daydreams, memories; all the minor actions of a day take on the proportion of significant events.

The idea of writing a novel may be terrifying and inhibiting. It was for me. So I tricked myself into believing that I was writing short stories rather than a novel. I made each chapter of the novel into a short story. I linked the short stories through setting and characters and overarching events. Once I had enough for half the novel, I no longer feared the size of the form. In fact, I used the notion of the novel to liberate me from another anxiety. In a short story, most elements must connect—you mustn't have obvious loose ends. In the novel, you need not worry about this as much. Ideally you should connect the narrative elements, but since nobody can remember all the details, the question of their interconnectedness will not be held against you. (And when you make connections in a novel, you'll get credit for the endurance of your own attention span.) So, once I accepted that I was writing a novel, I could allow my chapters loose ends and plan to connect them several hundred pages later (accumulating perhaps a tension of expectations regarding whether the connections would take place). If I forgot to connect everything, the reader would probably forget to worry about it too, as long as I made most of the connections. I did not need to write perfect endings (the hardest part of the short story) in the sense that everything would fit neatly. Not having to worry about perfect coherence—because there's hardly ever such a thing—made writing the novel easier for me than writing short stories. Of course, you still must integrate a great many details. I guess what makes it easier in the novel is that you have more time and more opportunities to do so.

Still, many short story writers ask, "How do you make a narrative that long?" "Well," I ask, "how do children grow? They eat many slices of bread." A novel routinely eats many slices of life to fatten up and grow longer, but more important, to make us as readers get to know the characters, settings and plots—the unsummarizable aspect of plots: the intricacies of perceptions and motivations.

PLOT VS. PLOT OUTLINE

I have used the word *plot* in the broad sense: to mean a story plan. But some writers think that plot cannot be separated from the story and still be plot. To use the example of the nervous system with which we began this chapter—you can't have nerves functioning outside the body. Notice how Vladimir Nabokov plays with the notion of separateness of plot in *Laughter in the Dark*:

> Once upon a time there lived in Berlin, Germany, a man called Abinus. He was rich, respectable, happy; one day he abandoned his wife for the sake of a youthful mistress; he loved; was not loved; and his life ended as disaster.
>
> This is the whole of the story and we might have left it at that had there not been profit and pleasure in the telling.

Nabokov plays a gambit opening: He shows us the plot right away, giving up suspense that might come from one aspect of plot, that is, from the uncertainty as to what will happen. Yet, the novel is as suspenseful as a thriller. Perhaps Nabokov wanted to show that the plot is not the driving force of a story. In this summary of the novel, however, Nabokov does not give us the full plot. We have one explanation: The man left his wife because of a young mistress. As I read I knew what would happen, and why it would, but I did not know how—and the drama took place mostly in the how, in the details of seduction and deception, which Nabokov handled with marvelous descriptive skill. Nor did I know fully why the man would leave his wife for a younger mistress. Many men fall in love with a younger mistress yet do not leave their wives. To give all the psychological motivation, which causes action, you must show the man's way of thinking, feeling, perceiving—through details. And exploring the motivation takes much more than a paragraph, probably most of the novel. Plot and story are not two separate entities. Nabokov shows that plot cannot be properly summarized and still be plot; it becomes a plot outline.

I used to find myself in this predicament: I have a "plot," I write it down, and then I say, "So what?" The story has not come to life; I failed to generate the details, the scenes. I thought too much in terms of plot outline rather than in terms of character and place and event. Sometimes students ask me, "What do you think of this story?" And they proceed to tell me a plot outline.

I tell them I'd be able to say what I thought only after I read the plot outline developed in a drafted story. The plot outline is like a game plan in basketball or football. It can look good on a chart, but once the ball flies, it does not suffice. You must have the players. If a player trips, other players may have to come up with a new plan. The plan is not sacred: it shifts, depending on the position of the players on the field and on the flight of the ball in the wind.

Although plot outline is not the same as plot, it's good to have a guide as you go through all the story details. Image-making is a forest in which you can easily get lost unless you have a map and compass—an outline. Some people don't work from outlines, yet they conceive plots because they have interconnected their characters, places and events.

If you don't write from an outline, once you have finished a story, you still should be able to see its outline, the way after a touchdown it's easy to draw a chart of what happened in the play. Something must happen, and in the end, we must know why it has happened. Plot is partly what you discover in the writing of a story, not what you "insert." You raise questions and seek answers, connect your sentences into paragraphs, paragraphs into chapters, chapters into novels. This thread of investigation may be a thin one, but you must have it to give yourself and your readers something to look for.

Keep in mind that though you may write happily without a plot, the reader may not enjoy reading a plotless story.

EXERCISES

1. Two to three pages. Outline a story from the example on page 75 of the parents who don't want their pregnant teenage daughter to have an abortion. Briefly sketch the daughter first, then her parents. Out of the conflict, brainstorm several possibilities, and select three possible outcomes. For example, this conflict could become a Woman against Society plot, Woman against Woman (mother) or Woman against Self. If you continue to write

the story, you will, of course, narrow the selection to one outcome, but it still may contain the three lines of conflict.

Objective: To practice exploring the possibilities of a conflict. From one basic conflict, you can derive several plots. Recognize your best possible plot from the sketches.

Check: Did you let the plot work as cause and effect? Characters and their conflicting desires are the cause. Have you found the right effects? Do your outcomes follow smoothly and reasonably from the characters in the conflict?

2. No more than three pages. Imagine a strange situation that begs to be explained. Instead of explaining it, plot a story about it. For example, an investment banker—before making a deal that would earn him two million dollars in commissions—cancels his engagement to a supermodel, joins a Benedictine monastery, and takes a vow of poverty, chastity and obedience. The story would investigate why the banker made this decision.

Objective: To learn how to work from wonder. Make your stories puzzles, more for yourself than for your reader. This will make you ask the most relevant questions related to the plot: Why? How?

Check: Have you offered a plausible solution to the puzzle? Have you given your protagonist sufficient motivation for his actions? "He just felt like doing it!" won't do, since it does not offer a genuine explanation. Let's first learn how to write a coherently plotted story; arbitrariness is easy—no need to learn how to do it. But to make connections among different events, so they work like logical arguments, requires thought and trial and error.

3. Three pages. "Ivan Ilych's life had been most simple and most ordinary and therefore most terrible." Using this summary statement from Tolstoy's "The Death of Ivan Ilych" as a model but using a different character, in an American town, write the crisis point of the story, a scene in which your character discovers that he's ill.

Objective: To learn how to make connections between one

part of a story and another—somebody's lifestyle and its consequences.

Check: In Tolstoy's story, because Ilych leads an empty life, he pays attention to surface details too much. He fusses around the house so much, making sure the furniture looks perfect, that he trips and injures his kidneys, it turns out, fatally. Does your scene have a similar connection between the lifestyle and illness so that the illness is not a pure accident but a consequence?

4. Two to three pages. Write a parody of a western story climax, preferably a duel. Take a look at what Stephen Crane does in "The Bride Comes to Yellow Sky." Recall the plot of a western story or movie and parody it. Exaggerate and make fun of the elements.

Objective: To practice writing parodies. When we write, sometimes we unconsciously imitate and parody the forms of stories we are familiar with. There's nothing wrong with that, but for a change, do it consciously. This way you gain distance and an overview of what the genre is about. And this also can become a conscious technique for irony. Some of the best literature has been written this way. Cervantes wrote *Don Quixote* as a parody of chivalric lore.

Check: Did you include enough elements of a traditional western? Have you added an untraditional element, as Crane does with the wedding?

5. Two to three pages. Recall the plot of the last romance novel you read. (If you don't read romances, use a murder mystery.) Outline it. Is the plot novelistic? How many important events occur, how many characters are involved, how much time elapses? Could the novel be reduced to a short story? Try to write the climax of the story, parodying the original, and introducing an untraditional element.

Objective: Same as in Exercise 4.

Check: Similar to Exercise 4. Make sure you've used enough traditional elements of the genre.

6. Three pages. Plot three variations of a realistic short story, one page each, starting with a character's conflict in a setting.

From the same conflict, think up three different resolutions. In each case make an honest effort to create a good story outline.

Objective: To learn how to express what happens in a story succinctly and simply. Something must happen in the story, and it must be clear. If you start with a character, make the character want something that makes sense given the setting. Frustrate the desire, and see where you can go from there to satisfy it. For example, Gogol's "Overcoat" opens with a clerk's wanting a warm coat because a St. Petersburg winter is approaching and his old coat is falling apart. The character's desires work with the setting.

Check: Have you set up the conflict clearly? Do we know why your character wants whatever he wants, and does this make sense in the setting you've chosen? Is it clear what results could evolve from this conflict? Now read what you've done and choose the best outline. (Could you write a full story from this? Try when you have enough time, outside of this course.)

7. Four pages. Outline the plots of two of your favorite novels and two of your favorite short stories, centered around the traditional scheme of conflicts (Woman against Woman, Woman against Society and so on).

Objective: To learn how to summarize the plots of the stories you write—or are about to write. Learning how to summarize the plots of novels you've read may make this easier. You may change the summary once you're into the story, but it's certainly good to have some kind of plan.

Check: In each story summary, did you explain why the main event happens? For each novel summary, did you have at least three major characters and three major events? (Some novels have fewer than three characters, but these are exceptions.) What are the main conflicts in the novels?

8. Three pages. Write a journey story that climaxes in a life-altering insight. Recall a journey you've taken and use yourself as your fictional persona. Make the story autobiographical and topographical. If you haven't experienced a big realization on a journey, don't worry—take any important insight you've had

elsewhere and make it come to you at the end of the journey.

Objective: To experience the journey-story form. Paint with your words, and make the sights correspond to thoughts.

Check: As you read, did you get a feeling you were traveling? Make sure you haven't simply relied on unexpressed memory and its associations so that it would be you alone who would get that feeling. Have you communicated it to us through engaging our senses and thoughts? When the big insight comes, does the landscape change from ordinary to extraordinary? See how Diane Johnson in "Great Barrier Reef" makes stars out of starfish.

9. Look up the character and setting sketches you did in the previous chapters. Summarize the best sketches and write them down on blank index cards. Summarize the plot outlines from above. Mix the cards the way Art Corriveau did, until you find a workable combination. Be playful. You need not know the whole action in advance.

Objective: To learn how to enhance your imagination. Imagination is simply the ability to make strange connections seem plausible.

Check: Have you integrated the action with the characters into the locales? In your scene, do we see bits of the setting and characters? Do we get a feel for what the people are like?

10. Three to four pages. Continue this story (from "An Occurrence at Owl Creek Bridge" by Ambrose Bierce):

> A man stood upon a railroad bridge in northern Alabama, looking down into the swift water twenty feet below. The man's hands were behind his back, the wrists bound with a cord. A rope closely encircled his neck. It was attached to a stout cross-timber above his neck. . . .

Tell us how and why the man got into this predicament, and where, if anywhere, he goes from here.

Objective: To work from a strange situation. Learn how to

jump into the story right at its crisis moment and work from there—forward, backward, whichever way you see fit to explain what's going on.

Check: Does your story make sense? Have you convinced us that a real man, with realistic thoughts, feelings, perceptions, is there?

11. Three pages. Steal this plot from Herodotus' *The Histories*. Croesus, the king of Lydia, thought that he was the most fortunate man on earth. He heard that a powerful kingdom, Persia, was expanding from the East, under its ambitious king, Cyrus. Croesus asked an oracle whether he should advance his forces against Persia and got an answer that if he did so he would destroy a powerful empire. So he attacked. But it was his empire he thus destroyed. Here's a scene immediately after the defeat:

> Cyrus chained Croesus and placed him with fourteen Lydian boys on a great pyre. . . . Croesus remembered with what divine truth Solon had declared that no man could be called happy until he was dead. Till then Croesus had not uttered a sound; but when he remembered, he sighed bitterly and three times, in anguish of spirit, pronounced Solon's name.
>
> Cyrus heard the name and told his interpreters to ask who Solon was. . . . Croesus related how Solon the Athenian once came to Sardis, and made light of the splendour which he saw there, and how everything he said had proved true, and not only for him but for all men and especially for those who imagined themselves fortunate. . . .
>
> While Croesus was speaking, the fire had been lit and was already burning round the edges. . . . The story touched Cyrus. He himself was a mortal man and was burning alive another who had once been as prosperous as he.

Now, write this story in more detail. You might go back in time and construct a one-page scene in which Solon laughs at

Croesus' wealth and Croesus is tempted to punish Solon. Then write a page in which something terrible happens to Croesus after Solon's departure. (In Herodotus' story, Croesus adopts an exiled nobleman, and the nobleman kills Croesus's son by accident in a hunt.) Next, write a page that would immediately follow the text above. Don't worry if your details aren't quite authentic for ancient Asia Minor. (If you like the story and want to adopt it, you might research in history books to make sure that your details are authentic.) Make Croesus and Solon communicate in simple English. Plunge into the story imaginatively. (Don't be discouraged if the writing turns out to be slow and difficult. It often does!)

If you don't like Herodotus' story, find some incident in a history book that intrigues you and begin a three-page story.

Objective: To learn how to borrow plots. Having a plot (plot outline) may not be enough. Give life to the story by bringing in your interpretations, themes, and insights into people's motivations. Learn how to project your imagination into a different place and time and make it come to life.

Check: Do your pages sound like excerpts from a story? I mean, have you gone beyond the summary, so that you bring us into the story with details and dialogue? Have you lingered on motions, descriptions, thoughts? If you answer most of these questions "no," go back and rewrite according to the criteria I've given you.

12. Three pages. Modernize the plot you used in the previous exercise. Instead of two kings, have two investment bankers—or two military officers, one American, the other Vietnamese—go through something similar.

Objective: To learn not only how to steal but how to transplant and transform plots so they suit you. Adopt them, make outlandish plots land in your culture. For example, Jane Smiley adapted the plot of *King Lear* for a novel set on an Iowa farm.

Check: Same as in Exercise 11.

13. Four pages. Take a character, a place and a time, and write three one-page plot outlines of potential stories. In the first case,

place the right person, at the right place, at the wrong time. In the second, the right person, at the right time, at the wrong place. In the third, the right time, right place, wrong person. In the end, choose the outline that promises to become the best story, and write one page, plunging into the main action in detail (even with dialogue, perhaps, if you construct a scene that warrants it), testing whether there's life in this for your imagination.

Objective: To learn how to make outline permutations out of several basic elements for a story, and to put the best story outline into practice to see whether it'll work.

Check: In your outlines, did you have clear conflicts? Were they realistic? Can you make them plausible?

14. Three to four pages. Can you plot a murder mystery? Choose the murderer, the victim, and the motive for the murder. Outline first how the murder happened, and then how the investigation will proceed and who'll conduct it. Let the investigator have her motives—not simply solving the mystery. Then parallel these two plots. Open with finding the body. Keep the investigation going forward, following some wrong clues and some right ones, until the resolution occurs.

Objective: To outline a piece of fiction with a dual time motion—one current, another past—until the two meet.

Check: Does your plot make sense? Is it plausible? If not, how could you make it plausible? Different motives?

CHAPTER FIVE

POINT OF VIEW

Where does the story come from? Who is telling it? To answer these questions, writers use the point of view (POV)—the vantage point(s) from which the story is observed. News stories are filled with, *he said*, *she said*, *according to*, and other indicators of information sources. Fiction is under hardly less obligation, even though the sources are invented. The fictional source of information corresponds to the POV.

FIRST-PERSON POV

The most natural POV is the first-person singular, since all stories and trials originate with someone, an "I," witnessing what happens. All other POVs spring from this mother of all POVs.

Here is an example of the first-person POV from "Sister Imelda" by Irish writer Edna O'Brien:

> I had met Sister Imelda outside of class a few times and I felt that there was an attachment between us. Once it was in the grounds, when she did a reckless thing. She broke off a chrysanthemum and offered it to me to smell.

The telling of a story usually occurs after the events; in the above example it comes years later. Although the "I" character was a school child, the narrative first person is not, and therefore tells the story in an adult's language. We must distinguish between the author and the narrator (between Edna O'Brien and the first-person adult narrator), and between the narrator (the adult looking back) and the character (the child).

The first-person character and the first-person narrator can appear to be one and the same, as in Mark Twain's *Huckleberry Finn*:

> Miss Watson she took me in the closet and prayed, but nothing come of it. She told me to pray every day, and whatever I asked for I would get it. But it warn't so. I tried it. Once I got a fish-line, but no hooks.

Huck Finn the narrator sounds the same as Huck Finn the boy, and the novel sounds like something spoken. Mark Twain invented the child's voice as his narrative means of perception for his fiction. But Mark Twain is *not* Huck Finn. The first-person POV in fiction does not represent the author. The first person is a persona; *persona*, as discussed in chapter two, means "mask." This POV should be different from you; he should be free to have his own religion, politics, aesthetics, that may, but need not, coincide with yours. You as the author should not be blamed for what your persona does. If your persona is a serial killer, nobody should assume that you are a serial killer. If your fictional "I" performs acts of kindness surpassing Mother Teresa's, this will not qualify you for the Nobel Peace Prize. E.L. Doctorow says that "a novelist is a person who can live in other people's skins." Writing in the first person helps you identify and empathize with characters who are very different from you.

This does not mean that you can't write about your essential concerns. On the contrary, now that you have a persona, a mask, you can bring out your demons and angels. As we discussed earlier, fiction is a carnival; behind your mask you can express yourself much more freely than with a straight face.

When the first-person protagonist is really you and the events in the story are taken directly from your experience, you are probably writing an essay or autobiographical fiction, which sounds like—and to some extent is—a contradiction in terms. Of course, you can cross the boundary between fiction and nonfiction. There are no German shepherds and barbed wires, no

Berlin Wall, between the two branches of writing. The Berlin Wall has collapsed in many ways. But make sure that this collapsed wall expands your world, rather than shrinks it.

The first-person narrator can tell a story with herself as a central character or she can be one of the minor characters. Or she can tell somebody else's story, barely mentioning herself except to show where the information comes from. Some literati argue, however, that the carrier of the first-person POV must always be a central character. Ostensibly we may follow and observe somebody else, but it's the story carrier's epiphanies and insights that matter to us most because we have identified with her vision. This may not always be true, but if your first-person POV carrier is an observer of somebody else's action, your readers *will* ask, "And what about this guy watching all this? Isn't he responsible too?" Gear your narrative, then, to answer these questions, no matter how subtly.

First-Person Multiple POV

In this variation of the traditional, first-person approach, you use several first-person narrators and alternate among them, usually beginning a new chapter with each change of narrator. This strategy offers a diversity of voices, viewpoints and ways of thinking. It allows you to convey just as much as through an omniscient narrator, without the arrogance of the omniscient sound and with the advantage of diverse voices.

Since the same event means different things to different participants and observers, the event could be presented richly, without an artificial extrapolation of what actually happened. Let the reader jump to conclusions and form an objective picture. William Faulkner explained his reasons for using this narrative strategy in *The Sound and the Fury*: "I tried to tell it again, the same story through the eyes of another brother. That was still not it. I told it for the third time through the eyes of the third brother. That was still not it. I tried to gather the pieces together and fill in the gaps by making myself the spokesman. It was still not complete. . . . I never could tell it right, though I tried hard and would like to try again, though I'd probably fail again."

For short pieces, too, first-person multiple POV may be a fine way to write, especially in a story centered around a sharp conflict. Still, since a short story must establish a focus quickly and maintain the focus, jumping POVs might disrupt its flow.

Epistolary Fiction

Letters are almost always written in the first person. Many novels—especially in the nineteenth century, such as Johann Wolfgang von Goethe's *The Sorrows of Young Werther*—have been *epistolary*, or written in the form of correspondence. We as readers become voyeurs prying into these "personal" revelations.

The advantage of writing letters is that you can visualize a correspondent and aim your voice at him as your audience. This might be a good model for any POV. Rather than writing for "posterity" and a "national" audience, find one trustworthy ear to talk to. John Steinbeck, author of *The Grapes of Wrath*, said: "Your audience is one single reader. I have found that sometimes it helps to pick out one person—a real person you know, or an imagined person—and write to that one."

Akin to epistolary fiction, the *diary* form also uses the first-person POV. The narrator writes to come to grips with an event and perhaps to keep it preserved for memory. The advantage here is that you may get rid of all self-consciousness and establish a frank voice.

Nowadays, fewer people write personal letters, so the epistolary novel is not a frequently used form. But a similar means-of-communication form has sprung up, the *phone novel*, which has the appearance of a telephone conversation transcript—Nicholson Baker's *Vox* and parts of Evelyn Waugh's *A Handful of Dust* use this approach. This is an objective—or theatrical—POV, since we as readers get the experience of being an audience, listening to conversations.

First-Person Narrator's Reliability

Philosophically, the first-person POV is the least problematic: The narrator has seen something, and now tells us about it.

However, when the source of information is singular, there are no checks for the truth of what's said. We can wonder if the reporter is telling the truth. (Of course in fiction nothing is reliable, but we strive to appear reliable.) We find the simplest paradigm of the unreliable narrator in the sour grapes fable: The speaker says that he did not want the grapes anyway, they were too green, when it's clear that he wanted but could not get them.

Here's an example of a self-conscious unreliable narrator, from Fyodor Dostoyevski's *Notes From Underground*:

> I was lying when I said just now that I was a spiteful official. I was lying out of spite. I was simply amusing myself with the petitioners and with the officer, and in reality I never could become spiteful. I was conscious every moment in myself of many, very many elements absolutely opposite to that.

What can you believe here? Reconstructing the true motives beneath the surface presented by the narrator is a part of the pleasure of reading an unreliable narrator. The narrative becomes a study of a split personality, a hypocrite or a liar. Since quite a few people fall into these categories—we probably all do at least now and then—this narrative strategy is often the perfect choice for a story.

Pros and Cons for First-Person POV

The first-person POV offers advantages and disadvantages that you should be aware of before using it in your fiction. The advantages include the following:

1. It's technically the least ambiguous. The reader always knows who is seeing and interpreting the narrative action. No artificial objective knowledge is assumed. If the first person makes faulty inferences, the reader will accept them as part of the narrator's unreliability.

2. In our era, subjectivity—even in the sciences—seems to be the prevalent mode, so we need an option for telling a story

subjectively, and first-person POV certainly gives you that option.

3. In first person, you can choose a voice most freely. While third-person narrative basically restricts you to standard English, in the first person you may use slang, bad grammar, everyday language to arrive at an authentic narrative voice.

4. First person offers smooth access to a character's thoughts. You don't have to worry about awkward switches in pronouns, like "He opened the door and thought, I better thaw the chicken."

Here are the disadvantages to the first-person POV for you to consider:

1. We can't take an outside look at our carrier of POV, unless we place a mirror somewhere, and mirrors have been overused in fiction. Avoid them unless you find no other solution. (Compensate for the inability to look directly at your character by reporting her thoughts about her appearance.)

2. From the first-person POV, faithful reproductions of diverse dialogues may be implausible. Your first person may appear to be a theatrical genius with an amazing ear. On the other hand, to render almost every dialogue in one or two voices may be monotonous. Generally, it's better to err toward the interesting side—good reproduction of dialogue.

3. That an "I" tells the story implies that the "I" is still alive. Thus, one source of possible suspense—whether the character will survive—vanishes in the first-person POV.

4. It's hard to create a compelling new voice for each story. Many productive short story writers find it easier to write in the third person because they don't have to invent voices so frequently. Once you create a strong voice, you might want to stick with it for a series of short stories or a short novel.

THIRD-PERSON POV

In third-person POV, the writer uses "he," "she," or "they" rather than the first-person "I." After choosing third person, the writer must then select which type of third-person strategy best fits the piece of fiction.

Third-Person Omniscient POV

In this POV, which is used infrequently in contemporary writing, the author knows everything about all the characters, places and events involved. Since not everything can be presented simultaneously, the author jumps from inside one head to another. We observe from many angles. The "camera" is conveniently set wherever the action is, akin to television coverage of a basketball game.

In the example below, from *Middlemarch*, which is mostly in third-person omniscient POV, George Eliot frequently makes comments in the first person, taking a panoramic view of the narrative, sweeping through history, philosophy and individual minds:

> At present I have to make the new settler Lydgate better known to anyone interested in him than he could possibly be even to those who had seen the most of him since his arrival in Middlemarch. . . .
>
> Lydgate's spots of commonness lay in the complexion of his prejudices, which, in spite of noble intention and sympathy, were half of them such as are found in ordinary men of the world: that distinction of mind which belonged to his intellectual ardour did not penetrate his feeling and judgement about furniture or women or the desirability of its being known (without his telling) that he was better born than other country surgeons.

As you can see, the author seems to knows everything. She can tell us more about a settler than anybody, including himself. She tells us about human nature; she makes no bones about this being an artificial narrative. She intrudes on the exposition of the narrative, saying what she plans to do with it. *Intrude* may not be the right word, though, in the omniscient narrative—since the reader is invited to share the omniscience and is given the credit of being constantly aware of the novel's artificiality.

Here's a contemporary omniscient narrative, from *Einstein's Dreams* by Alan Lightman:

> At some time in the past, scientists discovered that time flows more slowly the farther from the center of earth. . . .

> Once the phenomenon was known, a few people, anxious to stay young, moved to the mountains. . . . People most eager to live longest have built their houses on the highest stilts. Indeed, some houses rise half a mile high on their spindly wooden legs. Height has become status. When a person from his kitchen window must look up to see a neighbor, he believes the neighbor will not become stiff in the joints as soon as he, will not lose his hair until later, will not wrinkle until later, will not lose the urge for romance as early. . . . Some boast that they have lived their whole lives high up, that they were born in the highest house on the highest mountain peak and have never descended. They celebrate their youth in the mirrors and walk naked on their balconies.

The narrative here does not enter into specific people's heads. The narrative voice knows everything—science, customs—but the author does not ostensibly jump in to tell you about his stance. Jumping into the minds of two or more people and showing their thoughts is the standard feature of most omniscient writing. Here's an example, from "August 2002: Night Meeting" by Ray Bradbury.

> "Good lord, what a dream that was," sighed Tomas, his hands on the wheel, thinking of the rockets, the women, the raw whiskey, the Virginia reels, the party.
>
> How strange a vision was that, thought the Martian, rushing on, thinking of the festival, the canals, the boats, the women with golden eyes, and the songs.

Properly speaking, most omniscient narratives have the nature of a series of third-person limited omniscient with occasional essayistic explanations of what the world is like in the interim.

Third-Person Limited POV

This POV—and its variants—is the most common one used nowadays. There are at least three kinds of third-person limited POVs:

Third-person subjective POV. This POV resembles the first-person POV except usually it's done in standard English rather than in the character's voice. For example, "As Judy watched monkeys jump on trees, she thought about getting into shape and remembered that her mother wanted to buy her a ski cap." Here we have access to a person's thoughts and feelings just as we do in the first person.

Third-person objective POV. We observe what our "she" is doing without entering her head, and we don't attribute the observation to another character. You don't reveal the viewer—the way you don't see the person holding a camcorder. "As she faced the monkey cage, she rubbed Chap Stick over her thin lips."

Third-person limited omniscient POV or *third-person flexible POV.* This is a contradiction in terms. If the POV is limited, it can't be omniscient. However, since this term is so widely used, we could use it too, though I prefer to call this a *third-person limited flexible POV.* The two names for this POV are interchangeable. Both are in currency. This combines the objective and the subjective approaches. "As Judy watched monkeys jump on trees, she rubbed Chap Stick over her thin lips and remembered that her mother wanted to buy her a ski cap." We can see Judy *and* learn what she thinks. (For possibilities of irony in this approach—the author knowing more than the character—read Flaubert's paragraph about Bovary's gambling at the end of this chapter.) Although a narrator is not revealed, there must be an incognito narrator. It's hard to distinguish between the third-person POV narrator and the author. You may assume that most readers will interpret whatever the hidden third-person narrator says to be the author's viewpoint.

Here's an example of a third-person subjective POV from Doris Lessing's "Habit of Loving":

> But he would not go to the hospital. So the doctor said he must have day and night nurses. This he submitted to until the cheerful friendliness of the nurses saddened

> him beyond bearing, and he asked the doctor to ring up his wife . . . She promised to find him someone who would not wear a uniform and make jokes.

And later, from the same story, after the man marries a freelance nurse:

> "But you are nothing but a child," he said fondly. He could not decipher what lay behind the black, full stare of her sad eyes as she looked at him now; she was sitting cross-legged in her black glossy trousers before the fire, like a small doll. But a spring of alarm had been touched in him and he didn't dare say any more.

From an objective distance the narrative jumps into the main character's head and from there we observe how other characters look and behave, and decipher how they feel, without entering their heads. We are limited to one third person's knowledge.

Despite some initial distance toward the character, this POV resembles the first-person POV: We follow the thoughts of one person and see from that person's POV. Lessing's approach is mostly subjective—our vantage point does not step out of the main character's head for us to be able to observe him. Later in the narrative, when she needs to describe the man, she brings up a mirror so she would not leave his vantage point.

Conventionally, in the third-person limited perspective, the author should not intrude by having the narrator step in and tell something about himself or offer some universal truth. This authorial intrusion is more irksome than in the omniscient narrative, because the additional jump here will be from the limited to the omniscient POV.

Because it offers the leeway to say whatever the author pleases, the third-person omniscient is the most flexible, and in a way, the most forgiving POV. So it's surprising that it's not in fashion. Perhaps since we have good reasons to be skeptical about nearly everything, the omniscient voice may sound too dogmatic. Yet, because of the freedom to point out that the narrative is an artifice, third-person omniscient could sound less dogmatic than the third-person flexible.

Third-Person Multiple POV

This sounds like omniscient POV, and the difference may be subtle, but it's best to see it as a series of third-person limited POVs minus authorial intrusions. Czech writer Milan Kundera alternates two POVs from chapter to chapter in "Let the Old Dead Make Room for the Young Dead."

> [Chapter I] He was returning home along the street of a small Czech town, where he had been living for several years. He was reconciled to his not too exciting life. . . . [II] She knew the path to her husband's grave from memory, and yet today she felt all at once as if she were in this cemetery for the first time. [III] Not long ago he had turned thirty-five, and exactly at that time he had noticed that the hair on the top of his head was thinning very visibly.

The narrative follows the protagonists' POVs—we know what they think and what they see—so it's an alternation of two third-person subjective POVs.

Objective POV

Sometimes this perspective is blurred under the third-person objective POV, but we should distinguish an objective POV, which does not focus on one person, from the limited objective POV. Another name for this is the *theatrical POV*. We observe the action of two or more protagonists, favoring none of them with an exclusive focus, as though in a play. The author does not comment on anything, does not enter people's heads, but merely presents to us the drama as objectively as possible. Ideally, no hidden third or first person lurks anywhere. Of course, there are limits to objectivity; some people consider everything subjective. No doubt, the author will taint the narrative, but as long as she does it with subtlety, the scene will appear objective. Ernest Hemingway's "Hills Like White Elephants" is one of the most popular examples of this narrative stance:

> The warm wind blew the bead curtain against the table.
> "The beer's nice and cool," the man said.
> "It's lovely," the girl said.
> "It's really an awfully simple operation, Jig," the man said. "It's not really an operation at all."

The narrative offers a recording of a conversation in which a couple is probably discussing an abortion. The reader is allowed to be the judge of what's going on but, of course, must work harder than usual to infer the meaning of the narrative.

UNUSUAL POVS

Occasionally you may get tired of using the basic first- and third-person POVs. After much use, the first may sound too individualistic, and the third too distant and objectifying. Or you may feel stuck in a routine. For a fresh angle of vision, or for a special effect, you may resort to less frequently used POVs. The names for POVs come from the personal pronouns, so besides the ones we covered, there are *we* (first-person plural POV), *you* (second-person singular POV—and also plural in the sense of "Y'all"), and various permutations of these and of the ones we've already covered. After excursions to the less frequently used POVs, you'll probably want to return to the prevalent first and third person, which will become fresh again.

Second-Person POV

The author makes believe that he is talking to someone, describing what the person addressed is doing. But the "you" is not the reader, though sometimes it's hard to get rid of the impression that the author is addressing you directly. Here's an example of this POV, from "Main Street Morning" by Natalie M. Patesch, a contemporary American short story writer:

> Your knees are weak as you lean against the freshly painted red, white and blue fire hydrant. Your impulse is to run toward them, crying out, *me too! me too!* You can now taste your own long denial; you want to run and tell her all about your thirty-one years without her and have her cry out with absolving certainty: *Oh what a beautiful daughter you are!*

I find it a little confining to be told what I am doing and what I am thinking and what I am to do, as though I were following a recipe. If I get rid of that impression, the "you" can be quite engaging. Since the plea of this POV is for immediate attention, most often it is told in the present tense. The present brings us into the time of action, suspends any knowledge of the future, and you as the reader are invited to identify directly with the character. This POV can sound too insistent, as if the writer is grasping for the reader's attention. It can also sound journalistic, since much travel reporting is done in second person.

First and Second Combined

You can combine the second-person POV with the first, as does Margaret Atwood in "Hair Jewellery":

> Between my fits of sleep I thought about you, rehearsing our future, which I knew would be brief. Of course we would sleep together, though this topic had not yet been discussed. In those days, as you recall, it had to be discussed first, and so far we had not progressed beyond a few furtive outdoor gropings and one moment when, under a full moon on one of those deserted brick streets, you had put your hand on my throat. . . .

Here the first- and second-person POV, are combined to an excellent effect. This is the type of POV combination, or address of me to you, frequently found in love poetry, and Atwood's story is a love story of sorts, so the story benefits from the tradition. Yet, strangely enough, this POV combination is rare.

First and Third Combined

You can also combine first- and third-person POVs, as does Russell Banks in "Sarah Cole: A Type of Love Story":

> I felt warmed by her presence and was flirtatious and bold, a little pushy, even.
>
> Picture this. The man, tanned, limber . . . enters the apartment behind the woman.

This combination of points of view helps to develop the theme—a narcissistic man's affair with a homely woman. The narcissist switches the narrative into the third person to take a look at himself, the way one might like to see oneself on a screen; he also deals with his cruelty in the affair like that, projecting himself into another person, to understand his guilt. You could use first- and third-person combined POV for other kinds of characters, especially those with a personality dichotomy, where you want to look at a character from different angles.

Third-Person Plural Observer POV

Here the perceptions of an event do not come from the angle of the central character, but from a group of characters who watch the protagonist, as in "Mother" by the Italian fiction writer Natalia Ginzburg:

> One day when they were out for a walk with Don Vigiliani and with other boys from the youth club, on the way back they saw their mother in a suburban cafe. She was sitting inside the cafe; they saw her through the window, and a man was sitting with her. Their mother had laid her tartan scarf on the table. . . .

"They saw her through the window." We see the mother from the standpoint of the boys.

For the theme of the story, a mother's adultery, this is an effective angle. Her children's observation keeps her imprisoned in the role of motherhood, from which she tries to escape by becoming a lover. The story is secondarily about the boys, too, and our observation of their elusive mother through their eyes creates an effective narrative distance—appropriate because the boys are about to become orphans.

First-Person Collective Observer POV

This POV is ideal for small town narratives, where an individual lives under a communal scrutiny. This is how William Faulkner uses it in "A Rose for Emily," after an incident in which Miss Emily claims that her dead father is alive:

> We did not say she was crazy then. We believed she had to do that. We remembered all the young men her father had driven away, and we knew that with nothing left, she would have to cling to that which had robbed her, as people will.
>
> She was sick for a long time. When we saw her again, her hair was cut short, making her look like a girl, with a vague resemblance to those angles in colored church windows—sort of tragic and serene.

The reader follows the motions and the acts of one person through a group's viewpoint; somebody in the group, as the narrator, speaks for the group, never drawing attention to his identity, as though he does not have any, other than belonging to the group. Faulkner never individualizes the "we" observing Miss Emily, so he keeps the narrative distance between "us" and "her." This first-person plural POV fits the theme of a woman living under the oppressive communal gaze. If you set your stories in a small community—schools, towns, churches, families—and you focus on a secretive individual in conflict with the community, try this POV.

Stream of Consciousness

This technique evolved from cognitive theories about consciousness. In *Principles of Psychology*, philosopher William James, in striving to describe the thought process, coined the phrase "stream of consciousness."

Here's a segment of a stream of consciousness, in *Ulysses* by James Joyce, written as a direct interior monologue. Note that for the sake of approximating the mental verbal flux, Joyce omits punctuation, since in our thoughts we probably don't punctuate. Joyce presents the stream of consciousness as Molly Bloom's thoughts, not as a piece written for an audience:

> Father Corrigan he touched me father and what harm if he did where and I said on the canal bank like a fool but whereabouts on your person my child on the leg behind high up was it yes rather high up was it where you sit down yes O Lord couldnt he say bottom right out and have done with it what has that got to do with it and did you whatever way he put it I forget no father and I always think of the real father what did he want to know for when I already confessed it to God he had a nice fat hand the palm moist always I wouldn't mind feeling it neither would he Id say by the bullneck in his horsecollar I wonder did he know me in the box I could see his face he couldnt see mine of course he never turn or let on still his eyes were red when his father died theyre lost for a woman of course must be terrible when a man cries let alone them Id like to be embraced by one in his vestments and the smell of incense off him like the pope besides theres no danger with a priest if youre married. . . .

Molly Bloom recalls a confession and a confessed sexual encounter with a boy, daydreams about the priest, thinks about euphemisms and about men crying. The thoughts may seem random, but at the same time they have a narrative coherence. We find out what and how Molly thinks, what she did, what she'd like to do. Joyce communicates a rich texture of Molly's experience in this rush of consciousness. This technique is basically the first-person POV, a direct interior monologue. To follow the principle "show, don't tell," you directly show thoughts. Most often, we simply summarize thoughts without showing them, but in crucial moments of your narrative, you may want to show them.

You can resort to the stream of consciousness whenever you want to bring us intimately into a character's experience, so this is potentially an excellent way to characterize. The technique is well suited for moments of indecision, waiting, pondering, quiet contemplation, as well as for moments of violent crisis (such as being wounded or shocked). Stream of consciousness may have slow-motion effect if you use it amid action. Naturally, if you overuse this method you will not increase but, rather, decrease suspense, since stream of consciousness tends to meander into the future, past and present, without a sharp focus.

The major drawback of stream of consciousness is that it's cumbersome to read in large chunks. While writing it is often fun, it usually isn't fun to read. Be considerate to your reader, and edit your streams of consciousness so that there's always something interesting going on, in terms of language, images and thoughts. Use the stream of consciousness in small doses, in fairly brief passages (perhaps no more than a page at a time) to enhance rather than kill your narrative tension.

SHIFTING POVS

Switches in POV irritate some readers and certainly most editors unless you establish the pattern early as the form of the narrative. So, if for no other reason than the practical one of getting published, most writers must respect the conventions of POV. Beginning writers often write pages from the perspective of one person and then suddenly, mid-sentence, they might switch like this: "While he bit his nails and thought that she did not understand him, she brushed her hair and thought that he needed therapy." In one sentence we enter two heads. If this narrative is not otherwise omniscient in form, this switch jars us. If the POV switches throughout, it still should not take place within the same sentence. Conventionally, when you switch from the thoughts of one person to the thoughts of another, you'd start a new paragraph or more often, a new chapter. Otherwise, your narrative will be jumpy.

Consistency is one guideline. If you plan to use multiple POVs, make this clear as early as possible. After chapter (or paragraph) one, in which your POV focuses on Jim, open chapter (or paragraph) two with Julie's POV. Then you can shift back and forth with each new chapter or paragraph, if necessary. You have prepared the reader for these shifts.

Sometimes POV shifts can be effective. This is what E.M. Forster said about switching POVs—from omniscient to limited and to objective: "A novelist can shift his viewpoint if it comes off, and it came off with Dickens and Tolstoy. Indeed this power to expand and contract perceptions (of which the shifting viewpoint is a symptom), this right to intermittent knowledge:—I find it one of the great advantages of the novel-form, and it has a parallel in our perception of life. We are stupider at some times than others; we can enter into people's minds occasionally but not always, because our own minds get tired; and this intermittence lends in the long run variety and colour to the experiences we receive."

Switching POVs can establish the source of knowledge that we discussed in the beginning of the chapter. So for example, we can derive information about an event initially in the first person. After the story has been assembled from several witnesses, and enough inferences have been made to cover even what has not been told by the witnesses, the event may be described without reference to the sources; things can assume an objective third-person perspective—and a composite report can be written about the motives of everybody involved.

Gustave Flaubert employs this strategy in *Madame Bovary*. He starts in the first-person plural (or collective):

> We were in class when the headmaster came in, followed by a new boy, not wearing the school uniform, and a school servant carrying a large desk.

After Bovary and his background have been introduced, the first person observers drop out, and Flaubert gives us information, confident that we will have the impression that it has been gathered from witnesses, such as we had in the beginning. So after the first chapter, until the last, when the first-person plural POV reappears, the novel is narrated in a variety of third-person POVs, depending on what the novel needs to cover. For a while we follow Mr. Bovary. Sometimes we get his thoughts, other times we observe and analyze him.

> To shut himself up every evening in the dirty public room, to push about on marble tables the small sheep-bones with black dots, seemed to him a fine proof of his freedom, which raised him in his own esteem.

Notice the duality of perception of Bovary's action. We learn that he derives a sense of freedom from playing dice. At the same time, the distant and hidden carrier—author?—of the third-person POV gives us an ironic angle on that freedom with the phrase, "push about . . . small sheep-bones with black dots." The dice are reduced to their banality, something Bovary does not see, and thus we are invited to see Bovary as bovine and banal. In many other chapters, the narrative focuses on Madame Bovary. In some passages, the narrative gives us the setting, the town of Yonville, with its history as a given knowledge. The novel employs many strategies. It would be too simple to say that it's written in the omniscient POV, although in sections it is. In other parts, it's written in a succession of different third-person flexible POVs, with authorial interpretations. I won't call it intrusion because the interpretations are done gracefully enough not to stall the narrative.

Unusual Shifts of POV

If you carefully read even some of the best fiction, you will find unusual switches. For example, in the much-praised objective POV by Hemingway in "Hills Like White Elephants," from which we read a brief section above, these two sentences occur:

> The shadow of a cloud moved across the field of grain and she saw the river through the trees.
>
> He looked up the tracks but could not see the train.

You can see that someone is looking, from the outside. But to report what someone is seeing means you are in the person's head. How do we know that she saw the river? Perhaps she looked at the trees without seeing the river. In the second sentence, how do we know that he could not see the train? These brief POV shifts may be inadvertent, but perhaps Hemingway intentionally switched from objectivity to subjectivity, for one reason or another—maybe to make a disclaimer of objectivity. Who knows? Maybe we need an omniscient critic to explain this to us.

If you switch POVs, be in control, and don't apologize or try too hard to cover your tracks because that will either intrude on the narrative or slow it down. Simply do it in a regular enough fashion. Propel the reader into the new angle.

Here's an example of doing it gracefully, from Leo Tolstoy's "The Death of Ivan Ilych." The POV shifts from one character's thoughts to his appearance, from subjective to objective:

> Peter Ivanovich, like everyone else on such occasions, entered feeling uncertain what he would have to do. All he knew was that at such times it is always safe to cross oneself. But he was not quite sure whether one should make obeisances while doing so. He therefore adopted a middle course. On entering the room he began crossing himself and made a slight movement resembling a bow.

Tolstoy takes us from the character's thoughts to the appearance of his action—"a slight movement resembling a bow"—economically, with the help of one word, *resembling*. This is a good model, particularly in the third-person limited. After Peter Ivanovich spends some time observing Ivan Ilych's corpse and musing on Ilych's life in the first chapter, the second chapter opens with the history of Ilych's life. The transition takes place in a sharp way: The second chapter opens with Ilych as the subject. A new chapter as a new beginning opens up the possibility of starting from another angle. First, Ilych's history is objective, in the form of summaries, but in later chapters, the narrative focuses on Ilych's feelings, becoming quite subjective. The subject—the experience of dying—justifies the method of contracting the focus from the outside in.

Virtual Shift of POV

There's a way of getting into other people's thoughts without jumping POVs. Here's an example from Anton Chekhov's "Lady With a Dog." The story is told from a man's POV throughout, but at a crisis point, the narrative POV seemingly switches to the woman.

> She glanced at him and turned pale, then glanced again with horror, unable to believe her eyes, and tightly gripped her fan and the lorgnette in her hands, evidently struggling with herself not to faint.

Note that once we have the woman's perspective, the author lets us know that we are not actually in her head, that we have reconstructed what must be going on in her mind. One word does the trick of distancing the POV: *evidently*. "Unable to believe her eyes" may be inferred from observation; or at any rate, our third-person POV, still with the man, could infer this. So in third-person limited, if you seemingly switch, indicate that we haven't actually switched POV but have observed deeply.

EXERCISES

1. Two pages. First, in one page, describe an event—stealing a fake gold ring in a department store—in the first-person POV. Use the language that would come most naturally to the character you choose, preferably slang.

Then write another page, describing the same event from the POV of the sales clerk in the first person.

Objective: First, to gain experience constructing a primary, protagonist first-person POV. Then, experience constructing an observer/minor participant POV.

Check: In the first example, have you given us thoughts, feelings and perceptions of the thief, using *I* as in "I was sure that I could slip the ring onto my pinkie"? Does she know that the ring is fake? She shouldn't—why would she bother otherwise?

In the second example, have you used *I* as in "I could tell that this clown was about to make the move. She was out of breath and her cigarette-stained fingers shook"? The clerk should know, of course, that the ring is fake, and perhaps he should be ironic about the thief because he knows something she doesn't.

2. Two pages. Describe in one page the event in Exercise 1 in the third-person subjective POV, focusing on the thief. Since this will be similar in the scope of knowledge and angle of vision to the first part of Exercise 1, you might simply rewrite what you've done there, now in the third person. In addition to changing pronouns, change the diction to standard English.

Then write another page, describing the same event in the third-person limited flexible POV, focusing on the thief. Write both an outside description (how the action looks) and at a different point, an inward one (what the character thinks and how she perceives the sales clerk).

Objective: To gain experience writing in the third-person subjective POV, with its concentration on the experience of the protagonist; and then try out the third-person limited "omniscient"—or flexible—with its freedom to present the protagonist from whatever angle suits you.

Check: For the first part, make sure that what you described can be seen from your thief's angle. For the second part, do you have a dual perception, typical of a flexible stance? For example, have you indicated that the gold ring is fake but that the thief does not know it?

3. Three paragraphs. Describe an event on a battlefront, in which a soldier accidently—or not so accidently—kills his brother in "friendly fire." Describe this from the omniscient POV. Open with a paragraph about the history of the war, perhaps musing on the nature of wars. Second paragraph: Describe the actions and thoughts of the friendly fire soldier—up

to pulling the trigger. Third paragraph: Describe the actions and thoughts of the soldier right before and during being shot at. As he gasps a final breath, give him an insight into the afterlife.

Since you are free to cover the field from any vantage point, external and internal, strive for an orderly succession of angles of vision.

Objective: To experience the multiple nature of the omniscient POV.

Check: Make sure that you have not shifted from one character's thoughts to another's in midsentence. Have you described how these soldiers look, what they think and feel, and what dying is like? Even though subjective insights about death are inaccessible to the living, make one up, playfully, if need be.

4. Three pages. Event: A male doctor examining a woman patient may be sexually harassing her. She cuts his ear with a scalpel. A nurse watches and does not rush to help the doctor. Describe the event, three times, in the third-person subjective POV, using all the characters present.

Objective: To practice writing different interpretations of the same event, depending on the POV. Try to make the event appear different in each.

Check: Does the event appear radically different from each character's experience? If not, go back, and write at least two different interpretations. The nurse and the patient could have a similar interpretation, for example, but the doctor, a different one.

5. Two to three pages. Construct an unreliable narrator. (You could do this in the form of a letter, as part of an epistolary story, or in a diary entry, as part of a diary story.) You might use the ring thief from Exercise 1 or the friendly fire soldier from Exercise 3. Let the thief retell the incident, not only denying that she'd stolen the ring, but telling us why she had never even been interested in rings—how in fact she had always despised them. But let her tone contradict her statements.

Objective: To learn how to write in the unreliable first-person POV.

Check: Have you managed to portray the narrator's betraying the real meaning of her statement? For example, before or after saying that she despised rings, has she gotten carried away, describing the ring lyrically, showing her desire for it?

6. Two pages. First, write a one-page description of an important event from your childhood from the child's first-person POV. Use a child's language. Then write another page, in adult language, describing the same event from the perspective of an adult looking back.

For the first part, Huck Finn could be your model; for the second, Edna O'Brien's "Sister Imelda," (see page 99). Don't worry if this turns out to be more nonfiction than fiction.

Objective: To learn how to cover a single event from different angles of language and vision.

Check: Did you use poor grammar in the first part? Maybe you should. Is the perspective adequately naive?

In the second part, do you have a dual perception of what happened? For example, the adult narrator could recollect the childhood naiveté without using childhood language (though some for flavor might not hurt) and at the same time comment in adult language about how naive it was.

Do the different POVs offer you different insights and observations?

7. Two pages. Write an autobiographical story—perhaps the one from above—so that it doesn't sound autobiographical. Cast it in the third-person limited POV and use a character different from you. In the end, after you change characters, make up new details and lines of dialogue, and exaggerate the drama. The actual event from which you started should be simply a scaffold for building your story.

Objective: If you write from experience, the first person will only strengthen the nonfictional origin of your story. The third-person POV should help you distance yourself from the event psychologically. Now that you are looking at it from far away, why be bound by what actually happened? You are free to look for story possibilities in the initial situation.

Check: Has something other than the pronouns and diction changed? Namely, have you fictionalized the event? If not, go back and change the town in which this took place, create a different set of parents, and make the character's desires and fears quite different from yours.

8. Two pages. Using first-person POV, write about a fantastic event and make it believable. For example, write about the Great Flood from the standpoint of one of Noah's daughters. Don't use fancy biblical language, but familiar, simple English. Make sure to avoid anachronisms, such as reference to Oprah or some other pop culture icon.

Objective: To familiarize a distant event and a distant person by using the first-person POV in an informal way.

Check: Examine your vocabulary to make sure you haven't used anachronisms. For example, in this sentence, within the context of the Great Flood, there would be several inappropriate expressions (italicized): "Wow, when the doves flew out, it was *postcard-pretty* out there, just like *Daytona Beach* during *spring break*." And for believability, do you have mosquito bites (or something similar)? With all that water around, it would make sense.

9. One page. Write about a scene of misunderstanding in a love story, using the combined first-and second-person POV. If you like, write this in the form of a letter. (See the excerpt from "Hair Jewellery" by Margaret Atwood, page 111).

Objective: To practice this POV strategy. For a love story, this is a particularly well-suited POV. So give it a try.

Check: Have you given approximately the same amount of playing time to "you" as to "me"? Balance the two.

10. Two pages. First, write a page of a story from the standpoint of a horse in the first person. Let the horse kick a visitor, an IRS agent.

Then, on another page, describe the same incident from the standpoint of the horse's owner, a farmer.

Objective: To fail in the first instance, and get rid of the impulse to write from an animal's POV. (This is a common, and misguided, impulse in aspiring writers, perhaps because it offers an opportunity for cute and clever observations.) To succeed in the second instance. Animals' lives can be fascinating—a good subject for stories, provided we avoid anthropocentric assumptions about what they think.

Many beginners are drawn to an animal POV, and instead of the animal, they create some human in disguise, often moralizing about how bad people are to their environment. While the objectives of such writing may be noble, the execution usually isn't.

That does not mean that you can't write an animal story from a human POV, but let the human watch the animal, without jumping into the animal's head. You also can write animal stories from the third-person objective POV. But be cautious with the third-person animal subjective and the first-person animal POVs.

I don't want to be dogmatic about this, despite my never having encountered a successful animal POV story in the workshops I've taught. After all, Richard Bach successfully used an animal POV (third-person subjective) in his novella fable, *Jonathan Livingston Seagull.*

Check: In the first part of the exercise, is your horse consistent in what he knows? Does he know what tractors are but does not know other vocabulary, such as *barn*, *rifle*, *telescope*? Either make your horse know all this vocabulary and don't worry about it, or reduce it to a minimum. Good luck!

In the second part, if you've described the horse's thoughts and feelings, have you modified them with phrases such as *seemed to wonder* and *evidently felt* to indicate that these statements are inferences, not shifts of POV?

11. Three to five pages. Write about a disagreement you had with somebody from her POV, in the first person, in her voice. Don't make her an unreliable narrator. Take an external look at yourself, in this case in the third person, although you might want to do a first- and second-person POV combination if you prefer.

Objective: To learn how to see from other people's POVs. This exercise is good not just for writing, but for getting along in friendships, marriages, societies.

Check: Has your antagonist become the protagonist of the story? Have you found weaknesses in your position and shown them? If not, go back and reveal them.

12. Four paragraphs. First, write one paragraph from the third-person subjective POV, then switch to describing the feelings of other people, relying on *seemed, obviously, clearly* and other indicators that the POV has remained external. Look at Chekhov's example, from "Lady With a Dog," on page 119.

Then write another paragraph. From the third-person subjective POV—describing a person's feeling—switch into the objective POV, describing the person's actions externally. Look at Tolstoy's example from "The Death of Ivan Ilych," on page 118.

Then write two more paragraphs. End one paragraph with the thoughts of one person in the third-person subjective POV. Start a new paragraph, with the third-person objective POV focused on another person.

Objective: To practice switching POVs smoothly.

Check: For the first paragraphs, have you started with the thoughts of the POV person, then switched to an objective outside look? For a switch, do you use *seemed to* and similar indicators for the thoughts of the observed person?

13. Three pages. Mark has been hired to burn down buildings. After burning down the fifth building, he's caught. Now give us his story. For the first page, start from the POV of the arsonist's ex-roommate, Eric, in the first person, giving Mark's character portrait. Eric tells us what Mark was like and how he assembled Mark's story—from letters, message machines, police, firefighters, and Mark's brother-in-law. Then switch for the second page to third-person objective, dropping Eric from the narrative and focusing on Mark setting his first fire at a liquor store. For page three (the climax), use the third-person subjective POV, describing Mark's fear of being caught as he runs away from his fifth building, a rent-controlled apartment complex. No

need for transitions between these pages. New page, new chapter, new POV.

Objective: To create shifts that would account for the source of the knowledge of the story. Though these days it's not necessary to trace the assembling of the story from definite sources of information, it's still healthy to keep in mind how information is gathered, and what could be known, and what may be made up. For example, it might seem illogical that starting from Eric's POV we could find out exactly how Mark felt and what he thought; but if it's clear that Eric imagines and reconstructs the story, the way a historian reconstructs a culture from archaeological finds, the story will become acceptable, and perhaps the shifting POV will make the narrative more—rather than less—convincing.

You need not write your first novel like this, but don't get stiff in the joints before you make such shifts. Be sure that you know how to make POV transitions, even if you don't need them in a particular story.

Check: Proofread to make sure that you have stuck with Eric's subjective POV in the first page ("I thought," "I felt," "I wondered" and so on); with Mark's limited objective in the second page (e.g., "His back hunched, dressed in a black business suit, Mark tiptoed among aluminum garbage cans."); and for the last page, that you bring us into Mark's way of seeing (e.g., "Mark was sure that this was not a dog's shadow.").

CHAPTER SIX

DIALOGUE AND SCENE

A *scene*—a term taken from drama—is a continuous action set in one place. Actors move on a stage, talk, fight, make love. But unlike theater, in fiction you don't have to supply all the furniture, paint, heat. You supply a bit of background, and the reader constructs more out of it. As we've seen in the chapter on setting, it's enough that you list the details that comprise a setting. From your concrete nouns, your reader will visualize the setting.

To construct a good scene, you must be able to describe the setting, evoke characters, and clearly present their actions. These elements already have been covered in previous chapters. However, before we can discuss how to write scenes, we must consider one more key element: dialogue.

DIALOGUE

Writing dialogue probably is the most essential skill you need. Since most big scenes, and many minor ones, rely on dialogue, you must be able to write it well. Writing dialogue should be easy for most of us. It astonishes me how many people believe they are no good at writing dialogue (even the people who are good at it)—yet they spend hours per day talking and listening to others talk. In fact, the narrative aspects of writing fiction should be more difficult, because how much time do we spend listening to narratives? Not much.

Many writers, however, claim that dialogue is the easiest

aspect of writing fiction. For example, James Jones, author of *From Here to Eternity*, said, "Dialogue is almost too easy. For me. So much so that it makes me suspicious of it, so I have to be careful with it. . . . There are many important issues and points of subtlety about people, about human behavior, that I want to make in writing, and it's easy to evade these—or do them superficially, do them halfway—by simply writing good dialogue."

Two points regarding this quote. First: Dialogue does not accomplish everything, so don't despair if you don't trust yours. Some writers—Gabriel Garcia Márquez, for example—depend much more on narrative than on dialogue and yet write great fiction. Just as you can avoid narrative, you can avoid dialogue, though in either case, you handicap yourself. However, it's possible to write well with a handicap, just as it's possible to play a sport with one. For example, Ivan Lendl won the European junior tennis championship without a competent backhand. He ran around the balls on his left and hit them with his forehand, or chopped them on the backhand. You can avoid dialogue, summarize, describe, and have a chopped line here and there, but why handicap yourself? It was only after Lendl developed a tremendous backhand that he won a U.S. Open.

On the other hand, even with good dialogue, you will need some narrative, to stage your scenes and to connect them to other parts of the story. Dialogue alone rarely constitutes a scene. Look at the example from Donald Barthelme's story "Basil From Her Garden," in the section "Forms of Dialogue" (page 133). That's not a scene. You may turn it into one, with an imaginative effort, but you have no props to go by right away—no stage clues. We need to see the characters and their stage. So don't expect that all you need is great dialogue, and forget about description, setting, and the rest that we have talked about so far.

The second point regarding Jones' quote: Dialogue is easy. It's what you've been doing almost every day, most of your life.

Dialogue as Conversation

Dialogue is basically conversation. Your characters talk to each other. They should sound like real people. This could mean that all you need to do is to transcribe people's conversation. Unfortunately, it's not that simple—or rather, fortunately, it's not that complicated to write dialogue.

Real conversation may sound like this:

> "Er, Jim, have you heard the latest thing, on, what's his name, you know, er, I mean the guy who's so much like in the news—"
>
> "This coffee sucks. Well, I've been too busy lately, all the job applications and all—"
>
> "Shit, he's a pop singer, oh jeez, why can't I remember his name, like, he's like real famous, I mean, er, you know?—"
>
> "Uhuh."
>
> Pause. A cough. "He's hiding, you know who I mean, er, he's got an—damn it!—"
>
> "Sure, it's easy for those guys, they're all millionaires. Well, where's the waitress?"
>
> "Uhuh."

Even in a direct transcription resembling this one, you can't indicate where both characters speak at the same time, where vowels drag, consonants double and so on. Moreover, in real speech, you get a person's melody of voice, see his body language, and so you might suffer all the hesitations and indirectness and irrelevancies much better than when you read the transcript in print. You can't reproduce real speech. You can approximate it now and then, but your dialogue should be quicker and more direct than real speech.

"Dialogue should convey a sense of spontaneity but eliminate the repetitiveness of real talk," said Elizabeth Bowen. It may be effective to use "or something's," "I mean's" and "sort of's" for the sense of realism and spontaneity, especially where hesitations simulate not only the sound of real speech, but psychologically indicative moments. But use these fillers sparingly.

Moreover, your character needn't talk unless there's a point to be conveyed. Eudora Welty says that "only the significant passages of their [characters'] talk should be recorded, in high relief against the narrative." So make your talk matter and find the right balance between realism and economy of speech.

To make realistic dialogue, create a distinct voice for every character. By his diction (word choice) you reveal a character's region, class, education, and style of thinking (logical, impulsive, spiteful, etc.).

Give each character a voice with a distinctive level of diction. Let some speak in fragments, others in complete sentences; some in slang, some in professional jargon, others in standard English; some with fashionable and others with idiosyncratic vocabulary—of course, all within the reasonable limits of what kind of story you write. Where do you get people's voices? Listen. Remember. If you need to, record. Some people are fortunate because they remember sounds rather than images. The sound more than compensates for the lack of image. Frank O'Connor, for example, said, "I just notice a feeling from people. I notice particularly the cadence of their voices, the sort of phrases they'll use, and that's what I'm all the time trying to hear in my head, how people word things—because everybody speaks an entirely different language. . . . I cannot pass a story as finished . . . unless I know how everybody in it spoke, which, as I say, can go quite well with the fact that I couldn't tell you in the least what they looked like. If I use the right phrase and the reader hears the phrase in his head, he sees the individual."

If you are primarily a visual person, you may rely on vivid images with great success, but you still need the sounds. Get them any way you can. Record people, study their talk, study dialogue and dialects.

Dialect. When using dialect, don't alter your spelling radically. To evoke a drawl, don't triple vowels. Don't skip consonants. Here and there, you might alter a word or two, but don't overdo it, because most readers resent having to slow down. Create a dialect through unique word choices and syntax. For example, in this scene from Bernard Malamud's *The Assistant*, the words, *insurinks* for *insurance* and *macher*, a jack of all trades gives us a flavor of Yiddish and helps to evoke a New York immigrant ghetto.

"I make a living." The macher spoke soundlessly. "I make fires."

Morris drew back.

The macher waited with downcast eyes. "We are poor people," he murmured.

"What do you want from me?"

"We are poor people," the macher said, apologetically. "God loves the poor people but he helps the rich. The insurinks companies are rich. . . ."

Also, the macher's fondness of proverbs—"God loves the poor people but he helps the rich"—gives us a sense of the person speaking.

To be safe, use the dialects you are familiar with, but don't fear them. I must admit that since I did not grow up speaking English and since my visuals are stronger than my sounds, I feared dialects for years. But I realized that Faulkner and Steinbeck hadn't used any region's dialect exactly. They made their own variations of dialects. Every person, in a way, speaks his or her own dialect. So after you study a regional dialect for a while, you could make your own variation of it. I lived in Nebraska for three years and instead of writing about the people there I wrote about animals. When the writer Rick Bass asked me "So why don't you write about Nebraskans?" I said that as a stranger I couldn't do their dialect. "Come on," he said. "Who knows how people in Lynch, Nebraska, talk? Make up your own Lynch dialect. Who's gonna question you?" He was right. I don't have to use every Nebraskan's deviation from the standard English to feel that I have rendered Nebraskan farmers. On the other hand, just using a couple of regional words won't do the job. *Y'all* and *reckon* aren't enough to make a Southerner. If you need a Southerner, find a few elements of the dialect's grammar, syntax and word choice (other than clichés such as *reckon* and *y'all*) that evoke the sound of Southern speech.

When you write in dialect, here and there you may change the spelling of a word, to create a realistic sound, as does Norman Mailer in the following scene from *The Naked and the Dead*:

> Ridges laid down his shovel and looked at him. His face was patient but there was some concern in it. "What you trying to do, Stanley?" he asked.
>
> "You don't like it?" Stanley sneered.
>
> "No, sir, Ah don't."
>
> Stanley grinned slowly. "You know what you can do."
>
> . . . "Aah, fug it," he said, turning away.

"Ah" for a Southern way of saying "I" works. Now that we can begin to hear the Southerner, Ridges, we don't need every word rendered in dialect—an occasional one will do. If the reader knows the dialect, she'll fill in the drawl and other Southern sounds for herself; if she doesn't, she probably won't appreciate odd spellings anyhow. So be a minimalist with regional expressions, unless you have a special reason to be ultrarealistic and to accomplish a speech reproduction.

Obscenities. What about "fug" in Mailer's dialogue? Mailer wrote this a while back, when using obscenities in fiction was unfashionable if not illegal. I'd still say it's good to be conservative. Obscenities have been overused, so the shock value is gone, and the boredom of valuelessness has set in. Anthony Burgess said: "When I wrote my first Enderby novel, I had to make my hero say 'For cough,' since 'Fuck off' was not acceptable. With the second book the climate had changed, and Enderby was at liberty to say 'Fuck off.' I wasn't happy. It was too easy. He still said 'For cough'. . . ." Obscenities are easy, and people resort to them when they need an easy solution. You rarely need to be overly realistic, just as you don't need to reproduce every "er."

Child's speech. Sometimes it's enough to reproduce a child's logic rather than the sound of a child's speech, as does Vasily Aksenov in "Little Whale, Varnisher of Reality." Although this is a translation, the child's logic makes a realistic scene—in which a child cuts in between an adulterous couple.

> She lifted her hand and put the palm of this hand to my cheek . . . stroked . . .

> Just then Whale came squirming in between us. He tugged the pretty lady by the sleeve: "Hey, take your old umbrella and don't touch Daddy. He's my Daddy, not yours."

Only a child could make this confusion—to see a woman as another child competing for parental affection. And children at a certain stage are extremely possessive, so Whale's intrusion, by its realism, adds credibility to the story. There's charm in how children make odd, and yet obvious, connections.

Forms of Dialogue

Dialogue can range from straight dialogue, without any interpretation between the lines, to hardly any lines and a lot of exposition between them. In "Basil From Her Garden," Donald Barthelme strips the dialogue for the sake of absurdity, perhaps to mimic the impersonality of a psychiatric session:

> Q- What do you do, after work, in the evenings or on weekends?
> A- Just ordinary things.
> Q- No special interests?
> A- I'm very interested in bow hunting. These new bows they have now, what they call a compound bow. Also, I'm a member of the Galapagos Society, we work for the environment, it's really a very effective—
> Q- And what else?
> A- Well, adultery. I would say that that's how I spend most of my free time. In adultery.

You can vary dialogue, using a combination of direct and indirect addresses, as I did above in reporting my conversation with Rick Bass. I put his words in direct quotations; I report my words indirectly, using *that* to introduce the content of what I said. These shifts in the form of address emphasize his points more than my objections.

In theater, actors can show you the shades of meaning

through the intonation of their voices, body language and other means. In Barthelme's example we have no indication of body language and setting, so the dialogue is not really a scene.

A writer need not despair at not being able to render intonations and voices perfectly because he can, between the lines, describe action, as does Irwin Shaw in "The Girls in Their Summer Dresses":

> "Look out," Frances said, as they crossed Eighth Street. "You'll break your neck."
>
> Michael laughed and Frances laughed with him.
>
> "She's not so pretty, anyway," Frances said. "Anyway, not pretty enough to take a chance breaking your neck looking at her."
>
> Michael laughed again. He laughed louder this time, but not as solidly. "She wasn't a bad-looking girl. She had a nice complexion. Country-girl complexion. How did you know I was looking at her?"
>
> Frances cocked her head to one side and smiled at her husband under the tip-tilted brim of her hat. "Mike, darling. . . ."

Good dialogue often manages to evoke intonation, as does the last line from the above example, but there are serious limits to that, so the tone can be described, and body language can turn it into a scene.

Body Language, Character and Dialogue

Sometimes the more important part of dialogue takes place in body language and in the exposition between the lines, as in "The Real Thing" by Doris Lessing:

> He was more on guard than he knew, although he had said to himself before arriving, Now, careful, the slightest thing sets her off. Every line of him said, "Don't come too close." He leaned back in his chair, even tilting it as she leaned forward towards him.

The dialogue here is summarized, with emphasis on its essential quality, body language.

In a scene with dialogue, the words may run contrary to the general meaning of the scene. In the following example—"The Last of Mr. Norris" by Christopher Isherwood—a character, eager to mask his nervousness at a German border crossing, speaks about Greek archaeology quite out of context:

> He spoke so loudly that the people in the next compartment must certainly be able to hear him.
>
> "One comes, quite unexpectedly, upon the most fascinating little corners. A single column standing in the middle of a rubbish-heap. . . ."
>
> "*Deutsche Pass-Kontrolle*. All passports, please."
>
> An official had appeared in the doorway of our compartment. His voice made Mr. Norris give a slight but visible jump. Anxious to allow him time to pull himself together, I hastily offered my own passport. As I had expected, it was barely glanced at.
>
> "I'm traveling to Berlin," said Mr. Norris, handing over his passport with a charming smile; so charming, indeed, that it seemed a little overdone.

The dialogue establishes a dramatic scene, with suspense, and at the same time it characterizes Mr. Norris—his duplicity, pomposity, timidity. In the excerpt from "Sally Bowels" by Christopher Isherwood on page 61, the contrast between Sally's sophisticated speech and her appearance (dirty hands) portrays her more vividly and insightfully than summary could.

Good dramatic dialogue is multilayered, so that in addition to body language and direct meaning, there's another parallel meaning to what's being said. The dialogue below—in "Four Meetings" by Henry James—establishes two characters (the aloof narrator and a trickster posing as a painter), and it raises tension of an indirect confrontation:

> "Composes well. Fine old tone. Make a nice thing." He spoke in a charmless vulgar voice.

> "I see you've a great deal of eye," I replied. "Your cousin tells me you're studying art." He looked at me in the same way, without answering, and I went on with deliberate urbanity: "I suppose you're at the studio of one of those great men." Still on this he continued to fix me, and then he named one of the greatest of that day; which led me to ask him if he liked his master.
>
> "Do you understand French?" he returned.
>
> "Some kinds."
>
> He kept his little eyes on me; with which he remarked: "*Je suis fou de la peinture!*"
>
> "Oh, I understand that kind!" I replied.

Simplistic dialogue, which strives to accomplish only one thing, often falls flat because it is too transparent. Complex dialogue like James' creates drama; it's complex. And there's a subtext—what's not said directly.

The narrator sometimes tells us how what's said is said: "I went on with deliberate urbanity." At other times, he implies and shows indirectly. He is cynical. That could have been made explicit by adding a modifier: "Oh, I understand that kind!" I replied *sardonically*. This adverb would summarize the tone, but the diction accomplishes the meaning without the writer's spelling it out. "I replied" suffices. With the choice of detail, between the lines of dialogue, the narrator expresses his attitude toward the artist: "He kept his little eyes on me." *Little eyes* conveys that the narrator despises the artist and deems him cunning and petty.

Dialogue and Information

Every sentence in a piece of fiction conveys some kind of information. Dialogue brings us close to the characters and their conflicts. If you need history, philosophy, biology, and most other sorts of information, put them in the narrative part, unless your characters are historians, philosophers and biologists. If you set a story in the Vietnam War and you need some background history, don't put it all in dialogue between two soldiers. That would sound unnatural and, moreover, would be much slower than giving the history in narrative. Don't let your characters sound like a bunch of journalists pumping people for information (unless that's what they are).

Since dialogue does convey information about people's struggles, make sure you don't give us banal and irrelevant information. Avoid realistic dialogue introductions; summarize the introductory pleasantries and move on:

> After shaking hands, Jim asked Bill about the loan.
> "Oh, that."
> "Yes, what else? I've got kids to feed, and you're. . . ."

Now every line will advance rather than stall the story because we have jumped into the essential part of the conversation.

If a conversation pattern—verbal abuse, for example—occurs many times, and that's the main point, don't give us all the instances. Give us a dramatic one, when it counts, and summarize the others.

SCENE

So that we can properly discuss how to create a scene, go back to chapter one and reread the scene—the German soldier giving aspirin to the boy—from "The Burning Shoe." The story describes the village before the scene, but even during it we get the wooden floors, the bucket of water in the kitchen, the down cover. These sparse elements of the setting keep us seeing the stage.

In a scene, almost all the elements we've discussed so far come together. You portray characters dynamically—characters whom you may have sketched in summary before the scene.) They express themselves by what they do and how they do it, what they say and how they speak, and by what they think (if they carry the POV). In "The Burning Shoe" scene, we see that the boy, although scared, is lusty—he wants more honey cakes; the soldier, although surprisingly benevolent, is strict and practical—he says "Nein!" when he thinks he has erased the boy's bitter taste of the aspirin. The action taking place as part of the scene shows us what the characters are like. There's no need to tell it now.

In a scene you advance the plot. Whatever conflict evolves must culminate eventually in a scene, where the protagonists and the antagonists meet and clash, as the boy and the soldier do. The introductory statements lead us into the scene and raise our expectations—the Germans, since they had killed the boy's father, threaten to do more harm. So when the soldier walks into the bedroom, stamping with his boots, and pulls the down cover, there's tension. Will he strangle the boy? The question hovering in the slowed-down action creates the tension. It's essential to slow down even quick action, if tension is going to work, and in the "The Burning Shoe" scene this is accomplished with concentration on the sensory details and thoughts (stamping, cold hands, creaking throat, bulging eyes, "I thought, to strangle me") and with outright delay. The soldier withdraws his hand and pours water into the glass and puts some substance into it. Our old question recurs—will the soldier kill the boy? Again sensations keep us engaged and wondering—the glass pressing the lip against the teeth, the shudderingly bitter liquid, and the boy's thinking that this must be poison.

And now, at the culmination point, the surprise occurs. We find out that the bitter liquid is aspirin. The soldier gives the boy honey cakes. Not that every culminating scene must have a twist, a surprise, but you must raise expectations and delay answering them. The answer must come gradually, through sensory details (or a dialogue exchange, or both) of the action. Keep your reader guessing.

To construct a scene, you must bring a conflict to it—the characters must want or fear something that might happen during this scene. In other words, a scene must have a plot of its own, which of course must relate to the overall plot of the story. Everything that concerns the characters—who they are, how they relate to each other, how they conflict—must be fleshed out, embodied, dramatized, seen (that is, scened). You must dramatize whatever abstract plans and plot outlines you have, so that the reader will be able to play the drama in her mind.

Although the scene in fiction resembles the scene in theater, it is usually easier to do in fiction. You don't need to worry how to get a character off the stage, and you can fast-forward, summarize, tell, reveal characters' thoughts without speech and grimaces. But theater still remains a paradigm of what scenes are. A play is impossible without scenes. So is fiction, except perhaps for experimental fiction. In theater, characters act in a certain time at a certain place. This applies in fiction, too: Unless you specify the time and location of the action, your action is unrealized, abstract.

How to Prepare for the Big Scene

For a piece of fiction, you need at least one fully realized scene, taking place here and now (or there and then). The essential story is an event—what happened, who did it, to whom, where, when, how, why. You may prepare for the event without making scenes and without concretizing scenes in a time and space, but the event itself must be created on the page: continuous, like a piece of music, and spatial, like a painting. And the event must make sense—that is, all the characters, places, conflicts and other elements must plausibly connect here.

The most dramatic moment of your story usually will combine dialogue, scene, description, and the other elements of fiction. But before this scene can take place, you often need to introduce the necessary background, characters and conflicts, so that once the big scene—the culmination of the story—occurs, you won't need to interrupt the action and take us off stage to fill us in.

In preparation for your culminating event, you can use several minor scenes and summarize several potential scenes into a generalized one. For example, "Every Sunday morning she walked to the Unitarian Church. As she walked, she would spit at the hedges." "Every Sunday" dissolves the action into a blurry repetitive scene as do *would, often, always*. Instead of constructing many small scenes to show us that she walks every Sunday, we have simply summarized this.

Such generalized scenes do not offer sharp detail, because on different occasions, the repeated action would be somewhat different. One Sunday it would be sunny, so the woman could walk in sandals; another Sunday it could snow, so she'd walk in boots; and so on. We reduce the amount of detail when we make summary scenes of repeated action.

Of course, as usual, there are exceptions to this rule. In a summary scene you can come close to a realized scene, with many details, as in the case below, from John Cheever's "O Youth and Beauty!":

> Then if the host had a revolver, he would be asked to produce it. Cash would take off his shoes and assume a starting crouch behind a sofa. Trace would fire the weapon out of an open window, and if you were new to the community and had not understood what the preparations were about, you would then realize that you were watching a hurdle race. Over the sofa went Cash, over the tables, over the fire screen and the woodbox. It was not exactly a race, since Cash ran it alone, but it was extraordinary to see this man of forty surmount so many obstacles so gracefully.

We can imaginatively reconstruct this action, see it acted out without a gun and with a gun, in different yet similar houses.

This type of habitual action can set up the pieces—character, setting, conflict—but it will not do as a climax. In the climax of the above story, Cash's wife kills him with a gun. There are no "ifs" and "woulds" there. It takes place only once. A miracle is not a usual event, and a story works like a miracle; so it must take place as a here and now, only once. If it happens many times, it's a custom, not a miracle. You can introduce and develop a conflict through nonscenic narrative—but *the culminating point of your story inevitably must be laid out as a scene or several scenes.*

If you don't need to mention every Sunday, don't. Get us right into a scene to show us the characters and places on one crucial Sunday when our main event takes place. However, especially in a long piece of writing, you probably will need to compound and summarize scenes. So learn to summarize the auxiliary action and dramatize the key moments. P.G. Wodehouse advised: "I think the success of every novel—if it's a novel of action—depends on the high spots. The thing to do is to say to yourself, 'Which are my big scenes?' and then get every drop of juice out of them."

Silent Scenes. In preparation for the big scenes, many writers use silent scenes. These are not necessarily summary scenes, but descriptions of actions.

Certainly many war, crime, horror and erotic scenes don't need to contain dialogue. Consider the following scene from *All Quiet on the Western Front* by Erich Maria Remarque:

> Suddenly in the pursuit we reach the enemy line.
>
> We are so close on the heels of our retreating enemies that we reach it almost at the same time as they. In this way we suffer few casualties. A machine-gun barks, but is silenced with a bomb. Nevertheless, the couple of seconds has sufficed to give us five stomach wounds. With the butt of his rifle Kat smashes to pulp the face of one of the unwounded machine-gunners. We bayonet the others before they have time to get out their bombs. Then thirstily we drink the water they have for cooling the guns.

From what goes on before this scene we know exactly where we are, and the action here is timed, gruesomely vivid (as is appropriate for a war story), concrete, yet not tremendously detailed. Smashing a face to pulp is vivid enough to make you wince. The image of drinking water for cooling guns lets us even taste the scene. Remarque does not need to describe the metallic watery taste in aluminum cups—we probably have these sensory associations anyhow. This appeal to our taste buds makes the scene powerful, although there's no dialogue.

In *One Hundred Years of Solitude,* Gabriel Garcia Márquez uses no dialogue in the following erotic scene:

> Jose Arcadio's companion asked them to leave them alone, and the couple lay down on the ground, close to

> the bed. The passion of the others woke up Jose Arcadio's fervor. On the first contact the bones of the girl seemed to become disjointed with a disorderly crunch like the sound of a box of dominoes, and her skin broke out into a pale sweat and her eyes filled with tears as her whole body exhaled a lugubrious lament and a vague smell of mud. But she bore the impact with a firmness of character and a bravery that were admirable. Jose Arcadio felt himself lifted up into the air toward a state of seraphic inspiration, where his heart burst forth with an outpouring of tender obscenities that entered the girl through her ears and came out of her mouth translated into her language.

This scene engages our sensory imagination (hearing, touch, sight, smell, even balance), even though many things are metaphoric ("seraphic inspiration"). The lovemaking is not given to us blow by blow, but yet it is concretized enough in time—"the first contact"—and place—"on the ground, close to the bed." This scene may not be erotically thrilling—most readers probably don't get into an amorous mood reading this. But the exquisite language and imagery give you an aesthetically strong experience. In writing good erotic scenes, the beauty of the writing matters most.

Although Marquez's scene indicates some kind of talk, this scene has no dialogue. Many such scenes could be useful to show what's going on before the major conflicts escalate into big, fully realized scenes, which should usually contain dialogue.

The Big Scene

Once we know enough about the characters and their conflicts, we can enter big scenes. Here's a big scene from "The Blue Hotel" by Stephen Crane. We have seen the paranoid Swede in other chapters. He expects snowy Nebraska to be the wild West where everybody cheats at cards; he trembles with fear that someone will kill him, thinks he sees people cheat at cards, gets into a fist fight with an innkeeper's son, wins, and then becomes cocky and moves to another bar. And just when he celebrates his being a tough guy, this is what happens. He insists that the bartender drink with him but the bartender refuses.

> "Well," cried the Swede, "listen hard then. See those men over there? Well, they're going to drink with me, and don't you forget it. Now you watch."
>
> "Hi!" yelled the barkeeper, "this won't do!"
>
> "Why won't it?" demanded the Swede. He stalked over to the table, and by chance laid his hand upon the shoulder of the gambler. "How about this?" he asked wrathfully. "I asked you to drink with me."
>
> The gambler simply twisted his head and spoke over his shoulder. "My friend, I don't know you."
>
> "Oh, hell!" answered the Swede, "come and have a drink."
>
> "Now, my boy," advised the gambler, kindly, "take your hand off my shoulder and go 'way and mind your own business." He was a little, slim man, and it seemed strange to hear him use this tone of heroic patronage to the burly Swede. The other men at the table said nothing.
>
> "What! You won't drink with me, you little dude? I'll make you!" The Swede had grasped the gambler frenziedly at the throat, and was dragging him from his chair. The other men sprang up. The barkeeper dashed around the corner of his bar. There was a great tumult, and then was seen a long blade in the hand of the gambler. It shot forward, and a human body, this citadel of virtue, wisdom, power, was pierced as easily as if it had been a melon. The Swede fell with a cry of supreme astonishment.
>
> The prominent merchants and the district attorney must have at once tumbled out of the place backward. The bartender found himself hanging limply to the arm of a chair and gazing into the eyes of a murderer.
>
> "Henry," said the latter, as he wiped his knife on one of the towels that hung beneath the bar rail, "you tell 'em

> where to find me. I'll be home, waiting for 'em." Then he vanished. A moment afterward the barkeeper was in the street dinning through the storm for help and, moreover, companionship.
>
> The corpse of the Swede, alone in the saloon, had its eyes fixed upon a dreadful legend that dwelt atop the cash-machine: "This registers the amount of your purchase."

We have nearly all the elements of storytelling here. Besides dialogue, we have action. "The Swede had grasped the gambler frenziedly at the throat, and was dragging him from his chair."

Body language: "He stalked over to the table, and by chance laid his hand upon the shoulder of the gambler."

Vivid similes and metaphors: "pierced as easily as if it had been a melon."

A steady POV. This is told from an objective POV, from a short range: "and then was seen a long blade." We are watching this. We don't see the action from any participant's mind and we don't know who the narrator is. This is a theatrical POV.

Most of the story comes together in the image of the lonely Swede's corpse with its eyes fixed on the sign reading, "This registers the amount of your purchase." This scene seemed inevitable throughout the story, yet in a previous seemingly climactic scene, the Swede had won; our old expectations—which have driven the story forward suspensefully—have been fulfilled after we nearly quit them. But so that this would not be a linear plot, another chapter follows. From witness accounts it turns out that the innkeeper's son *was* cheating at cards. The Swede was paranoid but not wrong.

This scene, while excellent, is not perfectly graceful. Although the third-person narrative is not an omniscient one, the narrator is not quite hidden, because we get the interpretation of the scene: "human body, this citadel of virtue, wisdom, power. . . ." But by this point in the story, the reader has accepted Crane's foregrounded narrator, who carefully observes and makes interpretative forays into the narrative. This kind of authorial presence is not in fashion today, and modern readers probably find it distracting. The objective distancing from the narrative actually reveals a subjective interpretation of the story's theme.

Earlier in this chapter I said that using adverbs with dialogue tags usually doesn't work. But in this scene, we have an exception: " 'How about this?' he asked wrathfully. 'I asked you to drink with me.' " *Wrathfully* augments the tone; the anger would not be sufficiently visible without the adverb. A well-placed adverb may enhance your showing of an action.

This outline—summary scenes, minor scenes, and silent scenes leading up to the big scene—is a classical story structure, but certainly not the only one. Many stories work differently. They may open with a big scene, then supply background, then go on to other big scenes. Some stories take place as a single continuous scene. And some big scenes may not contain dialogue—for example, the aspirin scene from "The Burning Shoe" contains only one spoken word, *Nein*. How you prepare for the big moments in your fiction and how you construct the big scenes depends mostly on your subject matter. Having said this, I will also say that the classical story structure—with alternation among small scenes, narrative, and big scenes with dialogue—probably is the best choice whenever your subject matter allows it. The advantage of this structure is its variety of approaches: the changes of pace (from slow to quick, with both a quick pace and slow-motion effects in the climax action) and the changes in focus (from distant to close-up). This variety increases the possibility that the reader will stay fresh from page to page.

EXERCISES

1. One page. Write a composite scene of a woman and a man living happily together—their weekend routine. Use constructions such as "Every Sunday they would go out for brunch."

Objective: To learn how to make chronologically composite scenes. You might need these to build toward a dramatic change. There'll be a Sunday, perhaps, in which the story crisis takes place, when they won't be able to go out for brunch. There you'd switch from the usual "every" scene to the specific "once" scene.

Check: Is your scene vivid? If it isn't, it's not a scene but a narrative summary. Let the reader smell the java, taste the butter on the croissant. On the other hand, is the scene too specific? You shouldn't have time-bound sentences, such as, "It's awful that the earthquake split our bedroom in half a couple of hours ago, isn't it?" This is too specific, too dramatic, too unrepeatable, to characterize a usual brunch.

2. One page. Describe a lovemaking scene, without being too explicit. A good erotic scene depends more on suggestion than on complete revelation. This may be hard to do. Avoid statements like, "She was excited" and, "He moaned with pleasure." Namely, steer away from clichés and summaries. Try to be fresh.

Objective: Not necessarily to arouse your reader. Instead, dazzle him with exquisite images. Learn how to combine vivid imagery and graceful sentences.

Check: Have you engaged our senses? Make sure this is not all visual. Touch and smell. Do you have staple expressions such as, "She was swooning in ecstasy"? Delete them. Use fresher language, the way Marquez uses "seraphic inspiration" for ecstasy. And since the reader can't hear the ecstasy, offer an image that suggests it, such as words entering the girl's ears and coming out of her mouth translated in her own language.

3. Two to three pages. Describe a war scene, showing us a horrible deed without mentioning that it is horrible.

Objective: To show rather than tell. In a scene, more than anywhere else, this is crucial. Telling is a summary. Showing is a scene. "It looked horrible" tells and does not show. Here it's not so important that your sentences be graceful; on the contrary, construct some joltingly choppy ones, to reflect the subject matter.

Check: Have you engaged our senses? If not, go back and surprise us. Let us taste something, the way Remarque lets you taste gun-cleaning water at the end of his scene. Let us feel something, like salty mud in our nostrils.

4. One page. Write a scene with your protagonist engaged in some kind of activity just before she is ambushed or assassinated. Let the protagonist notice and misinterpret the clues of danger; and let her hesitate with the intuition of the danger and still go into the trap. You could play with atmospheric details and character's thoughts to achieve foreshadowing and suspense.

Now write the same scene from the perspective of the antagonists who are setting the ambush. Create the uncertainty of a hunt.

Objective: To prepare for the climax scene, with foreshadowing and suspense. Excite the reader with the sensation of impending danger (with skillful choice of details and clues), and yet don't make it too obvious what will happen, so that the reader genuinely won't know in advance. It's good that you keep your mind open so that although you may drive the narrative toward an assassination, something else could happen instead. If you surprise yourself, you will surprise the reader, too.

Check: Did you insinuate what's to appear through sensations—smells, sounds, visual clues? Saying, "I had a sense of foreboding as I approached the cave," or "The dark evergreens looked ominous against the pale sky" won't do. "Foreboding" and "ominous" is what you're striving to achieve—not mention. If you strike "ominous" from the sentence, you could rewrite and improve it: "The evergreens, dark against the pale sky, appeared like a brotherhood of monks clad in black robes and sworn to silence." That would not be particularly subtle either, but at least you would not glaringly state, "ominous." In fact, pointing sharply toward what's ahead may not be bad. The same sentence could be rewritten, "The dark evergreens appeared like moist knife blades poking into the pale sky." The notion of murder and a knife will be raised. The main goal is to create expectations, which need not be fulfilled neatly.

5. One page. Write a scene from the POV of a woman who comes home from work and is about to discover her boyfriend's lover.

Objective: Similar to Exercise 4, though not necessarily as suspenseful. Let the woman misinterpret—at first—the clues that somebody might be around.

Check: Did you provide enough sensory clues giving us a notion that somebody might be present in the house? Smells? Sounds? Keep them subtle.

6. Two pages. Use a dictaphone or a tape recorder and record a dinner conversation. (If you don't have such gadgets handy, listen carefully and write quickly.) Transcribe the conversation. Then read what you have. Most likely the transcript will be cumbersome to read, with all the pauses, fillers and so on. Edit it. Take out all the repetitions. Read it again. Perhaps now it's too spare. So put back a few repetitions for the natural sound, and here and there, describe minimal actions between spoken sentences—slurping the soup, clanking the china—so the dialogue does not appear to be suspended in a vacuum. These little details will turn the dialogue into a scene. Now the conversation should read smoothly, if for no other reason than because you've read thousands of dialogues done in that vein.

Objective: To learn to distinguish between real conversation and written dialogue. In your final dialogue, keep the best parts of the actual conversation, and the best artificial props—if any—you came up with in rewriting.

Check: Since this is an exercise in revision, the check is included in the task description.

7. Two pages. Reproduce a quarrel you've had. Don't edit for diversity of insults, subtlety of word choice, dignity of the scene. Just give it to us, raw.

Objective: A quarrel is a paradigm of dynamic dialogue. Conflicting motives drive word choices. Even if there's no quarrel in your dialogue, use a conflict to propel the conversation.

Check: Is it clear what the quarrel is about? It may be about two issues, one on the surface, another beneath it, but at least let the theme of the surface quarrel be clear. If it's too confusing, it won't work. Anger probably more than any other emotion helps the mind simplify problems into sharp outlines.

8. Four one-page dialogue scenes. Write probing dialogue between (a) a demented psychiatrist and a client, (b) an evangelist

and a philosophical homeless person, (c) a police officer and a burglar who pretends to live in the apartment from which he is stealing, and (d) a mother who's just miscarried and her four-year-old who wants a baby sister.

Objective: To practice writing different people's dialogue. Let characters speak spontaneously, pulling you in and saying things almost on their own. Perhaps once you begin hearing a voice, the voice will write and you will merely record.

Check: Do the characters sound different from each other? They should. Do your characters talk at cross-purposes? They should. Let them evade answering questions. Sometimes a question should be countered with another question. Sometimes, the answer should have nothing directly to do with the question.

9. One page. Describe body language during a conversation without reproducing any of the dialogue. Have a party of three at a table, two men and a woman. One man is in love with the woman, the woman is in love with the other man, and he's in love with himself. Describe their postures, inclinations of their bodies, hand motions and so on—the way Doris Lessing does in "The Real Thing," on page 134.

Objective: To learn how to show bodies talking. Some ambiguity of gesture is all right. Some psychologists think that even the direction a crossed leg points with its foot indicates who the leg-crosser likes most in a circle. Of course, these social psychologists don't make it any easier to attend a party because they expand the potential for self-consciousness, but they do make your task of writing easier. Even if they are wrong, they do what you should do in fiction: They make gestures meaningful.

Check: From the social dynamics you've given us, is it clear who's after whom? Is it clear that the second man is a Narcissus? Does he constantly glance at mirrors and touch up his fragile hairdo?

10. Two pages. Now let us hear what these people from Exercise 9 talk about. Intersperse their words into the description you already have.

Objective: To learn how to mix body language and dialogue.

Check: Do all your characters sound distinct from one another? Could you tell without direct dialogue tags who's talking? Does the content of what's said reveal who's after whom? Is Narcissus boasting? Is the first man insulting him?

11. Two pages. Write a dialogue, without using "said" or any other words indicating speech. Rely on punctuation marks and all the strategies for avoiding "said" that we've discussed in this chapter.

Objective: To practice avoiding direct dialogue tags.

Check: Is it always clear who's talking? If not, go back and insert *said* and other tags, to make it clear wherever needed.

12. Two to three pages. Write a dialogue between a father and daughter. She is looking forward to a trip to Alaska, which he's promised, provided that she got all As on her finals. However, the father has lost all his savings gambling that afternoon when she comes home with her transcript. He can't afford the trip, yet he doesn't have the heart to tell her. Meanwhile, she got a C in English but forged an A on the transcript. Let him marvel at her improvement in English and ask to see her brilliant essay on honesty; and let her keep evading his request, asking about Alaska and going about her business, packing for the trip.

Objective: To practice constructing dialogue that serves to avoid giving information, to mislead, and to forestall dreaded questions.

Check: Is there a lot of cross-purpose conversation? There should be. Are there irrelevant things said out of context? There should be, like in Christopher Isherwood's "The Last of Mr. Norris" (page 135). Is there body language to show anxiety? Defensiveness? Faked emotion? Pauses? Ignored questions?

CHAPTER SEVEN

BEGINNINGS AND ENDINGS

A good piece of fiction resembles a multicourse meal. You begin with an aperitif or an appetizer. If you can afford it, of course, you'd like a delicacy, before you get down to the nitty-gritty of knife-handling and chewing.

Some story beginnings offer the burning quality of cognac; others, the salty allure of caviar; and some we prefer to skip as though waiting for fast food.

Some writers, write the beginning last; others write it first. Gabriel Garcia Márquez labors over his first paragraph for days, and when he has it down, he says the rest comes easily. Some writers need to know the end before they begin; others need to know only the characters, whom they set into motion to find their own endings and beginnings. Others, like Jerzy Kosinski, have both the ending and the beginning before they do the rest: "I always start a novel by writing its first page and its last page, which seem to survive almost intact through all the following drafts and changes." Experiment and see what works for you.

As you write, you need not despair if you don't have a brilliant beginning. Perhaps your ending will become your beginning in the final version. Maybe you will chop off both the draft ending and the beginning, and a passage from the middle of the story will emerge as the dynamic beginning. Many writers assume we have had enough beginnings and endings, and they spare us. This minimalist approach—give me just the story without the decor—is possible in short stories, but in novels, it's harder—probably impossible—to do.

I admire graceful beginnings and endings, so although my aesthetics in other respects might be minimalist, I see no reason why you should deprive yourself (and your readers) of their grace.

BEGINNINGS

After the cover art and the title, beginnings are your first impression, or rather, expression. The cover may be beautiful, the title sonorous, but if the first lines sound dull, the first impression will be dull. From social psychology, we know that the first impression is often the most important one, that after all kinds of other impressions settle, the last impression will probably resemble the first. Because of this notion, many writers belabor their openings, to make them "stunning."

While it's important to be interesting in the first lines, beginnings must accomplish much more. To resort to a prolonged comparison: In a chess opening, you try to win—and control—the greatest amount of space with the fewest moves possible. You open and develop your pieces, place them in striking distance of the opponent's pieces, with a view to the engagement—the middle game, in which you'll maneuver toward the winning end game. You might aim to have a preponderance of pawns on one side, so once all the heavy pieces are exchanged, you advance a single pawn. A good player never aims to play a trick in the first five moves if she respects her opponent. Likewise, if you respect your reader, you don't resort to tricks in the opening, for these are short-lived. Like a sound chess opening, an opening of fiction must accomplish more urgent goals than "brilliant combinations." (Reserve those for the climactic action.) Introduce your characters, give us the place and time where the story occurs, and raise a question, complication or crisis, that we are to follow—something to intrigue us, so we want to keep reading.

Unlike bombastic journalism, which relies on opening with a bang, fiction can open less loudly. Here's an example of a bang opening by Truman Capote in "Children on Their Birthdays": "Yesterday afternoon the six o'clock bus ran over Miss Bobbit."

Yes, this catches our interest, but what next? It'll be hard to match the intensity of the beginning in what follows. The story starts with a climax rather than working toward one; instead of looking forward, we look backward, and the whole story might be an anticlimax. (Actually, despite the drawback of bombast, Capote does manage, with considerable skill, to make a good story. But that's a feat, not something a beginner can be expected to emulate.)

Some bangs may work effectively, provided they are timed well and delayed a bit, as this from George Gissing's *New Grub Street*:

> As the Milvains sat down to breakfast the clock of Wattleborough parish church struck eight; it was two miles away, but the strokes were borne very distinctly on the west wind this autumn morning. Jasper, listening before he cracked an egg, remarked with cheerfulness: "There's a man being hanged in London at this moment."

This is a skillful jab—not an outright bang in the first sentence, but in the second. The first one draws characters and an orderly setting (useful, for we need to know where and with whom we are) in lyrical strokes, so the hanging announcement startles us. It's harder to startle in the first sentence because there's nothing prior that the sentence could contrast. Still, if the punch has been delayed, its intensity has been only intensified, and the problem remains: Where do we go from here, if our hero's already hanged in the second sentence?

If you open without murdering anybody on the first page, you have less to live up to, and you still might create intrigue, as does Heinrich von Kleist's beginning of "Marquise of O—." Not only does this have the quality of a hook (not a punch)—raising a question of what to look for in the story—but it also introduces a crisis and a character:

> In M—, an important town in northern Italy, the widowed Marquise of O—, a lady of unblemished reputation and the mother of several well-brought-up children, inserted the following announcement in the newspapers:

> that she had, without knowledge of the cause, come to find herself in a certain condition; that she would like the father of the child she was expecting to disclose his identity to her; and that she was resolved, out of consideration for her family, to marry him.

The introduction—"lady of unblemished reputation"—contrasts to what follows five lines down. The question is raised, which we will follow through most of the novella: who's done it? Who has impregnated the lady? We are not hooked as fish but as fisherman, to stare into the stream of words to come, and to catch the guy.

True, the action must go pretty high to surpass the shock of an incognito impregnation; and von Kleist does deliver the escalation of the action—plunder, rape and murder. We start high, slow down, and go higher. In terms of music, we could express this as allegro-adagio-allegro vivace. The good opening facilitates this dynamic structure. Whenever you have a dramatic hook, you must live up to it.

I've quoted another brilliant opening by von Kleist, from *Michael Kohlhaas*, on page 50, where the startling moment occurs at the end of the first paragraph, rather than at the beginning. The virtuous man, driving his virtue to an extreme, has become a murderer. We have motivation to find out how such a paradox could occur. And the murder is not the culmination of the story; the climax is that a peasant war will start and Dresden will burn.

Von Kleist has managed to keep up with the high expectations that his opening hook created.

Rather than with a dazzling hook, you might open with something more essential: character, setting, theme and style. If the point is to invite the reader into your story, it's usually good to open with fine writing—show the reader that he can trust the narrator, that the narrator has the skill, the mischief, the humor and the charm, to tell a good story—as Charles Dickens did in *Little Dorrit*:

> Thirty years ago, Marseilles lay burning in the sun, one day. A blazing sun upon a fierce August day was no

> greater rarity in southern France then, than at any other time, before or since. Everything in Marseilles, and about Marseilles, had stared at the fervid sky, and been stared at in return, until a staring habit had become universal there. Strangers were stared out of countenance by staring white houses, staring white walls, staring white streets, staring tracts of arid road, staring hills from which verdure was burnt away. The only thing to be seen not fixedly staring and glaring were the vines drooping under their load of grapes. These did occasionally wink a little, as the hot air barely moved their faint leaves.

If this opening were to show up in a fiction workshop as a student's work, I suppose most participants would jump at it and demand that the repetition of "staring" be diminished. But the repetition works stylistically—Dickens carries the staring theme the way a musician might sustain a theme, weaving it through a long passage, accruing a mood and a playful rhythm. Staring and glaring and winking—clearly, he's had fun writing. At the same time, he introduces us to the setting (Marseilles) and an important theme (scrutiny).

If you don't manage an opening that announces a theme explicitly, in a paradoxical fashion, as does von Kleist in *Michael Kohlhaas* (or Dickens with, "It was the best of times, and it was the worst of times"), don't despair. Consider laying out a theme and raising an anticipation implicitly, on a metaphoric, poetic level. Here's one effective opening—from Stephen Crane's *The Red Badge of Courage*—that works through images rather than ideas:

> The cold passed reluctantly from the earth, and the retiring fogs revealed an army stretched out on the hills, resting. As the landscape changed from brown to green, the army awakened, and began to tremble with eagerness at the noise of rumors. It cast its eyes upon the roads, which were growing from long troughs of liquid mud to proper thoroughfares. A river, amber-tinted in the shadow of its banks, purled at the army's feet; and at night, when the

> stream had become of a sorrowful blackness, one could see across it the red, eyelike gleam of hostile camp-fires set in the low brows of distant hills.

This opening sets up expectations. The quality of images persuades me to keep reading, and the promise of finding something (rather than getting it right away) sets me fishing. The hook may not be visible, but that's fine—the worm is. Thematically, from the title, I know I will read about courage, and from the first paragraph, that I will read about fear—"*tremble* with eagerness." "Eyelike gleam of hostile camp-fires set in the low brows of distant hills" tells me I am listening to a skillful narrator.

And notice that the paragraph takes its time. It's not a bang opening. From my observation and informal surveys with students and friends, it seems most people read at least half the first page when browsing. This means two things to me. First, you don't need to open with a bang or a trick. Your command of the language and images will assure the reader more than a glistening image out of context. Relax, and concentrate on leading into the story most appropriately in terms of your theme.

Second, if you do have something bizarre and fantastic going on, state it by the end of that half page, or even right in the beginning. In the first several sentences, readers will accept almost anything, which will work as a premise for the story. If your character is an angel or a thoughtful shoe, say so right away, while the grace of laying out the premises and promises still covers you. Of course, what follows had better be convincing.

Ways to Begin

There are many ways to begin a story. Learn and use these various methods just as a good chess player does not rely on only one opening. Different openings may encourage you to write in a variety of ways, which I think is important especially as you experiment, looking for your best work pattern.

Setting. Here's an example of opening with a setting, by F. Scott Fitzgerald from *Tender Is the Night*:

> On the pleasant shore of the French Riviera, about halfway between Marseilles and the Italian border, stands a large, proud, rose-colored hotel. Deferential palms cool its flushed facade, and before it stretches a short dazzling beach. Lately it has become a summer resort of notable and fashionable people. . . ."

This sets the stage and raises our expectations—high society members will show up here and play. "Lately" may indicate that we are going to deal with the newly rich; there may be an ironic quality to the adverb. "Flushed facade" may lead into questions of shame amid glamour. The advantage of this opening is that we know where we are, and we have begun to anticipate the actors, but we don't have any definite questions yet. We are easing into the novel, which is fine, perhaps in the spirit of the theme.

Ideas. If you open with an idea, you take a risk—the piece might promise to be too intellectual, dry, essayistic. However, ideas sometimes, especially if expressed in the first person or in dialogue (or monologue), serve multiple purposes, as you'll see in this example from Charles Dickens' *Hard Times*:

> "Now, what I want is, Facts. Teach these boys and girls nothing but Facts. Facts alone are wanted in life. Plant nothing else, and root out everything else. You can only form the minds of reasoning animals upon Facts: nothing else will ever be of any service to them. . . ."

The idea of facts being everything indirectly portrays the speaker (a principal) and the place (a boarding school). And the idea becomes a theme, nearly a leitmotif for the novel. So far from a dry abstraction, an idea may accomplish as much as a well-chosen image.

Strong Sensations. Sensations quickly invite your reader to begin experiencing your narrative, and therefore many writers favor sense-oriented beginnings, as does Jessica Hagedorn in *Dogeaters*:

> 1956. The air-conditioned darkness of the Avenue Theater smells of flowery pomade, sugary chocolates, cigarette smoke, and sweat.

This opening may contain an overload of sensations, but it works. The reader receives a strong impression of the setting. And a part of the setting, time, we get immediately—"1956"—even before we have begun to look for a sentence. The introduction follows two questions: *when* and *where*. *When* is immediately and unobtrusively given as an abstract information, and *where*, as a sensory atmosphere.

A single strong sensation gives our imagination clear entry into the story. We don't have to start working right away, to try to sort out a complex image. William Faulkner in "Barn Burning" focuses on a single smell: "The store in which the Justice of the Peace's court was sitting smelled of cheese." We are in the scene at once, experiencing, without having to decide on which sensation to concentrate. No need to cajole us to get there.

A Need or Motive. Nothing propels the characters and the readers as efficiently as a definite need, and the sooner the need is identified, the better. Katherine Mansfield in "Marriage a la Mode" introduces us to the characters' wishes right away:

> On his way to the station William remembered with a fresh pang of disappointment that he was taking nothing down to the kiddies. Poor little chaps! It was hard lines on them. Their first words always were as they ran to greet him, "What have you got for me, daddy?" and he had nothing.

We learn what the characters want right away. It may be equally effective to open by stating what the character does not want.

Action. Our animal eyes most quickly notice movement. Starting a story with action will catch your reader's attention. Look at how Irwin Shaw does it in "The Eighty-Yard Run":

> The pass was high and wide and he jumped for it, feeling it slap flatly against his hands, as he shook his hips to throw off the halfback who was diving at him.

Sex. Sexual images excite some people and tire others, but overall, the tactic of opening with sex has worked for many writers—it certainly does for Tama Janowitz in *Slaves of New York*:

> After I became a prostitute, I had to deal with penises of every imaginable shape and size. Some large, others quite shriveled and pendulous of testicle.

This opening promises a great deal of (fictional) self-revelation; and since many people read fiction to find out about the aspects of people's lives that aren't otherwise easily observable, this is a good hook. But sometimes the use of a sexual image may sound like a desperate plea for attention. Opening with sex has the advantage of grabbing a reader's attention, and the potential disadvantage of appearing cheesy.

Symbolic Object. If in your first sentence you describe an object, whether you intend it to be a symbol or not, most readers will treat it as a symbol, and they'll probably ask, "Why do we start with this thing? What does it mean?"

The expectations created by a described object could give you an effective opener. For Jean Stafford this technique works in "A Country Love Story":

> An antique sleigh stood in the yard, snow after snow banked up against its eroded runners.

A sleigh evokes all kinds of associations—Santa Claus, freedom, travel, and the quaintness of a bygone era. And the eroded runners indicate that the bygone perhaps can't be recaptured.

The advantage of opening with a symbol is that besides giving us thematic expectations the object gives us something concrete to visualize and play with. The disadvantage is that this prominent position may bring an overload of reader's expectation and interpretation to the object, so that the opening might appear overly subtle.

Character Portrait. Your opening could provide an external look at a character, such as this one from Charles D'Ambrosio's "Her Real Name":

> The girl's scalp looked as though it had been singed by fire—strands of thatchy red hair snaked away from her face, then settled against her skin, pasted there by sweat and sunscreen and the blown grit and dust of travel.

The story centers around a terminally ill girl; although we don't know yet that she's dying, we begin to see that something is amiss, and our unease will grow throughout the story, until her death.

The disadvantage is that it'll take a while before the action starts—first we'll go through a summary with various thoughts and generalizations before a scene can begin. The main advantage is that we go straight for the character; we learn right away what the character does; we hear her voice. The advantage is probably greater than the disadvantage—for when the story's action begins, we will be prepared. We'll know the character—her main concerns and themes.

Question. Like Ivan Turgenev in *Fathers and Sons*, you can begin your narrative with a question:

> "Well, Peter, any sign of them yet?" This was the question addressed on the 20th of May, 1859, to his servant—a young and lusty fellow with whitish down on his chin and with small dim eyes—by a gentleman of just forty years of age, in a dusty overcoat and check trousers, as he emerged hatless on the low steps of a posting-station on the X highway.

Most motivation for reading comes from questions. Reading becomes a search for answers. So asking a question is the most direct way to get the reader to work with you.

The advantage is that the question, if it's part of a dialogue, leads us immediately into a scene—we jump into the middle of the action, something is going on in the first line. However, that may prove to be a disadvantage, too, because we don't know the speaker yet, nor the place where he speaks, and supplying this background quickly after the question may appear stilted, as it does in the above example. Still, this can be an effective opening, because it's important for your reader to have questions.

Scene. A scene naturally combines action, setting and character. Even a brief scene may do all this, as does Alexander Pushkin's opener of "The Queen of Spades":

> Card-playing was going on in the quarters of Narumov, an officer in the Guards.

One simple sentence introduces all three elements. The advantage is that an action will be in progress as we join it; we skip preparations. We jump into the middle. Yet unlike in an opening with a common hook, nothing extreme has happened, so the action can escalate, not decelerate.

Travel. In this type, the character and the reader share the same experience: both arrive as strangers to a place. This shared experience is an effective lead, and if it hadn't been done so many times, I'd certainly recommend it as one of the best ways to start a story. Even so, if your setting is interesting enough, this technique should be effective.

Travel as a background can set the mood, as in Reidar Joensson's *My Life as a Dog*:

> The snowflakes had a hypnotic effect on me. I was getting more and more drowsy, but I needed to keep my eyes open. What if I missed my station and got off at the wrong one, rushed out into the white arctic tundra,

> totally dazed, only to be met by wolves who were ready to tear me to pieces! Now, that would be unforgivable and unworthy of a true Trapper.

This works—because we experience the narrator's thoughts and perceptions. The setting we see in travel gives us access to the character.

Character's Thoughts. Saul Bellow opens his novel *Herzog* with the main character's thoughts:

> If I am out of my mind, it's all right with me, thought Moses Herzog.

We are in the character's mind, which is where the reader probably wants to be; it makes sense to get there right away, especially in a psychological novel. The disadvantage of this method is that thoughts are abstract—we don't see anything yet. But the thought is interesting and paradoxical enough that it could make us curious; we may ask, "What kind of guy is this, who doesn't care whether he's crazy?"

Prediction. Richard Yates opens his novel *The Easter Parade* with a bit of foretelling:

> Neither of the Grimes sisters would have a happy life, and looking back it always seemed that the trouble began with their parents' divorce.

This evokes an ominous tone of prophecy, so that you tend to read it with a sense of foreboding, which, dramatically, can work. The downside is that this opening might reveal the end (in general terms), thus perhaps decreasing suspense.

Anecdote. Anton Chekhov opens "In the Ravine" with the following paragraph:

> The village of Ukleyevo lay in the ravine, so that only the belfry and the chimneys of the cotton mills could be seen

> from the highway and the railroad station. When passers-by would ask what village it was, they were told: "That's the one where the sexton ate up all the caviar at the funeral."

The entertaining anecdote lures the reader into the story. The humor, however, does not prepare me for the spirit of the story—a tragic one with a baby's death. But maybe the humorous mood struck in the beginning intensifies the tragedy, and perhaps caviar and funerals have symbolically to do with the death of a baby. Still, this example reminds me that some openings function to entice the reader into the story, without necessarily setting the key mood, theme and so on. Perhaps too much can be made of all that. Most readers, after all, probably say, "Come, entertain me!"

A Final Comment on Beginnings

Obviously, you can start your novel or story in many ways, some of which we haven't mentioned. You might come up with some unique approaches, although it's not uniqueness that's most necessary in the beginning, but an orientation for the reader. To prepare your reader for your story, you must—not long after the first sentence—introduce the setting, character and problem (or crisis)—something that the rest of the piece will solve. And while you introduce these elements, make the reader begin to see, hear, experience, get involved in your story. Entertain your reader.

How you'll accomplish all this should partly depend on the subject matter, and partly, of course, it'll be arbitrary. Many people think there's only one possible—"right"—opening for each story, and sometimes I agree. But often, I think, you can enter a story—a description of an event—in many ways, and several of them may work. "All the roads lead to Rome," the old saying goes. You may enter the city from nine directions, and although where you enter will shape your experience of Rome, once you reach the Colosseum, all this may not matter much. You are with the lions now. (But you'd better remember where you entered if you want to leave the Colosseum and Rome.) So while it's healthy to learn how to open in many ways, it's also healthy not to get lost. Use openings for what they are: entrances to something larger than themselves. The beginning must lead somewhere. The threads you start here must continue. The beginning (besides the ending) is the least forgiving place for loose ends. Here you commit yourself to themes, places, characters. If you can't keep the commitment, find another beginning, another door that leads in.

THE END GAME

Thomas Fuller said, "Great is the art of beginning, but greater the art is of ending." It seems many writers agree that endings give them more trouble than beginnings do. That's partly because in the ending—especially in short stories—everything needs to fit; in the beginning we don't yet know what needs to fit, so almost everything appears acceptable.

It is particularly true that short stories must end adequately; all the strings must tie in. David Lodge says in *The Art of Fiction*: "One might say that the short story is essentially 'end-oriented,' inasmuch as one begins a short story in the expectation of soon reaching its conclusion, whereas one embarks upon a novel with no very precise idea of when one will finish it."

With novels, while it's essential to resolve the conflicts you raise, frequently the last page does not matter much—it's a kind of exit two-step jig. If the series of conflicts has resulted in many deaths and births, how one waves good-bye after all this won't matter. Some good friends of mine don't like good-byes, and after we spend days talking, we part quickly, almost in mid-sentence. Nothing will now change the good times and conversations we've had. I'm not saying that your novels don't need to reach a resolution, but in many cases it does not matter much how they end after the resolution—you may spend quite a few pages settling accounts and fading out.

In a novel, it is clear when the end will occur—the book ends, physically. You can't hide it, unlike in movies, in theater, in symphony.

Let's compare a long novel to Beethoven's Fifth Symphony: After the amazing music, we get a prolonged announcement of the end, and when the end finally comes every fool in the audience knows it's the end. Yes, you've given me a shattering experience, but I'll do fine without all this militaristic pomp after it. His end works as a kind of punishment, in the name of the idea of the End.

Now having said this, I do acknowledge that we still need to end somehow. In a novel, the prolonged announcements of the end are even more absurd than in the symphony hall, because the quantity of pages under my forefinger tells me when the end comes, so there's no point in playing hide-and-seek.

Both in the novel and the short story, once you reach the resolution, exit quickly. You might make one victory circle, like a skater with a medal on her neck, to part from the readers with a graceful exhibition, but this is not necessary. Or if your story cannot reach a resolution, exit it once this has become clear.

Types of Endings

Although there are many ways to end a piece of fiction, in all of them you may strive to achieve basically the same goal: Give us another look, or angle, or thought, on what has just taken place in your fiction, something that will put it all in perspective.

When you are about to end a piece, decide which image or thought you want your reader to carry as the last impression. I think that endings with striking sensory images are often preferable to abstract analysis. Even church services end either with bread and wine or with music, not with abstractions. In fiction, too, a taste of wine aged in centuries-old oak barrels may end the supper evocatively.

Circular Ending. I can't generalize about all endings, but in a great many pieces of writing, endings must give an answer to the questions, concerns and images set forth in the beginning. The beginning and the ending may sometimes tie together quite neatly.

In a novel, you sometimes find the first paragraph functioning as the last. We already know the beginning of *My Life as a Dog,* by Reidar Joensson, from page 161. The same paragraph serves as the ending of the novel. It makes sense, given that it is a *bildungsroman,* a boyhood of a future writer, so at the end he writes the first page of the book:

> One day I might tell somebody the truth. I know exactly how I'll begin: The snowflakes had a hypnotic effect on me. I was getting more and more drowsy, but I needed to keep my eyes open. What if I missed my station and got off at the wrong one, rushed out into the white arctic tundra, totally dazed, only to be met by wolves who were ready to tear me to pieces! Now, that would be unforgivable and unworthy of a true Trapper.

That type of circularity works in this case, but sometimes it may appear strained and artificial.

Matching vs. Nonmatching Ending. A matching ending is pretty close to a circular one; the first image, transformed, serves also as the last. The end answers the concerns of the beginning directly.

We quoted from the beginning of Jean Stafford's "A Country Love Story" on page 159. Now let's read the ending:

> She knew now that no change would come, and that she would never see her lover again. Confounded utterly, like an orphan in solitary confinement, she went outdoors and got into the sleigh. The blacksmith's imperturbable cat stretched and rearranged his position, and May sat beside him with her hands locked tightly in her lap, rapidly wondering over and over again how she would live the rest of her life.

The story starts in the sleigh and now ends in it, giving it an obvious unity.

I'll give several examples of such rounded-off endings under other headings below, but often such endings aren't a necessity. For example, Kafka's "The Metamorphosis"—whose beginning is perhaps (almost unavoidably) the most frequently quoted, and whose ending is rarely quoted:

> They [Mr. and Mrs. Samsa] grew quieter and half unconsciously exchanged glances of complete agreement, having come to the conclusion that it would soon be time to find a good husband for her. And it was like a confirmation of their new dreams and excellent intentions that at the end of their journey their daughter sprang to her feet first and stretched her young body.

The story does not end with the same character, Gregor. It's not in the fantastic mode any more. The end could hardly be more dissimilar from the beginning. But indirectly it's appropriate—it presents a contrast to Gregor's agony and intensifies the sensation of his being superfluous. The world could go on quite well—actually better—without him. This ironic, apparently unmatching ending probably works better than another cockroach image could.

Surprise Ending. This is occasionally called the O. Henry ending, although Guy de Maupassant, and other writers before him, practiced it. In "The Necklace," a woman named Matilda borrows a necklace, loses it, buys a glass replica, and works as a washer woman for fifteen years to replace the lost one with a genuine diamond necklace. She gives the genuine necklace to its owner, who says:

> "You say that you bought a diamond necklace to replace mine?"
>
> "Yes. You did not notice it then? They were just alike."
>
> And she smiled with a proud and simple joy. Madame Forestier was touched and took both her hands as she replied:
>
> "Oh! my poor Matilda! Mine were false. They were not worth over five hundred francs!"

Trick Ending. This is not the same as the surprise ending, although it may be a surprising one, too.

If Kafka had told "The Metamorphosis" without revealing to us that Gregor Samsa was in a cockroach's body, and he saved this line for the last, it would be a trick ending, or a cheat ending. I am hard-pressed to give you any examples from literature, because a trick ending is usually enough to ensure that a piece of writing will not be regarded as literature.

Ambrose Bierce's "An Occurrence at Owl Creek Bridge" comes close to it. A man is being hanged. But after this, we get the story of the man's escape, for most of the story, until the man reaches his home.

> Ah, how beautiful she [his wife] is! He springs forward with extended arms. As he is about to clasp her he feels a stunning blow upon the back of the neck; a blinding white light blazes all about him with a sound like the shock of a cannon—then all is darkness and silence!
>
> Peyton Farquhar was dead; his body, with a broken neck, swung gently from side to side beneath the timbers of the Owl Creek bridge.

Bierce tricks most readers into believing that the man has escaped. And then, bang, we are back, continuing the opening. This all makes sense now, when you think about hallucinations, theories of a mind racing before death and so on. He has tricked us for a worthwhile purpose. But it's not the ending that's a trick—it's the middle of the story. The ending fits the beginning perfectly. Thanks to the beginning, it works.

Summary Ending. You can summarize the outcome of the story.

For example, in Guy de Maupassant's "Mademoiselle Fifi," a French prostitute can't bear to be humiliated by a Prussian officer; she stabs him to death, runs and hides. These events are dramatically presented, but the outcome is summarized at the end:

> A short time afterward, a patriot who had no prejudices, who liked her because of her bold deed, and who afterward loved her for herself, married her, and made a lady of her.

The main dramatic event takes a couple of hours, so the rest is narrated summarily. In such cases, this strategy works better than dragging on with the story. However, the summary lends the story an air of a tale—which you may or may not want. Many movies have used this device, as a way of going outside of the frame of the event covered in the picture, without having to linger and decelerate—and therefore this device may seem too familiar. But, since it is used pretty rarely in current fiction, summary endings can be a good option. Tom Wolfe successfully uses a summary ending for *Bonfire of the Vanities*, as does Marilynne Robinson in *Housekeeping*.

Open Ending. Many writers object to a neat ending because it seems contrary to ordinary experience, which keeps going after an event is "over," and the repercussions of the event keep recurring in new experiences. Not even the death of one person ends the experience of others, and as long as you have at least two characters in a story, you might need to account for how the survivors keep thinking, feeling, experiencing. If you agree with this outlook, you might use open endings. Exit a piece of fiction while the action is ongoing. Much is said about beginning *in medias res*, but you can also exit in the middle of things.

For an example, let's take a look at *The Fixer* by Bernard Malamud. Yakov Bok, an apolitical Jewish man, has come to Kiev from his shtetel (Jewish village) around 1914. After he's unjustly accused of murdering a Christian boy, without indictment, he spends a couple of years in solitary confinement, undergoing all kinds of extreme torture. When a bogus indictment arrives, he's escorted by Cossack soldiers to his trial, where his chances are slim. However, the October Revolution might take place soon. These are the thoughts and images that end the novel, on Yakov's way to the trial, which we never reach:

> Afterwards he thought, Where there's no fight for it there's no freedom. What is it Spinoza says? If the state acts in ways that are abhorrent to human nature it's the lesser evil to destroy it. Death to the anti-Semites! Long live revolution! Long live liberty!
>
> The crowds lining both sides of the streets were dense again, packed tight between curb and housefront. There were faces at every window and people standing on rooftops along the way. Among those in the street were Jews of the Plossky District. Some, as the carriage clattered by and they glimpsed the fixer, were openly weeping, wringing their hands. One thinly bearded man clawed his face. One or two waved at Yakov. Some shouted his name.

We don't know how the trial will end. Will Yakov be sentenced to death and shot before the revolution takes place? Or will the revolutionaries free him? We are left in suspense as to the major events in the novel. However, one theme is resolved: Yakov is a changed man. He wants a revolution, while in the beginning he considered himself apolitical. So we have a character change, resulting from insights. But the major source of suspense, whether the character will be freed or executed, remains open, unresolved. As I read I did not worry whether he would start considering himself political, but whether he'd survive.

Still, I think this is a successful ending; it answers some psychological questions and yet leaves off without resolving the action. I remain anxious for Yakov, and I can start imagining different endings—the author's open ending invites me to become active, to imaginatively end the novel's action.

Some endings may be completely open, without answering any of the raised questions—which indirectly could point at the unanswerability of the questions. For example, *The Fixer* could have ended in suspense without any character change. Many absolutely open endings are actually anti-endings.

Ending with an Idea and an Image. This is how Milan Kundera ends *The Book of Laughter and Forgetting*:

> Everyone was delighted with the idea, and a man with an extraordinary paunch began developing the theory that Western civilization was on its way out and we would soon be freed once and for all from the bonds of Judeo-Christian thought—statements Jan had heard ten, twenty, thirty, a hundred, five hundred, a thousand times before—and for the time being those few feet of the beach felt like a university auditorium. On and on the man talked. The others listened with interest, their naked genitals staring dully, sadly, listlessly at the yellow sand.

The juxtaposition of the theory about Western civilization and genitals staring at the yellow sand works as irony. For a novel of ideas that deals with a communist dictatorship, this certainly makes a cynical closing statement.

Musing About Ending. Just as there are many self-consciously drawn beginnings, there are many endings that draw attention to themselves, with musings about what it means to end. Here's Naguib Mahfouz's ending of *Midaq Alley*:

> I will be patient so long as I live, for do not all things have their end? Oh yes, everything comes to its *nihaya*.
>
> And the word for this in English is "end" and it is spelled: END. . . .

A Final Comment on Endings

No matter what type of ending you use, you must end skillfully and gracefully because this is the reader's last impression of your piece, which will cast light on the whole piece retroactively. That's why it's good to end with an effective image or an interesting thought.

If you are not satisfied with what a brief ending can achieve and you still have the urge to explain something, you might write an epilogue. You might write a couple of epilogues for that matter, the way Tolstoy did in *War and Peace* (first epilogue, sixteen chapters; second, twelve chapters—totalling over a hundred pages) with musings about history, war and so on, if you are blessed with the reluctance to end your novels. You could also write a commentary and then decide where to put it, at the end or the beginning. Dickens playfully solves the problem of where elucidation belongs like this, in *Our Mutual Friend*, entitling his epilogue as "Postscript: In Lieu of Preface."

EXERCISES

1. One paragraph. Write the opening of a western, with an odd action involving several animals. Imitate Larry McMurtry's opening of *Lonesome Dove*:

> When Augustus came out on the porch the blue pigs were eating a rattlesnake—not a very big one. It had probably just been crawling around looking for shade when it ran into the pigs. They were having a fine tug-of-war with it, and its rattling days were over. The sow had it by the head, and the shoat had the tail.

But use different animals—burros, horses, roosters, hawks, cats, possum, skunk, sheep, bears, coyotes.

Objective: To lead into a setting in an active way, with something already going on; also, to entertain.

Check: Do we get a sense of place, through these animals and their background? Is your opening amusing? Pass it on to your neighbor (mother, spouse, whoever happens to be at your mercy) and see whether she smiles.

2. One paragraph. Write the opening of a romance, with the heroine meeting her lover-to-be. If you can't do this with a straight face, do it as a parody.

Objective: To play with a formulaic beginning, since most romances start this way. If you do this as a parody, the purpose is to practice the technique and have fun. When you exaggerate something, you might understand more clearly how it works.

Check: Have you portrayed the lover-to-be attractively enough? He mustn't be easy to get, nor be a slob (except in a parody), nor should he be too stereotypical (as, let's say, a handsome doctor with salt-and-pepper hair).

3. One paragraph. Write the opening of a psychological novel about a large family set in a small town. Lead us into the town as though we were in a train (look at the *My Life as a Dog* example on page 161) or in a car.

When you finish your paragraph, choose a quotation from the Bible, the Koran, the Baghavad Gita, or any literary work that seems to be appropriate, and use it as an epigraph.

You could, if you use a famous quote, paraphrase it, the way George Orwell does this one, in *Keep the Aspidistra Flying*: "Though I speak with the tongues of men and of angels, and have not money, I am become as sounding brass, or a tinkling cymbal. And though I have the gift of prophecy, and understand all mysteries, and all knowledge; and though I have all faith, so that I could remove mountains, and have not money, I am nothing."

Objective: To describe an experience of travel so that readers would feel they are getting to a place and are in the right mood for what follows. Also, to learn how to use quotes. If you've chosen the theme of your story, address it with a quote.

Check: Do you get a sensation of travel? Do you engage enough senses? Do you show mesmerizing effects of stripes on the road, or falling snow, or apparently revolving fields?

For quotations, be sure they relate to your theme, at least obliquely.

4. One to three pages. Begin a story of your own for a couple of paragraphs by continuing this opening from "Love Is Not a Pie" by Amy Bloom: "In the middle of the eulogy at my mother's boring and heartbreaking funeral, I started to think about calling off the wedding."

Objective: To use somebody else's energetic first sentence to begin your story. If you see a story emerging, keep going for at least a couple of pages. Later, if you finish the story, cut the first line, or transport it before the text, as a quote.

Check: Do you get ideas for a story? Do you have a scene that keeps you imagining? If not, paraphrase the beginning as "In the middle of the eulogy at my mother's boring and heartbreaking funeral, I started to think about accepting John's proposition." Does this work better? If not, try, "In the middle of the toast at my mother's boring wedding, I started to think about her impending funeral." If this does not work for you, find an opening, and play the game of variations, until you hit something that triggers thoughts and scenes.

5. Three to four pages. Open the story with its chronological end, either a wedding or a funeral. Make it a substantial scene—at least a page. Then start chapter two, at the story's chronological beginning, with where the romance started (for the wedding), or the disease occurred (for the funeral). Outline the rest of the story, and write the story's last paragraph, which should chronologically precede the beginning.

Objective: To learn how to open with the last event of the story, which will serve as the starting point and the goal toward which all your narrative will focus.

Check: Are you coming up with enough ideas about what could happen in the lives of the people involved? For example, if you chopped both the beginning and the end, would there be enough interesting material left in the middle? If so, when you finish a draft of the story, you might cut off the death or the wedding frame.

6. One page. Open a novel with the description of a birth, from the standpoint of the mother.

Objective: To practice opening a biographical novel at the chronological beginning. Especially if you are a man, imagining a story from a mother's POV, with the sensations, thoughts and so on, will do you a lot of good. You will have to fictionalize.

Check: Give it to a mother and ask her if you've described it well. Or find several accounts of births and, although each birth is unique, make sure that yours contains similar elements.

7. Three pages. Write the last three pages of a story of a love affair. A woman breaks into her boyfriend's apartment and discovers his message machine tapes. She listens to the messages, which cast a new light on the relationship. As she does this, a criminal breaks in, and she makes a bargain with him.

Objective: Same as Exercise 6 – to have the past and the present clash (or meet with a new insight and development).

Check: Are the tapes interesting? (After several tape-recorded messages, she could compare what they say to what she remembers, to heighten their importance.) Is the action dramatic – with scenes, staged, described, and fleshed out in dialogue?

8. One page. Write a deliberately upbeat ending of a romance, perhaps the romance from Exercise 2. But change the genders to vary the story from the usual romance formula; write from a male POV, and let the man overcome a temptation, and come back to his wife all the wiser.

If you don't like the formula or are tired of it, parody it, vent your mischief on it. However, if all your stories have unhappy endings, you could probably benefit from doing this exercise seriously. If the formula irks you, get rid of the temptation business, but end your story in an upbeat way.

Objective: To make money. I'm joking, but not entirely. To practice the varieties of religious experiences? Yes, as endings.

Check: Does your upbeat ending sound corny? It shouldn't, not in well-done formula fiction. It might help to use poetic images at the end, rather than obvious generalizations as thoughts. If you want to express thoughts, they should be interesting.

9. One to two pages. Write the beginning of a story (jumping into the complication of an action or a crisis) and the ending (coming out of a resolution), so that they reflect each other. To intensify the connection between the beginning and ending, use the same symbolic object in both. For example, Jean Stafford in "A Country Love Story" uses the antique sleigh as the first and the last image. When we come to the sleigh at the end, we realize we have taken a journey.

Objective: To practice matching endings with beginnings, in a concrete way, concentrating on objects as symbols. You don't have to know what the symbols mean—they'll work anyway.

Check: Did your object evoke many associations for you? Jot them down, without censoring them. Then analyze how these associations relate to the events in the story. You might make use of these associations to tighten the connections among the beginning, ending, and the rest of the story.

10. Write a story outline. Then write the first and last paragraph of the story so that the two have hardly anything to do with each other.

Objective: To practice contrasting the ending with the beginning.

Check: Does the ending make the beginning look like an orphan? It should, to show how much we have departed from it.

11. Outline a story and write its surprise ending.

Objective: To practice using a variety of endings.

Check: Is the ending truly unexpected? Does it make sense? Could it happen, given the plot outline?

12. One to two pages. Describe a character's death, accounting in detail the thoughts and perceptions of the dying. Imagine that you are ending a long novel that involves an exhausting life.

Objective: To be able to end in a traditional way yet with a new twist, some new description, analogy, image of what awaits all of us. Use insights from psychology and physiology to shape your description. Could you write an upbeat description of death?

Check: Is the description convincing, vivid, serious—not pompous, sentimental and preachy?

CHAPTER EIGHT

DESCRIPTION AND WORD CHOICE

Description should be a basic skill, your way of showing and seeing. You need vivid detail, not only to give life to your story, but to supply proofs. The more outlandish your plot, the more you must ground it in realistic detail to provide verisimilitude, similarity to truth. Gabriel Garcia Márquez claims that in a journalistic article one false piece of information is enough to invalidate the article, and in a piece of fiction one striking and true detail may be enough to lend credibility to the entire story. In "A Very Old Man With Enormous Wings," he describes an angel who lands on a beach. Why should we accept his fantasy? Because the details bring the celestial down to earth:

> There were only a few faded hairs left on his bald skull and very few teeth in his mouth. . . . His huge buzzard wings, dirty and half-plucked, were forever entangled in the mud.

And later:

> He was lying in a corner drying his open wings in the sunlight among the fruit peels and breakfast leftovers that the early risers had thrown him. . . . The back side of his wings was strewn with parasites.

How can we doubt parasites in the wings? The realistic description makes the fantasy acceptable, gives it credence. His style of writing is magical realism, and the magic does not go from heaven to earth first, but rather, from earth to heaven, from worms to angels. Especially if you are interested in writing fantasy, science fiction and historical novels, you must learn how to select the basic, authenticating detail in order to convince us.

As a fiction writer, however, you run into strong resistance against descriptions. Today's readers seek quick scenes, action and energetic dialogue. So why bother to describe, when description slows the pace of your fiction? The reader will probably leap over your poetic descriptions to get to the next drama. And how can your fiction compete with the stunning landscapes and awesome special effects of the movies? Impossible.

Perhaps. With well-chosen words, however, you have a chance to practice a real craft, to make much out of little, out of a dog-eared dictionary, alone, in an individual effort—and that is close to creation, which takes place *ex nihilo*, out of nothing. (Movies come into being out of millions of dollars, as team efforts with large staffs; movies make much—and sometimes suprisingly little—out of much.) Remember that a reader cooperates with you; the reader will daydream, free-associate and imagine, starting from your words. You only need to place the word correctly so it opens the internal movie houses, concert halls, restaurants and botanical gardens in your reader's head. More may happen in the reader's than in a movie-goer's head precisely because on the surface words are sketchy and incomplete: the reader jumps in and completes the work, actively imagining, not passively receiving. And if you describe succinctly, you need not fear that you will bore the reader. So there is no reason (except financial) for you as a writer to feel worsted by movies.

HOW TO DESCRIBE

Some writers try too hard when they want to evoke an image by mentioning every aspect of the object they're describing. This is not necessary. It is enough to list the key aspects of an image and then rely on the power of words to evoke. You don't need to supply all the colors and nuances. Márquez merely mentions the parasites in the angel's wings, and the reader's imagination does the rest of the work. Another common mistake in descriptions is to rely on adjectives—sometimes piles of them—to create pictures. (It's all right to use adjectives sparingly, provided we mostly rely on concrete nouns to show images.)

In description, you directly show what can be seen, and indirectly, what can be inferred, such as mental states. You must show even emotion: It's easy to say outright how your characters feel, but explanations usually flatten your narrative. You can get away with telling how your central character, the carrier of the POV, feels, since you have access to his mind, but we need evidence for the feelings of others. How do we know that Joan is bored, that Peter is ashamed, that Thomas is skeptical? Show how they look and behave, what their hands are doing, and the reader will infer the emotion.

Be especially descriptive with powerful feelings. If you use a vocabulary of passion to describe weak feelings and exaggerate what your characters should feel, you write sentimentally. André Gide said: "Often with good sentiments we produce bad literature." Dramatize, show, demonstrate strong feelings; *mentioning* strong feelings only cheapens them. Describing the symptoms of these feelings may evoke the impression of them for the reader, provided you don't resort to clichés, like *rivers of tears, swooning, racing of the heart.* Each strong feeling is a new sensation for the person experiencing it; so when you describe the feeling, you must create a fresh description.

Descriptions need not be long to show a great deal. For example, Charles Dickens describes a ruined and depressed person like this: "He looked like his own shadow at sunset." "Ruined and depressed" conveys information but evokes no picture; Dickens' sentence both conveys the information and paints a grim picture. A compact description that delivers convinces the reader that she need not practice speed-reading on your prose.

Descriptions are perhaps even more important for the writer than for the reader, because they keep the writer close to the scene and help him visualize, concretize and participate in the story. It's good not to interrupt the momentum of the fictional action when describing. John Gardner claims that good writing attains the quality of an uninterrupted fictional dream. Pause to describe, and you may lose the dream. It's best to use dynamic descriptions, whenever feasible, as Flannery O'Connor does in "A Good Man Is Hard to Find":

> She stood with one hand on her thin hip and the other rattling the newspaper at his bald head.

In the action of rattling the newspaper, we find that the man has a bald head. She does not pause to give us a separate sentence on that account.

Another example from the same story:

> She set him on her knee and bounced him and told him about the things they were passing. She rolled her eyes and screwed up her mouth and stuck her leathery thin face into his smooth bland one. Occasionally he gave her a far-away smile.

The descriptions are part of the dynamic scene. This is a good technique when an action takes place and when description can be brief. However, when you must describe many details, it may be best to pause the action and concentrate on the task at hand.

In the previous chapters, we have covered some aspects of description—setting and character—but we need to cover how these two elements can work together in a description. The setting can express a character's mind; and a character's mind can shape our perception of the setting. This interaction of the setting and character often amounts to a mood. In a description, you can create a mood. The visible world helps you express a psychological state. For example, in the following passage, from a story of mine, "Bread and Blood," I could have simply said that while marching in the defeated army, the character, Ivan, was doomed to the feelings of futility and fear. But mentioning futility and fear probably would evoke no images—these words would be abstract, the reader would not be invited to participate in the story. With descriptions I give body to the abstraction, to Ivan's mental state, and the reader can easily identify with this embodied mood:

> Past a burned-out and gutted steel mill, the decimated regiment of Croat Home Guards stumbled through a field of craters that bombs had dug. Out of the water-filled craters rough-skinned gray frogs leaped as beating hearts that had deserted the bodies of warring men and now roamed the doomed landscape. Ivan found the sudden leaps of so many hearts out of the gray earth unsettling. He could not see any of them, until they were in the air, so that it seemed to him that the earth was spitting up useless hearts and swallowing them back into the mud.

Ivan's anxious state of mind shapes our perceptions of the environment, which become almost hallucinogenic. A happy member of a victorious army would see the frogs differently, perhaps as a cheerful rhythm of the liberated land coming to life.

At the same time, the environment shapes our experience of Ivan's mind. Since I show bomb craters and leaping frogs—something for the reader to visualize—I am free to summarize Ivan's feelings, without fear that I am telling and not showing. I am doing both, while at the same time I mirror the mind in the setting and the setting in the mind. I can now tell that Ivan found what he saw "unsettling." I can guide the reader's perception of the scene through Ivan's eyes—the frogs appear as "useless" hearts. *Useless* is a summary, an evaluation of what's shown. If you create a mood through imagery, you are free to interpret the mood, to guide it explicitly, especially if you thereby clarify a character's perception. The descriptive scene here works as an expression and clarification of Ivan's state of mind. I think this is an essential technique in writing fiction—with a bit of expressive showing, you can advance the telling of the story. If I tried to show everything—without choosing several telling details, and without slanting the perception of the scene through metaphors and summaries—it would have taken me pages of landscaping, and the effect would have been diluted. And if I tried to tell and explain everything taking place—without showing where we were—the story would become abstract and lose its impact.

Through the details you choose, you can control the distance from which your reader watches the action. If you focus on a detail that is apparently peripheral to the action, you may create an ironic distance, the way Stephen Crane does in "The Blue Hotel" in the middle of describing a fight:

> Of course the board had been overturned, and now the whole company of cards was scattered over the floor, where the boots of the men trampled the fat and painted kings and queens as they gazed with their silly eyes at the war that was waging above them.

We aren't watching the fight directly, but through the eyes of the painted kings and queens; the qualification of these eyes as "silly" imparts a sense of silliness to the fight. Instead of heeding the blows exchanged, we pay attention to the cards, putting the blows into ironic perspective. We are not consumed by the scene: We have the leisure to observe and draw parallels between the cards and the players.

Finally, a good description—besides setting mood and establishing perspective—creates an aesthetic experience for the reader. As you read, the author's skillful strokes pull you right into the action. The continuation of the fight in "The Blue Hotel" achieves a dazzling cinematic quality:

> For a time the encounter in the darkness was such a perplexity of flying arms that it presented no more detail than would a swiftly revolving wheel. Occasionally, a face, as if illuminated by a flash of light, would shine out, ghastly and marked with pink spots. A moment later, the men might have been known as shadows, if it were not for the involuntary utterance of oaths that came from them in whispers.

A beautiful description like this will win your readers' trust and respect. They will keep reading because through the vivid flashes of description they have been experiencing the action you've created; they will want to find out what happens next in this fight. We have been watching the fight without knowing the result. This concentration on painting a scene makes it possible for you to suspend the action, as if in slow motion, and to enhance the scene's suspense and the reader's expectations.

WORD CHOICE

For description, a writer depends on word choice as a painter does on the selection of paint. In the following famous passage, Gustave Flaubert explained the importance of word choice: "Whatever you want to say, there is only one word that will express it, one verb to make it move, one adjective to qualify it. You must seek that word, that verb, and that adjective, and never be satisfied with approximations, never resort to tricks, even clever ones, or to verbal pirouettes to escape the difficulty."

Le mot juste is the French expression he used, and this is still a common way of describing the right word in English, giving it an aura of French finesse. But there's no need to mystify and treat as foreign the basic skill of choosing the right word.

Here are two examples of the right word choice, in one description from David Foster Wallace's story "Forever Overhead." Pay attention to how the words achieve vivid sensations:

> There is a huge exclamation point of a foam into your field of sight, then scattered claps into a great fizzing. Then the silent sound of the tank healing to new blue.

"Fizzing" evokes the sound of a pool after a splash. The tank "healing" to new blue is perfect. The hole in the water has filled; once the fizzing bubbles burst, the color returns to the water. The additional twist of the silent sound of the tank healing alerts your ear; as you visualize the white water becoming blue, you barely hear a murmur. All of these effects are accomplished through the right word choice—*fizzing*, *sound*, and *healing*, in synergy. Wallace certainly follows Vladimir Nabokov's maxim, "to caress the detail."

The way you choose your words should give you power. Words do not act alone, so you need to evaluate them in your syntax. The word *syntax* comes from a Greek word that means "to deploy." Deploy your words strategically, so they can attack as well as defend. An army needs fit soldiers, so use fit and vigorous words. Trust nouns and verbs, and modify them with adjectives and adverbs only when you can't find the right noun and verb, or when you want to sneak in a metaphor.

Verbs

You must be skillful with verbs to be, literally, verbally expressive. Donald Hall said in *Writing Well*: "Verbs act. Verbs move. Verbs do. Verbs strike, soothe, grin, cry, exasperate, decline, fly, hurt, and heal. Verbs make writing go, and they matter more to our language than any other part of speech." Since verbs act, use vigorous verbs, as in the following sentence from *Heart of Darkness* by Joseph Conrad:

> Going up that river was like travelling back to the earliest beginnings of the world, when vegetation rioted on the earth.

Rioted—what a lush verb!

For the sake of compactness and clarity, present verbs in the active voice whenever feasible. Instead of, "He was struck by the ball," say, "The ball struck him." Avoid weak connective verbs—*is* and *has* (and their variants)—because they stall action and impart a static quality to your writing. Instead of, "A painting is on the wall," say, "A painting hangs on the wall." Instead of, "There are many people in the room, having a lot of loud fun," say, "Many people in the room frolic." (Since no rules work consistently, use common sense. If trying to make verbs active makes your sentence stiff or odd, come up with another variation or revert to the passive and static constructions.)

But don't overdo the vigor of your verbs because your writing will sound cruel and sadistic. "I glued the stamp," should not become "I shoved the stamp onto the envelope." You can yank a plank of wood out of a fence, but yank thread out of a needle and you will not gain vigor but stupidity.

Even skillful and famous writers occasionally fail to measure the power of verbs. That's only natural—even top tennis players double-fault, trying to overpower the opponent; top basketball players miss dunks. It's impossible to avoid occasional slips in your writing, as in the following example from a novel by a famous novelist. I have italicized the words that I think are overly strong:

> January *knifed* through the heated Jaguar; a child sneezed as it *battled its way to freedom*, and Mrs. Dancey, *erecting* her fur coat-collar and sinking so far as might be down into it, *declared*: "I think I'll stay where I am." Eva did not reply: she had walked away. The children set off in the *reverse* direction—their mother, *impaled* on draughts, sent a whinny after them."

Knifed is too strong for air getting into a car. *Battled its way to freedom* is a little too much for a child getting out of the car; moreover, the expression is a cliché. *Erecting* may be all right, though its sexual implication may be too much. *Said* would have accomplished the job of *declared* without the stately formality, which may be ironic, but not enough to warrant the overblown vocabulary. *Reverse* of what? Eva's direction? This adjective is plainly vague. *Impaled* literally means to be executed by having a stick stuck through your anus, through your entrails, and into your head. The metaphor in the image may go in the right direction but way too far!

Use strong verbs, but beware of this potential to exaggerate to the point of absurdity. Rather than go for the "kill" verb (unless you have a kill going on), go for the effective word as does Larry Woivode in "Silent Passengers": "The boy stared out the windshield with an intensity Steiner couldn't translate. . . ." *Translate* is the right word. It implies that the boy's staring was a language different from Steiner's; that Steiner tries to understand but fails. Notice that the word is not pretty—it's a relatively long word with a foreign origin (a Latin root, so it could sound academic rather than direct), not a simple Anglo-Saxon one, yet since it's well chosen, it works. Many writers rightly seek, whenever they can, to use simple, short Anglo-Saxon words, for a punchy rhythm and a sensation of directness—like *crack, jump, do, shout*—rather than long Latin and Greek ones, like *accelerate, juxtapose, equivocate, obfuscate, metamorphose*. But these academic-sounding words with Latin or Greek origins do occasionally work best—for example, "With complex explanations you obfuscate the basic problem." *Obfuscate*—in the sense of deliberately muddying an issue—works better than *muddy*, which evokes a clear image. In the spirit of the loss of clarity, the word, as an oblique one, is the most effective.

Of course, it's good to place a simple word effectively. "A religious man, in the grips of dying, directed his gaze to the ceiling." This will become stronger if you write: "While air wheezed out of him, he looked up with such longing that his eyes seemed to scratch the ceiling." Instead of a cliché, *grips of dying*—air *wheezing out* gives us a more concrete and active picture of death. Instead of *directed his gaze*, *scratched* accomplishes everything: frustration, futility, beastly impotence. Though *scratch* is a common word, the way it's used here is uncommon. Use words unusually for effect. Inexperienced writers often use "unusual" words fashionably—that is, usually. For example, *awesome, vivacious, hellatious, serendipitous*—avoid such trendy words and nurture your odd words. Read a dictionary and copy words that intrigue you, the simpler the better, and use them accurately, even—and especially—if you have never heard them used that way.

Sometimes you can make a verb out of a noun to create action. "Loud clashes of iron *dominoed* the coaches as our train pulled wheel by wheel onto the broad Soviet tracks from the narrow Hungarian rails." Besides setting things in motion, the metaphor of train coaches as domino pieces is packed in the verb *dominoed*.

Mary Gaitskill uses this noun-as-verb technique in "The Girl on the Plane":

> There she stood with a hatchet, about to brain him.

Since we have an image of violence here, to *brain* him is the right verb, derived from a noun.

Leslie Silko, in "Yellow Woman," also uses this technique:

> He shook his head and pawed the sand.

Pawed is effective; the simple word creates an image of a hand as a paw in the sand. This could have been said in a longer way: "He shook his head and his hand, like a paw, passed through sand." Here's an example from Gary Soto's writing, of making a picture and metaphor from a noun used as a verb:

> I scissored my cigarette between fingers, very European.

To give your prose density, now and then you might pack your metaphors into image-oriented verbs.

Nouns and Concrete Description

Rely on concrete nouns, that is, names for things, because in fiction, you must give us the illusion of a world. Notice how Russell Banks gives us a world through concrete nouns, in "Sarah Cole: A Type of Love Story":

> The package of shirts on the table behind her, the newspapers scattered over the couch and floor, the sound of windblown rain washing the sides of the building outside, and the silence of the room, as we stood across from one another and watched. . . .

Notice that there is only one adjective here (properly speaking, a noun-verb combination functioning as an adjective), *windblown*. The rest are nouns and verbs. The concrete nouns evoke the room and its atmosphere better than a string of adjectives and generalizations could. To describe, you need concrete nouns more than adjectives, which are peripheral unless deftly used. Just listing things patiently may work. The reader will contribute colors and shapes from her imagination.

Be concrete rather than abstract whenever possible, unless you write philosophy. What an ugly-sounding word *concrete* is, especially if taken concretely: Cement with iron rods rusting in it. However, its Latin origin, *crescere*, means "to grow." Growth, like a crescent moon, enchants. You can't readily make a picture from abstract words—even the ones that people find important, like *emotion*. Become a little more specific—*loneliness* and *expectation*—and you still don't see much. If you can't accomplish the task with several words, create a scene to show, to concretize, the abstract.

Tim O'Brien gives us an excellent model of concreteness in "The Things They Carried":

> Until he was shot, Ted Lavender carried six or seven ounces of premium dope, which for him was a necessity. Mitchell Sanders, the RTO, carried condoms. Norman Bowker carried a diary. Pat Kiley carried comic books. Kiowa, a devout Baptist, carried an illustrated New Testament that had been presented to him by his father, who taught Sunday school in Oklahoma City, Oklahoma. . . . [W]hen Ted Lavender was shot, they used his poncho to wrap him up, then to carry him across the paddy, then to lift him into the chopper that took him away.

Here, each person is briefly characterized by what he carries; the items say much more than summaries, interpretations, thoughts and adjectives could express. O'Brien's orderly emphasis also offers an impression of military life. He also uses this example to develop the story's theme. We see life's cheapness during war, where even death is handled with cheap things—ponchos. The story demonstrates the power of concreteness.

Adverbs and Adjectives

These modifiers often diminish the effect of your verbs and nouns. For example, "He ran extremely fast," does not accomplish anything more than, "He sprinted." Actually, less, because it takes too long to read and therefore slows you down; the syntax of the sentence is not faithful to its meaning. To run fast means to sprint. What is extremely fast? The maximum speed of a 100-

meter dash is 36 kilometers (23 miles) per hour; what's the point of emphasizing the extreme when humans are fairly slow creatures compared to, say, cheetahs? If we *really* want—and "to really want" means nothing more than "to want"—to emphasize the speed, we could say, "He dashed."

"He ran very slowly," also wastes words. (The piled adverbs slow us down and thus the syntax reflects the meaning of the sentence, but that's a minor consolation for the awkwardness.) What's the difference between very slowly and slowly? Many writers have pointed out that *very* is the least "very" word in the language. You may be better off with, "He jogged."

Some purists conduct campaigns against adjectives and adverbs. Mark Twain advocated that after finishing a piece of writing, one should cross out all the adjectives and adverbs and take a second look, and then bring back the ones that are absolutely necessary. He guaranteed that this strategy would improve the prose. I don't think you need to be so strict about using modifiers, but do examine them. You might accomplish more by choosing verbs and nouns precisely.

Sometimes adjectives and adverbs add a good touch to your prose. It's like using paprika wisely. Paprika, though not strong by its nature, adds taste. (Strong verbs are like hot pepper. They sting.) Here are examples of well-chosen modifiers—first, from "The Demon Lover" by Elizabeth Bowen:

> The *passe* air of the staircase was disturbed by a draught that travelled up to her face. It emanated from the basement. . . .

Passe surprises here. You would not expect to see a French word for something that should basically mean stale, but this makes it sound staler than stale. *Passe* in the sense of outdated, no longer in fashion, is *le mot juste*.

Here's an example of a perfectly descriptive adjective from "Four Meetings" by Henry James:

> I saw her but in diminished profile.

Diminished—how visually true! When you look at a person's face at an angle from behind, you may see just a bit of the nose, a shortened mouth, certainly a smaller version of the profile; this word choice accomplishes all that.

Adverbs can convey a picture, too, as in an example from "The Girl on the Plane" by Gaitskill:

> He sat down, grunting territorially. . . .

Mary Gaitskill describes a man taking up a seat on the plane. *Territorially* conveys an attitude, a behavior, in a picture and a sound. In the three above examples, the modifiers are precise.

You can use adjectives and adverbs to express an image; you can even compress metaphors and likenesses into these seemingly peripheral words. Lorrie Moore does this with an adverb in her story, "Community Life":

> She wished to start over again, to be someone living coltishly in the world. . . .

Instead of saying, "living like a colt," which would be a likeness, Moore compresses the likeness into a quiet metaphor, conveyed in a single adverb, *coltishly*. Who says adverbs are weak? I did, didn't I? Well, let me retract it! Rules have exceptions, so be free, be coltish, when you write.

Peter Taylor strikes a metaphor with an adjective in this sentence in "The Old Forest":

> I found myself wondering for the first time if all this might actually lead to my beautiful, willowy Caroline Braxley's breaking off our engagement.

Two adjectives characterize Caroline. *Beautiful* alone would be useless, and it's not strong anyway. *Willowy* accomplishes a metaphoric compression, a picture of a woman as a willow tree—an expressionistic image of a mood. I imagine Caroline: She lets her elongated hands hang loose, effortlessly bent in the wrists;

her hair, skirts, motions, all are a melancholy yet graceful assembly of hanging. *Willowy* strikes me—it's not "precise," but it's right.

Metaphors and Similies

Aristotle said, "The greatest thing in style is to have a command of metaphor." In Greek, *metaphor* means "transport." (A Greek trucking company is called *Metaphora*.) You carry over a meaning from one realm to another—a human being becomes a willow tree or a horse—and thus expand your view. You borrow a strong impression from wherever you like and bring it into your picture, enriching and complicating, creating a dual reality, with a possible stereo effect, a sharper and deeper sound. Perhaps there's some kind of metaphysical assumption in using metaphors, that many things share one essential nature. A metaphor can make us see something in a way we never have before; it can make us wonder, break out of our habitual ways.

Metaphors make this shift directly, as in "heart of gold." Similes make the shift indirectly—"as busy as a bee," and "working like a madman." (*As* and *like* announce the comparison; *of* doesn't.)

Metaphors and similes are stylistic devices. If your metaphors explicitly draw attention to themselves, your prose will appear labored and mannered. That's why it's particularly effective to sneak your metaphors quietly into adverbs and adjectives, as in the above examples. Sometimes, of course, when you come up with an effective metaphor, you may wish to give it center stage and express it in verbs and nouns, as does Louise Erdrich in *Love Medicine*:

> She threw the oak pole singing over my head, through my braincloud.

The pole "singing" is one metaphor expressed in a verb. It's a metaphor because it transposes the activity of a living creature to an inanimate object. *Braincloud* is another metaphor. It transposes sky and cloud to your head. It's not only a metaphor, it's an image. Who would mind reading a string of metaphors like this? The metaphors are seamlessly interwoven into the sentence. If Erdrich had said, "She threw the oak pole, which seemed to be singing over my head, as though through a cloud around my brain," she would have acknowledged importing the images from elsewhere—*as*, *like*, *seemed* and other announcements draw attention to the comparison as an artifice.

Use metaphors bravely. But when you have many of them, squeeze some into modifiers, so your metaphors will have the humility of a footnote rather than the loudness of center stage. Even quiet bees make honey—often better than loud bees do.

Avoiding Clichés and Wrong Word Choices

Examine your words to make sure they achieve the effect you want. When they fall short of your goal, cross them out, and find the words that work. Mark Twain said, "The difference between the right word and the almost right word is the difference between the lightning and the lightning bug."

In metaphors it is essential that the transposition of one set of elements into a new context be fresh—that you see it for the first time like that. If you have seen a metaphor or a likeness many times elsewhere, don't use it. Otherwise, your metaphor will be a cliché, such as "as busy as a bee." No doubt, once upon a time, that used to be a fresh image, but no more. Other passé metaphors and likenesses:

heart of gold
pearly white teeth
steel will
strong as a bull
brilliant light
seamlessly interwoven (from my writing above)
pretty as a picture
drunk as a sailor
meek as a lamb
faithful like a dog
postcard pretty

illegible handwriting, like a doctor's
like zombies
chiseled features
clean as a bone
window of opportunity
broken heart
he is sweet
like an idiot
piercing eyes
she blossomed (it's good that the image is packed in a verb, but it's been done a zillion times, to use another cliché)

There are many other clichéd metaphors. Continue the list for fun, if you like.

Strive to create fresh metaphors—though *fresh* is not fresh in this context (would *crisp* be better?)—as Lorrie Moore does in "Community Life":

> The electric fan was blowing on him; his hair was moving gently, like weeds in water.

This example creates a picture I hadn't seen before reading her sentence. So she has shown me something, and I am tempted to say, Thank you! Okay, I did.

You can make something new and striking without belaboring it. See how Japanese fiction writer Mori Yōko creates an original image in "Spring Storm":

> "You were trembling like a drenched cat."

Simple, nicely done, and true to life. No doubt you have seen a drenched cat trembling. It's good to observe and jot down your observations, because sooner or later you might use them in your fiction. It's amazing how often we fail to notice things around us. There are many images like drenched cats trembling around us, but we fail to pay attention because our eyes are tired. This is one skill many poets possess—finding images that, once expressed, seem obvious. Read poetry (or, even better, write it) to sharpen the art of making images and choosing words.

Not all images need to strive for quiet simplicity. However, if in a sentence you can't come up with anything better than "chiseled features" use "chiseled features" and move on. Your main goal is to tell your story, and now and then to throw an image as refreshing as a snowball at your reader. Otherwise, keep moving. If you strive to be an original metaphorist in each sentence, you may either induce writer's block or write precious prose, which will take ten years to become a novel. Fear of clichés may be an even greater fault than using clichés, if you quit thinking of your conflicts and characters for the sake of beauty. As in most things, find the right measure.

Symbols

Many writers think that to deepen and embellish their writing they must "use" symbols. But don't worry about symbols. You've got better things to do: write, paint, play. The origin of the word is *symbolein*, which in Greek means to throw (*bolein*) together (*sym*). As you throw words together, you will *symbolein*, make symbols, meaningful connections between the concrete and the abstract; but the less you control how that happens, the better, because the connections will come from your unconsciousness or semiconsciousness, from the spring of words and images, spontaneous, free. Throwing together suggests, to me, a certain looseness.

I may be wrong in analyzing the etymology, but probably not in analyzing the usefulness of planning symbols in writing. I respect deliberately using and studying symbols in psychoanalysis, anthropology, religion and literature, but in writing fiction it's good to be spontaneous. A Ph.D. friend of mine can't mention fish without worrying about its symbolic relationship to Christianity, which he, as an academic neopagan, finds troubling. He can't mention a banana in a story without worrying that he has mentioned his penis. Consequently, he's got a huge writer's block and a small writing libido. So don't go around psychoanalyzing symbols in writing—yours or others'. Arranging symbols neatly will either inhibit you or will make your prose artificial. I don't know of any other single topic that obfuscates more and makes the craft of writing appear more complicated than it needs to. But, who knows, if they interest you, symbols may work for you. (After all, see what's happened to the gospel against adverbs in this chapter.)

EXERCISES

1. One page. Choose a fantasy figure—Dracula, Narcissus, Santa Claus, or one of your making—and convince us of his physical reality by using mundane details.

Objective: To learn how to "prove" the existence of fantastic characters. Regardless of whether you believe in Christ, it's tempting to believe in a god who sweats and bleeds. The details of his story stay with you because the spirit has become flesh, through the word.

Check: Have you mentioned enough real, daily stuff?—dandruff, toothpaste, a hole in the sock, bad temper, toothache, mosquito bite, bronchitis, whatever. If not, go back and do it.

2. One page. Pretend that you are an architect and make up a factory or a gym. Draw it first, if that helps you imagine it, and then write a description of it.

Objective: To practice visualizing something you haven't seen, and to bring it out in a description. You may benefit from a painterly and architectonic imagination.

Check: Have you described the building so that it seems "real"? Cover the tracks of your artifice so that the impression will be that you have actually gone out in the streets and sketched this building by looking at it. For realism, perhaps you need cracks in the mortar, pigeon stripes on the walls, some intrusions of "rude" reality.

3. Three paragraphs. Describe a horse, a dog and a cat. Don't mention the animal you portray and avoid anthropocentric ascriptions of thoughts and emotions. Try to engage all of our

senses; let us pet the beast with you. If you have animals around you, observe them, and describe them in detail. Otherwise, rely on pictures.

Objective: To practice accurate description from direct observation. Don't worry whether your writing is pretty, but whether it's precise, as though you were writing a nature textbook.

Check: Give what you've written to your brother, spouse, or whomever happens to be around, and see whether they can identify your animals. (For the test, avoid words that would identify your animal, such as *whiskers*.) If not, go back and try again.

4. Three to four paragraphs. Describe a flower shop, a bakery, a shoe-repair shop, and any other little store you come across. Concentrate on smells and sounds.

Objective: To work from auricular and olfactory imagination. If you have to resort to metaphors, so be it.

Check: Come back to the exercise a day or two after doing it. After reading, close your eyes, contemplate the words you used, not reading into them extra meaning, and see whether what you describe comes across.

5. One page. Describe the sounds you hear from your room at midnight. Don't strain; simply list the sounds and their probable sources. Then, rewrite the list of sounds and make ghosts, lovers, thieves and so on out of them. Exaggerate, dramatize, metaphorize. If you aren't naturally inclined to exaggerate, write from the POV of a highly paranoid and sensitive person, someone different from you.

Objective: To learn how to control usage of sounds, first for basic realistic description, then for making much out of little. No other sense can excite the creativity of imagination as much as hearing. This turning ants into elephants, the proclivity of the ear in the dark, can be particularly useful in psychological suspense.

Check: For the first half of the exercise: Have you mentioned enough sounds without making too much of them, or too little? For the second half: Have you moved beyond the banal into fantasy?

6. Write a sentence and use a simple word in an odd way—as, for example, in the following sentence, *scratch* is used: "The dying man's eyes seemed to scratch the ceiling." Write a dozen such sentences and save three or four that work best; revise them until you think they are perfect.

Objective: To learn how to put words together in new ways. Think of what your verbs can do, even if you've never seen them do it before. Experiment. When you describe something, run through a list of verbs, until something sounds interesting.

Check: Read slowly a day later, when you are fresh. Analyze the sentences and see whether at least one of your word usages surprises you.

7. Make a verb out of a noun in a sentence. (For example, "She *brained* him with a hatchet," "I *scissored* a cigarette between fingers," "She *hatcheted* him," "Her dog *treed* my cat.") You can make verbs even out of numbers—for example, "She *360ed* and fell."

Objective: To concentrate on the activity and the words in your sentences. Merge the noun and the verb into one word, giving it both the concrete power of a thing-oriented noun, and the energy of an action-oriented verb.

Check: Does your sentence achieve the concreteness and the energy of a thing in motion? Does it create an image? It should. Does it sound good? It should. (Some nouns used as verbs would sound ridiculous—for example, "I *villaged* for an afternoon"; "She *chemistried* all day.") Use your judgment and taste, as you should, ultimately, in all matters of writing.

8. Whenever you read, be on the alert for a well-placed word, *le mot juste*. Note these in your journals, or wherever, and analyze them.

Objective: To think of words. They reveal or evoke or create images. If you want to create, know your materials.

Check: Have you collected at least a dozen gems by the end of the week of your reading? If you haven't, keep hunting for them.

9. Three to five pages. Imitate Tim O'Brien's "The Things They Carried." Create a dramatic plot using a group of soldiers,

mountain-climbers, lovers, hunters, basketball players or some other group. Portray the drama through the items the group members carry.

Objective: To learn how to express yourself through concrete nouns. Objects placed together speak of people who put them together. The advantage of arranging objects to speak is that the reader may infer the causes and the characteristics of the people who have done it; you need not be judgmental, let the reader be. You can always say, You said it. (Another—peripheral—objective: Get in the habit of writing stories as a variation on a theme. Yours will be a variation on a theme by O'Brien.)

Check: Have you mentioned for each character one or two distinct objects, and for each group several shared objects (such as ponchos for soldiers)?

10. Write variations on Exercise 9, each one a brief paragraph: the things they wore, the things they threw into a garbage can, the things they ate. Make these items portray the characters who use them.

Objective: Same as in Exercise 9.

Check: Same as in Exercise 9.

11. One to two pages. Create images for abstractions: laziness, loneliness, envy, jealousy, joy, pleasure, lust, love, boredom, impatience. For example, for laziness, describe the room of a lazy student, and don't mention laziness. Try to render each feeling in a concrete sentence, which may be nothing more than a list.

Objective: To concentrate on the basics, things, what the world is made of.

Check: Does your list work like symptoms of a disease or evidence of a crime, corpus delicti, or like an airport basket into which you empty your pockets? Why not?

12. One page. Choose an abstract word from Exercise 11—*envy, jealousy, lust, joy, loneliness*—and construct a scene that would express and concretize the word's nature. Don't mention the word.

Objective: To practice concretizing abstractions through a long and rich description. This is a potential source of fiction—from the mood, you jump into a scene, and if there's enough tension in the scene, you can keep going until you have a story.

Check: Has the mood expressed itself naturally, giving shape to your sequence of sentences? The mood should be like a monkey in the jungle—the description should be the mood's natural habitat. (A single sentence may trap the mood like a cage.) Let the important moods live out their natures. Read what you've written. It should read like a fine part of a story. If it doesn't, rewrite, reshape, craft!

13. Twelve sentences. Write three sentences with similes. Rewrite them so that the likenesses become metaphors. Then rewrite so that the verbs would express the metaphors. Then rewrite the metaphors into adverbs. For example: (1) Joan lived like a colt. (2) Joan was a colt. (3) Joan colted around. (4) Joan lived coltishly. (If the initial likenesses cannot make the whole metaphoric journey, create new metaphors, so that you end up with three of each form.)

Objective: To learn how to control your likenesses and metaphors. Learn how to juggle them, so you can attain a flexibility with metaphors. No need to appear stiff and pompous when you can be nonchalant. This could be your method of finding the optimal placement of your metaphors. Let them find their syntactical level.

Check: Do your sentences work? If not, find new metaphors that do. Choose your three most effective sentences, one per metaphor. Some metaphors may be in the adverbial state, others in the verb state, whatever strikes you as best.

14. Six sentences. Write two sentences with likenesses. Rewrite the sentences, compressing likenesses into noun metaphors. Rewrite, squeezing the metaphors into adjectives.

Objective: Same as in Exercise 13.

Check: Same as in Exercise 13.

CHAPTER NINE

VOICE

St. Jerome figured out, centuries ago, that he could read without moving his lips. We don't need to move our lips while reading, but most of us still have a reading sound barrier. We hear some kind of voice, touching our tongue, slowing our eyes. I do, and that's why when I tried to learn speed-reading I always relapsed into the slow mode, listening to the words as though they were read aloud. In good pieces of writing I wouldn't want to have it any other way; where the voice takes over, fiction engages me most.

Many critics have made *voice* a mysterious term. Since it's a metaphor, I can't—at least not right away—give a definition of what it is. However, its being a metaphor does not mean that we must treat the phenomenon as a transcendental mystery, like God lurking in the burning bush, although many people treat "voice" in this religious way. Novice writers go around looking for their voices just as people used to go around "looking for themselves." At least the search has become more specific.

I see no reason to beat around the voice bush. The metaphor, taken directly, compares the written text with the spoken word. This is a good guideline: Write as you speak. Even better: Write as you'd speak at your best. In public readings, some writers show that they are better speakers than writers. When they interrupt the reading and improvise, they become more interesting. I wish that they had written with the same freedom with which they improvised. And some good writers are dull talkers; they come to life only on the page. This should be your goal—to make your text sound more natural and more engaging than you sound otherwise, no matter how much work and artifice this requires.

As a writer, you must be in command of at least one voice: yours. If you write in the first person, nonautobiographically, constructing personae, you must be able to create different voices, like an actor. For each persona, you might develop a different voice. But when you write in the third person, most likely you'll need only one narrative voice. In dialogue, of course, you must create many voices. But the most important voice will be yours, something that will carry the narrative in a confident and confiding manner.

Of course, you may have a "literary" voice, different from your daily conversational voice, but unless you are driven by some kind of theory or ideology (minimalist, maximalist or whatever), I don't see much reason for creating a dichotomy between what goes to your tongue and what goes to your fingers. Some writers do stiffen when writing, as though they were at a formal party or a job interview.

Since metaphors can be interpreted in several ways, I'll give you one more: Voice is a metaphor for a writer's vigor. To make sure that it's you speaking, take out all the tapes surrounding you. No dubbing. The tapes in your mind, something that sounds like somebody else, are mostly clichés. Get rid of them. There's nothing new that you need to discover about your voice. *Discover* means to uncover something that exists. Simply take the dirt and the lid off, and you'll see the precious earthenware. Get rid of the static in your writing, which hides your voice. *Static*: excessive use of adjectives, adverbs and passives, imprecise word choice, clichés. (Later you might like to muffle your voice and achieve a smokey sound with choice modifiers, but first make sure you can be loud and clear.)

Voice should not be confused with posturing, with trying to sound "different." With a cool attitude. When you take up a fashionable voice, you might sound like a "real cool dude," but we've heard enough "real cool dudes"—there's usually something smug and shallow about them. If you have something to say, there's no reason to *pretend* you have something to say. Write it! Yet, if you seemingly have nothing to say, don't be discouraged. Perhaps you have a lot to say once you start a story, once you deal with a place and its people.

You don't have to be a prophet – that is, a savior of a people – to speak. Of course, if you are an Alexander Solzhenitsyn or an Elie Wiesel it might help your voice, but it won't necessarily improve your prose. It might worsen it, since you might be tempted to write tracts. Still, I marvel at the power of Solzhenitsyn's and Wiesel's voices. As soon as they open their fountain pens, you feel they have had to stand up to huge forces. If you want a strong voice, face the crowd of your opponents and outshout them even if they stone you and jail you. (There's an exercise for you!) That's the surest recipe, which, if you have the courage and beliefs, you might consider. This may not be silly advice. Evelyn Waugh, author of *Brideshead Revisited*, said: "An artist must be a reactionary. He has to stand out against the tenor of the age and not go flopping along; he must offer some little opposition. Even the great Victorian artists were all anti-Victorian, despite the pressure to conform." So be combative, at least a little. In anger, people's voices naturally become stronger and louder. This is true of writing voices, too.

If your passions are strong and you are a fighter, the question of voice is a superficial one. You are eager to speak; you only need the podium. That is, you need the writing technique. But don't worry about voice. If you make sure that you say what you mean, you'll have a strong voice. However, "saying what you mean" means being graceful and clear, which may take a lot of labor. Being yourself when you write means to edit, go back, sharpen, to say precisely what you want to say.

EXAMPLES OF PERSONA VOICES

By creating a persona voice, the writer strives to create the illusion of someone speaking to the reader, in the first person. In autobiographical fiction in the first person, the writer uses her own voice. For nonautobiographical fiction in the first person, the writer creates a voice, usually different from the writer's. Like an actor, the writer has taken up a mask and a voice, a persona, who seemingly tells the story. The persona writes as though speaking to a listener. As you read, you listen.

See how much J.D. Salinger's persona in *The Catcher in the Rye* sounds like someone talking to us:

> I don't want you to get the idea she was a goddam *icicle* or something, just because we never necked or horsed around much. She wasn't. I held hands with her all the time, for instance. That doesn't sound like much, I realize, but she was terrific to hold hands with. Most girls if you hold hands with them, their goddam hand *dies* on you, or else they think they have to keep moving their hand all the time, as if they were afraid they'd bore you or something. Jane was different. We'd get into a goddam movie or something, and right away, we'd start holding hands, and we wouldn't quit till the movie was over. And without changing the position or making a big deal out of it. You never even worried, with Jane, whether your hand was sweaty or not. All you knew was, you were happy. You really were.

In this passage, we hear a clear voice. As a reader I am directly addressed in the phrase, "I don't want you to get the idea that. . . ." The word choice is conversational (*goddam, big deal*); and so is the syntax: sentences end with "or something." Some sentences are fragments: "And without changing the position or making a big deal out of it." "Jane was different," would be a fragment in standard English grammar; after *different*, the comparison should continue. But in spoken language, *different* has a different meaning, and the sentence is complete. This adolescent voice seemingly reproduces daily speech, but Salinger worked to achieve it. If you tape-recorded a kid (anybody) and transcribed the speech word for word, the text would be slow, much more fragmented, perhaps barely intelligible. As in dialogue, the "natural" sound is designed to be read. And as it is read, the syntax and word choice evokes the illusion of the spoken sound.

Mark Twain was among the first in American literature to create the illusion of the spoken word. He juggled different first-person voices, one framing another, in "The Celebrated Jumping Frog of Calaveras County":

> [*The frame narrator*]: In compliance with the request of a friend of mine, who wrote me from the East, I called on good-natured, garrulous old Simon Wheeler, and inquired after my friend's friend *Leonidas W. Smiley*, as requested to do, and I hereunto append the result.

Later, the narrator relays Simon Wheeler's speech, who talks about Smiley:

> So he set there a good while thinking and thinking to hisself, and then he got the frog out and prized his mouth open and took a teaspoon and filled him full of quail shot—filled him pretty near up to his chin—and set him on the floor. Smiley he went to the swamp and slopped around in the mud for a long time, and finally he ketched a frog, and fetched him in, and give him to this feller, and says:
>
> "Now, if you're ready, set him alongside of Dan'l, with his fore-paws just even with Dan'l, and I'll give the word." Then he says, "One-two-three-jump!" and him and the feller touched up the frogs from behind, and the new frog hopped off, but Dan'l give a heave, and hysted up his shoulders—so—like a Frenchman, but it wa'n't no use—couldn't budge; he was planted as solid as an anvil, and he couldn't no more stir than if he was anchored out. . . .

The frame narrator sounds like a formal lawyer, Wheeler like a good colloquial talker, and Smiley sounds like a folksy farmer. The result of these three voices working together in a polyphony is a yarnlike humor, with an ironic sound. It's interesting that to do a yarn, Twain resorts to this polyphony of speakers, three different personae.

Here is another example of a persona voice, achieved through the syntax and word choice, so that it sounds more like a diary than a speech. This is from Elizabeth Dewberry Vaughn's novel, *Many Things Have Happened Since He Died*:

> The Lord hates fornicators. I am not one I hate them too. I don't believe in it before marriage I really don't I don't know what happened. I had never before I was saving myself.

And later on in the same novel:

> But in a way it is His fault because He should have protected me more and I couldn't handle all that Daddy dying and no money and him pressuring me all the time and not knowing what to do and Mama practically having a nervous breakdown not able to help me when I needed it most when I always heard He won't give you anything you can't handle well He did. It was too much. And that is not my fault. It was just too much and I couldn't handle it I am not Superman sometimes I need help and nobody was there.

Vaughn has written exclusively in the first person in all her fiction. She works with grammar to give immediacy and urgency to her persona's voice: run-on sentences, commas and periods omitted. This resembles the writing of someone in a remedial English class—so we get a sense of a young person talking to us, a person rather than a writer, which is an advantage. By taking the liberties of someone who doesn't care about grammar, she is able to give us a mind's voice amid turmoil, doubt, passion, fear. This kind of voice is partly a matter of technique, though of course the writer makes it sound natural, not technical. If you want to write in the voice of someone who is not well educated, this may be a good model. Not having to worry about some aspects of grammar might free you to bang thoughts and impressions onto the page.

In *Normance,* Louis-Ferdinand Céline achieves a similar effect to the one above—a rush of thoughts and images—but a much faster one, through overusing punctuation, particularly his signature "! . . ." Generally, a voice can't carry over well in translation, but since his depends so much on punctuation, some of it does carry over from the French, enough to give us an idea of what punctuation can do:

> Look, the windmill's tipping! and so are we! our whole house! . . . a first rate eddy of air! . . . the one up there pitches toward the handrail, I think he's going to go right over . . . no! he stumbles against it, and chucks up on the other side! . . . before he was thirsty, our gondolier, but this might be just a little bit worse! he can't have a tongue left! . . . we may find ourselves cooking from the heat right here in our own rooms! . . . the eyes above all! the eyes! the lids won't shut any more! . . . a hundred shell-holes, sending sprays up into the sky! . . .

The rush of fragments fits the subject matter, the Allies bombing Paris. However, the roughshod appearance of this writing does not mean that little work has gone into it. Céline claimed that for some of his novels he'd write a draft of millions of words, which he'd edit down to a hundred thousand.

A constructed voice of a persona need not aim at the apparent simplicity of the spoken language. The voice in some pieces of writing may aim at an intense complexity. Here's an example, from Anthony Burgess' novel, *A Clockwork Orange.* Burgess' narrator, a young English gangster, uses Russian vocabulary as a cryptic gang jargon, which, at the height of the Cold War, exploits the fear that many people in the West had of anything Russian. At the end of the novel, Burgess gives translations of the words—(*britva* = razor; *litso* = face; *nozh* = knife; *vred* = hurt; etc.)—so unless you know some Russian, reading this novel takes additional work:

> It was stinking fatty Billyboy I wanted now, and there I was dancing about with my britva like I might be a barber on board a ship on a very rough sea, trying to get in at him with a few fair slashes on his unclean oily litso. Billyboy had a nozh, a long flick-type, but he was a

> malenky bit too slow and heavy in his movements to vred anyone really bad. And, my brothers, it was real satisfaction to me to waltz—left two three, right two three—and carve left cheeky and right cheeky, so that like two curtains of blood seemed to pour out at the same time, one on either side of his fat filthy oily snout in the winter starlight.

The mixture of the foreign vocabulary (liable to rouse xenophobia), familiar gang expressions (brothers), piled-up adjectives (fat filthy oily) and poetic images (winter starlight) creates a unique and cultured sadistic voice. Although nobody I know talks like the narrator in *A Clockwork Orange*, the voice is convincing, because the words are put together vigorously, in constant high contrasts. This is the type of writing that many critics like to call a *tour de force*. It works against the odds through the author's vigor, skill, labor.

Similar mixing of languages, in striving for the effect not of cruelty but gentility, particularly with French, has been done too many times. So if you suffer from the finesses of Frankophilia, be careful. Unless writing a satire of manners in which French is used for putting on airs, or deal with French-speaking peoples or the culinary arts, it's best to abstain. *Cool* will most often do for *nonchalant*.

Frequently bilingual writers, particularly Spanish-English writers, use many Spanish words, which add flavor and accent to their writing in English and enrich their voices. Since we all probably know some Spanish, this does not burden our reading, and may add color without pretentiousness.

THIRD-PERSON NARRATIVE VOICES

Some people construct their third-person narrative voices, others don't set out to do anything like that but may end up doing it anyway. Here, too, as with first-person narrative voices, you can play with syntax to achieve whatever texture you want. Whether T. Coraghessan Boyle crafted or spontaneously arrived at the following voice, from the novel *World's End*, is unclear; regardless, it exhibits a syntactical pattern:

> When they released him, when van den Post sauntered up to throw back the bars that pinioned him, he didn't fall into grandfather van der Meulen's arms or run home to where his mother sat stricken over a mount of flax and grandfather Cats anxiously paced the *stoep*—no, he took off like a sprinter, like a dog with a pair of sticks tied to its tail, streaking across the field and through the standing corn, hightailing it for the gap in the trees where his cousin had disappeared in the shock of dawn.

Boyle's voice depends largely on his maximalist syntax. Note that he doubles dependent and comparative clauses—"When they released him, when . . ." and, "took off like a sprinter, like a dog." He doubles his main clause with "or": "he didn't fall . . . or run home. . . ." He gives you both the negative (what didn't though could have happened) and the positive (what did happen.) Though this type of syntax runs the risk of turning cumbersome, the rich images and many strong, clipped words—"shock of dawn"—sustain a quick pace and make the novel dynamic.

James Joyce's voice evolved from a direct, economical one in his early short stories to an exuberant, playful and constant verbal high in *Ulysses*. Let's look at the economy in a passage from his relatively early work, *A Portrait of the Artist as a Young Man*:

> On a certain Tuesday the course of his triumphs was rudely broken. Mr Tate, the English master, pointed his finger at him and said bluntly:
>
> —This fellow has heresy in his essay.
>
> A hush fell on the class. Mr Tate did not break it but dug with his hands between his crossed thighs while his heavily starched linen creaked about his neck and wrists. Stephen did not look up. It was a raw spring morning and his eyes were still smarting and weak. He was conscious of failure and of detection, of the squalor of his own mind and home, and felt against his neck the raw edge of his turned and jagged collar.

The writing moves energetically, perhaps because of good sentence variety. The varied number of words in the sentences of the last paragraph—6, 26, 5, 14, 31—augment a sensation of unpredictability and tension, as do alterations between the declarative and the negative statements. Though he uses mostly direct sentences, Joyce does not avoid adverbs and adjectives, but uses them—*rudely*, *bluntly*, *heavily*, *raw*—and I think it's his adverbs that give tenor to his voice.

Later, in *Ulysses*, Joyce writes in larger strokes, in long giddy sentences, but his fondness for adverbs and adjectives has remained sufficiently for us to hear a similar voice after all:

> They passed the main entrance of the Great Northern railway station, the starting point for Belfast, where of course all traffic was suspended at that late hour, and, passing the back door of the morgue (a not very enticing locality, not to say gruesome to a degree, more especially at night), ultimately gained the Dock Tavern and in due course turned into Store street, famous for its C division police station. . . .
>
> You frittered away your time, he very sensibly maintained, and health and also character besides which the squandermania of the thing, fast women of the *demimonde* ran away with a lot of £.s.d. into the bargain and the greatest danger of all was who you got drunk with though, touching the much vexed question of stimulants, he relished a glass of choice old wine in season as both nourishing and bloodmaking and possessing aperient virtues (notably a good burgundy which he was a staunch believer in) still never beyond a certain point where he invariably drew the line as it simply led to trouble all round to say nothing of your being at the tender mercy of others practically.

Joyce depends heavily on the peculiar diction, which at any moment may include new coinages (squandermania), rare words (aperient), foreign words and, in other passages, old Anglo-Saxon words. His words keep coming, modifying each other, in a long breath, without a desire to stop. Joyce managed to get in touch with the basic joy of words, relishing each turn of syntax. *Ulysses* deals with many voices (in first and third person; in monologue and stream of consciousness), and they all can be recognized as Joyce's, through their exuberance.

Joyce's complex voice evolved through his obsession with language. Although the voice may sound artificial, I think it flowed out of Joyce's hyperverbal lifestyle.

SUBJECT MATTER AND VOICE

Your fictional voice in each piece should depend on who and what you write about. In the above examples, the subject matter invariably influences the writer's voice. Salinger's choice to write about adolescence certainly helped him shape the adolescent persona voice. Vaughn's writing about a confused person influenced her in choosing the diarylike, ungrammatical voice. Choosing war and madness as the subject matter, Céline appropriately constructs a disjointed voice. Burgess, writing about hooligans, constructs a fitting voice, filled with a gang jargon. In *Ulysses,* Joyce's complex voices fit his project of investigating how consciousness and verbal flux shape each other. Twain finds several voices to fit the subject matter of how yarns are created and disseminated.

In this chapter we have moved from the simple, relatively straightforward persona voices, like Salinger's, to complex ones, like Boyle's and Joyce's. I still think it's best to strive for simplicity and clarity, but if you must bring in various voice constructs—for the sake of realism, polyphony, experimentation, or complex subject matter—go ahead. However, it's probably best to find your direct way of putting sentences together, as did Joyce in the beginning, before experimenting. In the words of Oscar Wilde (a man who followed his own advice the least), "To reveal art and conceal the artist is the art's aim." Translated to voice, I think this means: Find a way of telling the story without drawing attention to how loud, varied, and complex in construction your voice can be—unless of course you need to construct a voice to fit the tale. But never do it the other way round.

Simplicity may scare you because of its potential blandness. Here's an example of a simple syntax with an exciting and quick voice, from Kate Braverman's "Tall Tales From the Mekong Delta":

> He fell in step with her. He was short, fat, pale. He had bad teeth. His hair was dirty. [After the man addresses her the narrative continues like this:] She didn't say anything. He was wearing blue jeans, a black leather jacket zipped to his throat, a long red wool scarf around his neck, and a Dodgers baseball cap. It was too hot a day for the leather jacket and scarf. She didn't find that detail significant. It caught her attention, she caught it briefly and then let it go. She looked but did not see. They were standing on a curb. The meeting was in a community room across the boulevard. She was not afraid yet.

The succession of short sentences creates a hurried pace and a matter-of-fact voice. All the sentences start directly, without conjunctions (*and*, *but*), without introducing auxiliary clauses (*with*, *although*, *when*, *if*); there are no auxiliary clauses anywhere. For example, most of us would connect the sentence ending with baseball cap with the following one, using *although*. "He was short, fat, pale." Usually, one would be tempted to put an *and* before *pale*, but omitting them accelerates the line. In terms of voice, we could say that this is writing with a short breath, as though the narrator were running uphill. And this shortness of breath fits the subject matter—threat.

The voice that suits you may vary from one piece of fiction to another, depending on the personae and the subject matters you choose. Experiment. Write in many modes, read out loud, see what your breathing tells you. Your breath, literally, can show you the beat, tempo for your sentences.

Most writers, of course, find one voice, closest to themselves, which they use in most third-person POV narratives and some first-person narratives. The way you think—whether hitting things directly or obviously—should, together with the way you breathe, reveal your "natural" syntax. And that is your voice:

your home in fiction. Sometimes you'll have to leave home and assume different personae, like an exile, and live in different skins, but that is the way you'll cover the most ground.

VOICE AND HUMOR

Humor in fiction, like spice in cooking, must be used in the right quantity, in the right places, and at the right time. You might think that the more humor the better, but beware. A friend of mine with a great sense of humor wrote four novels and couldn't publish any of them, he claimed, because his writing was too funny. A television audience may want humor insatiably, but editors of novels may be a particularly humorless lot. There's another explanation, probably more accurate. A humorous novel is tough to sell because humor is largely subjective. Since first novels are risky for publishers anyway, a humorous first novel may be even riskier. Humor, despite its innocent appearance, is a double-edged sword. If you jest at a key dramatic moment, you may lose the drama, especially if the humor in any way turns on the plot. If you don't take the plot seriously, why should the reader? Your tone sets an example for how to read.

On the other hand, if you have nothing playful, no humor, anywhere in your novel—how dreary! It's like a feast without wine. Joke as much as you can, especially in a comedy (not too much in a tragedy), and later, in revision, notice whether a joke is timed poorly, in which case, place it elsewhere. In transitional moments, jokes can maintain your reader's attention, and they can provide a new mood. If the emotional tone of your novel is grim, it's good to offer a break, because unrelieved grimness can grow monotonous. Using humor as a contrast will then deepen the tragic impact of your story.

Humor often stems from a writer's voice and attitude toward his subject matter. Think of Woody Allen. Sometimes when he gets in the groove of his voice, almost anything he says is funny. I noticed the impact of voice on humor when I was a kid. When called on by a teacher, I'd use a peasant dialect in a goofy way, and though most often I said nothing funny, my classmates and sometimes the teachers laughed at the voice.

We've seen how Mark Twain uses different voices humorously. Here's a simple example of a single humorous voice from *Huckleberry Finn*:

> The widow she cried over me, and called me a poor lost lamb, and she called me a lot of other names, too, but she never meant no harm by it. She put me in them new clothes again, and I couldn't do nothing but sweat and sweat, and feel all cramped up. Well, then, the old thing commenced again. The widow rung a bell for supper, and you had to come to time. When you got to the table you couldn't go right to eating, but you had to wait for the widow to tuck down her head and grumble a little over the victuals, though there warn't anything the matter with them. . . .

If you rewrote this passage to get rid of the dialect and the voice with its funny diction, you would lose some of the humor. It would still be funny, no doubt, because of Huck's way of seeing things, his logic, but the voice provides a crucial element.

Although I say the voice is simple and direct, it displays irony. Huck imitates Miss Watson—"called me a poor lost lamb." Here his voice uses touches of another voice. I think that's an important aspect of humor: ironic touches imported from someone talked about and adapted into the narrative voice.

Methods of Humor

Many people claim that humor cannot be taught and learned, that it's a natural character trait. Much humor takes place spontaneously, without being premeditated, but analyzing humor often reveals a method. You can learn how to apply various methods to create humor.

Absurdist Humor This excerpt from Samuel Beckett's novel *Molloy* is a description of lovemaking. This may strike you as too nihilistic to be humorous, but this is humor of a kind—absurdist humor. Beckett's humor, like Twain's, depends on the voice and a peculiar logic working together. While in Twain voice is perhaps more important than the logic, here logic is more important than the voice:

> And all I could see was her taut yellow nape which every now and then I set my teeth in, forgetting I had none, such is the power of instinct. . . . Anyway it was she who started it, in the rubbish dump, when she laid her hand upon my fly. More precisely, I was bent double over a heap of muck, in the hope of finding something to disgust me for ever with eating, when she, undertaking me from behind, thrust her stick between my legs and began to titillate my privates. She gave me money after each session, to me who would have consented to know love, and probe it to the bottom, without charge. But she was an idealist. I would have preferred it seems to me an orifice less arid and roomy, that would have given me a higher opinion of love it seems to me. . . . The other thing that bothers me, in this connexion, is the indifference with which I learnt of her death, when one black night I was crawling towards her, an indifference softened indeed by the pain of losing a source of revenue. . . . What I do know for certain is that I never sought to repeat the experience, having I suppose the intuition that it had been unique and perfect, of its kind. . . . Don't talk to me about the chambermaid, I should never have mentioned her, she was long before, I was sick, perhaps there was no chambermaid, ever, in my life. Molloy, or life without a chambermaid.

The narrative voice undermines whatever it touches with indifference. Beckett treats the first love and knowledge of love—traditionally topics of much sentiment—in a reductive manner, placing them in the context of a garbage dump. That reduction, in technique, may be the same as cynicism since it portrays a higher level of human life in animal, dog, terms. And it *is* cynicism. People often resort to cynicism in the hope of being humorous, for the two share much. Twain's humorous description of prayer—"to tuck down her head and grumble a little over the victuals, though there warn't anything the matter with them"—is a downshifting maneuver, bringing something in high regard—prayer—to something basic—grumbling. (Twain's humor sounds less cynical than Beckett's because of Huck's "disarmingly" charming voice.)

To make cynicism come to life as humor requires wit, cleverness. Molloy's trying to get rid of his hunger by finding something disgusting in a dump of discarded foods is a clever twist. That the narrator calls the woman an idealist because she pays him for lovemaking is another twist. Paying strikes us as materialistic, but you can find some logic in this—paying for a service is an idea that she sticks to even though he'd do it for free. That he gets carried away and sinks his teeth in her neck forgetting he has none—this surprises you with its logical impossibility, and evokes a potentially funny picture of naked gums biting. In the statement "perhaps there was no chambermaid," the narrator's doubt continues where we don't expect it. Perhaps there was no narrator? No life without a chambermaid? As you read this, I assume that the paradoxes and sometimes logical impossibilities laid out one after another create an effect.

Sundry Humor: Slapstick, Caricature, Exaggeration, Stereotypes. Nikolai Gogol, a versatile humorist, used all kinds of humor. Though much of his humor is lost and diminished in translation from Russian, some does come through.

In describing a giant in *Dead Souls*, Gogol jokes: "He was seven feet tall, in other words, a born dentist." This is a jab at Russian dentistry, another "trade," where strength to pull out teeth was the basic skill. The joke works through exaggeration and the stereotyping of a profession. Once when I visited a dental clinic in Novi Sad (Northern Serbia), three muscular dentists tied me to a chair and flexed their muscles on my jaws. I was reminded of the joke, but did not laugh.

Gogol uses stereotypes for a humorous effect. Earlier I wrote against the use of stereotypes, but sometimes they can work, if the humor is not malicious. Gogol also uses similes in an astoundingly simple way. The freshness of these metaphors works, for me, as humor. Speaking of a healthy man, Gogol says: "A lump of iron would sooner catch cold and start coughing than that wonderfully constituted landowner."

Here's another kind of humor Gogol uses. When Chichikov, the hero of *Dead Souls*, runs into an acquaintance, a landowner, their meeting goes as follows: "They immediately embraced each other and remained clasped in each other's arms for about five minutes. The kisses they exchanged were so powerful that their front teeth ached for the rest of the day. Manilov was so overjoyed that only his nose and his lips remained on his face, his eyes having completely disappeared."

This is perhaps the most common type of humor—slapstick. It depends on exaggerating and overdoing a simple social exchange. A hug with a greeting kiss becomes a major enterprise. Note Gogol's caricaturist skill. "Only his nose and his lips remained on his face, his eyes having completely disappeard." This wonderfully reductive image enhances the scene.

Gogol mostly uses typology, caricature, and exaggeration in his humor. It's not simple to reduce it to a formula, at least not as simple as in the following case study: Oscar Wilde's humor.

Substituting Opposites as Humor. Oscar Wilde's humor is like math. He creates it through substitution of values.

"The old-fashioned respect for the young is fast dying out."

"Divorces are made in heaven."

The technique is transparent yet effective. Wilde substitutes one element in a cliché for its opposite and the cliché becomes something new, surprising, certainly funny. You put in *young* for *old*, *divorces* for *marriages*.

In "The Decay of Lying" Wilde writes: "The ancient historians gave us delightful fiction in the form of fact; the modern novelist presents us with dull facts under the guise of fiction." Here we have a role reversal. Historians, who should give us facts, give us fiction. Novelists, who should give us fiction, give us facts.

You can apply this technique not only in one-liners, but in two (or more) sentences, as does Wilde in this case from *The Importance of Being Earnest*: "I hope you have not been leading a double life, pretending to be wicked and being really good all the time. That would be hypocrisy."

As though he's put a negative sign before a parenthesis, Wilde here switches things around: good/wicked. Everything else stays the same.

In the following example from "The Decay of Lying," Wilde has created a string of reversals of what's commonly expected, by the mechanics of custom:

> Many a young man starts in his life with a natural gift for exaggeration which, if nurtured in congenial and sympathetic surroundings, or by imitation of the best models, might grow into something really great and wonderful. But, as a rule, he comes to nothing. He either falls into careless habits of accuracy, or takes to frequenting the society of the aged and the well-informed. . . . In a short time he develops a morbid and unhealthy faculty of truth-telling, begins to verify all statements made in his presence, has no hesitation in contradicting people who are much younger than himself, and often ends by writing novels which are so life-like that no one can possibly believe in their probability.

"Careless habit of accuracy"—usually *accuracy* strikes us as something *careful*, and we accept the coupling of the two words quite mechanically. Wilde breaks the couplet, as he does with contradicting people much younger. Now this is not all formula. Part of Wilde's humor is his voice, the stylishly and ironically high-brow way of putting words together. "Frequenting the society of the aged and the well-informed," for example, strikes a tone of leisure, of the English upper-class, so Wilde's is a comedy of manners, besides being a humor of inversion.

Wilde's humor method is not unique. Much of Beckett's humor conforms to this "formula." (I put formula in quotation marks because nothing guarantees that all you write according to it will be funny. But some things will be.) Beckett's (Molloy's) softening indifference with the thought of losing revenue is a reversed phrase—we soften pain, in a cliché. He softens its near opposite, indifference.

George Bernard Shaw uses the same technique: "A drama critic is a man who leaves no turn unstoned."

Situational Humor. Much situational humor depends on timing and confusion. Here's an example from Bernard Malamud's novel *The Fixer.* In it Yakov, on the way to Kiev, must abandon his horse in order to cross a river:

> The boatman untied the boat, dipped both oars into the water and they were off.
>
> The nag, tethered to a paling, watched from the moonlit shore.
>
> Like an old Jew he looks, thought the fixer.
>
> The horse whinnied, and when that proved useless, farted loudly.
>
> "I don't recognize the accent you speak," said the boatman, pulling the oars. "It's Russian but from what province?"
>
> "I've lived in Latvia as well as other places," the fixer muttered.

The scene taking place is sad. Thus, the contrast, the fart in the solemn moment, "cracks" the solemnity, and it cracks up the readers.

Now take this phrase—"The horse whinnied, and when that proved useless, farted loudly"—and place it one line up or down, and you'll see that the joke won't work so well, or will be lost altogether.

Timing, however, is not everything. Something high is brought low, human speech to a nag's fart. This downgrading results in humor. I don't think there's an absolute recipe for humor, but if you practice this downshifting and timing so that one thing could be taken for another, you might create humor.

Notice one more point in Malamud's example. The protagonists don't laugh. They continue being serious, they don't notice the humor; to them the nag's fart has nothing to do with what they are doing. This increases the humor. You may take this as a paradigm: If a protagonist in your story cracks a joke, don't have him and others roll on the floor holding their sides; otherwise, your reader will get the impression that you are congratulating yourself. That's a bit like prerecorded laughter in a sitcom. Deadpan humor is the best. If it's funny, your reader will laugh. If not, all right, there was no promise of humor anyway. But if your reader encounters an orgy of laughter after a flat joke, she may resent not laughing. (Of course, when it's important that a character laugh at a joke, let him laugh.)

You can learn how to make humorous passages, from what I've told you so far, or from your own analysis. Analyze writings you find funny. If you persevere, in some of them you'll find an applicable method.

EXERCISES

1. One page. Construct the voice of an uneducated person (or someone who never paid any attention to writing classes) through playing with syntax. Rarely use a comma, but sometimes put one in the wrong place, and sometimes in the right place. Skip periods for long stretches, and here and there use sentence fragments. Take a look at Vaughn's example, but do it more extremely—misspell (not too much though, keep it readable), use possessives and contractions incorrectly. Combine this with repetitive expressions (end sentences with *or something*, like Salinger in *The Catcher in the Rye*, overuse *like*, and so on). Add to it some regional expressions. Let the character talk about her "date from hell."

Objective: To arrive at a voice through the basic syntactical technique. Can you begin to hear someone sounding like this? What's this person like? What does she wear, eat, drink? If grammar puts a strain on you, perhaps freedom from grammar will free you.

Check: Did you get a sense of character? You should. Voice without character is pale and impersonal; character without voice can hardly be alive.

2. One page. Construct the first-person voice of an immigrant from a language you are familiar with—Spanish, German, Italian—all right, even French. In every second sentence or so use one foreign word. Don't double or triple r's (verrry) in English to give us the accent with rolled r's, but now and then—rarely—make a change in spelling. Let the person talk about her getting married to an American for a green card. Describe the fake wedding in detail, with many asides. (If you're not familiar with a foreign language, use a regional dialect, and make the wedding a marriage of convenience.)

Objective: In our multicultural society, languages mix, "interpenetrate." This is a vast reservoir of voices. Tap it.

Check: Do the foreign words make sense in their context? If you didn't know what they meant, could you guess from their placement and tone? (Ask a colleague whether the foreign words sound convincing.) Do these words add color to the voice?

3. Two pages. Write a polyphonous story, after the example of Twain's "The Celebrated Jumping Frog of Calaveras County." Frame the story in the voice of an overeducated persona, who imitates an uneducated narrator, and let the narrator introduce a folksy character with her regional speech, in a yarnlike style. Don't worry if your narrators don't sound authentic in terms of regions and dialects. Invent your own regions and dialects, if you like.

Objective: To create an orgy of voices. If you can play different voices against each other, or with each other, you might attain a wonderful liveliness in your story.

Check: On the most basic level, do the voices sound different? Let them not use the same syntax, length of sentences, level of diction, fillers. Is each voice consistent? For example, a sales type of abbreviation ("As is" for "as it is") would clash with highly formal syntax ("Lest he should abdicate his primogeniture, grant him the seal.") Do all these voices sound spoken? They should.

4. Three pages. Write a rough draft of a story, with a theme of abuse. Let's say, a lawyer (or a doctor) exploits an elderly widow. Don't hide your tone of outrage about the injustice, but

don't preach. Give us the event only. Revise a draft of what you've written. Replace all the clichés with words that should address what you mean as directly as possible. Remove passive voice whenever possible. Cut redundancies, excess adverbs and adjectives. Make sure it's always clear where the action is: Who does what to whom? Who kicks whom? Once rid of the static, your piece should sound loud and clear. The combination of emotion (outrage) with clear writing must result in a strong voice.

Objective: Nothing sharpens a voice like a sense of wounded justice. See if you can drive yourself to a pitch of standing up for an injured person.

Check: Did you speak forcefully? In simple, direct, unmincing sentences?

5. Two pages. First, imitate Joyce's early style, which we discused earlier in this chapter. Offer a good variety of sentences, emphasize with concrete images energetic verbs and adverbs.

Then, imitate Joyce's style in *Ulysses*. Write two long, unrestrained sentences that have the energy to keep going, with odd words (find them in a dictionary or thesaurus)—at least half a page for each sentence.

Objective: Breathing exercises. See which carries more life for you, more thrill, without making you run out of breath.

Check: Read your exercises out loud. Which suits you better, the first or the second style? Give these sentences to a colleague of yours. Which style does he prefer? If both you and your colleague prefer one, maybe something in it might work for you. You might adapt this to your work—the adverbs, the sentence variety, the alterations between negative and positive statements, whatever.

6. Three sentences. Can you imitate T.C. Boyle's syntax of doubles? Perhaps we should call it stereo syntax. Analyze his sentence on page 208 and write three similar ones.

Objective: To experiment with sentences. Whether with T.C. Boyle or someone else, you might find a rhythm that works for you, that releases your imagination. Painters study other painters' strokes. Why deny yourself a basic learning technique?

Check: Do you have many doubles, expressed with *or, and, but*? Do you express some points in a negative and others in a declarative?

7. One paragraph. Can you imitate Kate Braverman's voice and syntax in the excerpt from her story on page 211? Make all sentences direct, and some factual. No conjunctions. Clip the sentences with commas, make many of them short, and end the paragraph with a negative statement, and yet create expectations for further paragraphs. This strategy builds a good forward momentum.

Now rewrite the exercise with many *althoughs, buts, ands,* and *becauses*. Put in more adverbs, and add several metaphors.

Objective: To find which way of writing suits you better. Some artists draw with many long, fuzzy pencil strokes, others with a few sharp, short ones.

Check: Which syntax suits you better? Read both exercises out loud, and feel the rhythm in each. Which moves better? Ask a colleague for her opinion.

8. One to two pages. Imitate Beckett's account of Molloy's first love. Write in the first person. Possible themes: trying transcendental meditation, getting a college degree, publishing your first short story, eating caviar, listening to "The Ode to Joy" at a glamorous concert hall, attending the funeral of someone who should be beloved. Treat each "high" with indifference. Overanalyze the experience into total banality.

Objective: To practice cynicism with a twist as a source of humor.

Check: Have you concentrated on the physical details? With TM, you might talk about twisting your knee, incense, etc. With the college degree, you might analyze the poor quality of the paper, sunstroke, sweat, hunger. (Of course, you can do better than this.)

9. One page. Take a list of proverbs, clichés and truisms, and insert the opposites for each subject. (*Marriages are. . . .*)

Objective: To learn the basic technique of Wilde's humor. Don't worry whether the reversals you create are funny. If you write enough of them, some will be. Even a computer could do this.

Check: Read the ones you think are funny to someone who laughs pretty easily. If you don't spark any laughter, find someone else. If nothing happens, choose another set of truisms, twist them, and check them with your hired laughers.

10. One page. Give a twist to familiar expressions. For example, "One more drink and I'll be under the table," becomes, "One more drink and I'll be under the host" (as a comedian has paraphrased this in a cartoon).

Objective: Similar to the purpose of Exercise 9, but here you don't have to substitute opposites. Host and table are not opposites, but the substitution works perfectly. Look for something that would make sense in the situation.

Check: Same as in Exercise 9.

11. Three half-page paragraphs. Imitate Wilde's quote about the decay of the art of lying. Can you write something similar on the decay of the art of jealousy, stealing, flirting, drinking, smoking, chocolate-eating, procrastinating? Take three of them, and tell us something against the grain of the common wisdom.

Objective: To create humor by upgrading an apparent vice to a virtue.

Check: Are you convincing enough? Wilde's arguments make sense. Constructing lies takes imagination, and it probably develops imagination, so it should be a useful skill for a fiction writer. Make sure that your arguments are sensible, at least at some level.

12. One page. In the proverbs and clichés from Exercises 9 and 10, reverse key adjectives and see what happens. Something is bound to turn out funny. Or at least twisted.

Objective: To learn that humor can take place almost at every turn of a sentence. If you examine many possible permutations, something will work. We call witty people "quick," because they can quickly think of enough permutations to light upon something interesting. This is a technique, and no matter how spontaneously a witty person applies it, he still does it.

Check: Have you made enough switches?

13. One page. Make up a dialogue in which momentary confusion occurs, at least in the reading, as in Malamud's examples. Take a heart-breaking departure, or a solemn rite of passage, and make a joke; let something from the "bodily substratum" (Mikhail Bakhtin's phrase) intrude on the solemnity.

Objective: To practice situational comedy. Learn how to place and time your intrusions. Create and exploit confusions. Your characters should not laugh.

Check: Have your buddies read this. Are they laughing? Or smiling? If not, shift your intrusive line up or down. Again, check with someone around you. Humor is in the ear of the reader, not in the eye of the writer.

14. Three pages. Choose three social conventions: a handshake, keeping the door open for the next passerby, and holding hands. Construct three slapstick scenes: exaggerating whatever can happen, so that it becomes funny. Pattern this after Gogol's example of friends embracing and kissing each other. You might augment your humor with dialogue and with caricatures of the handshakers' faces.

Objective: To practice basic slapstick as comedy of manners.

Check: Do you make the conventions appear ridiculous? Vivid? Your readers should get the sensation of doing all these things as though participating in the scenes. Have you managed to squeeze in a good caricature? And, most important, is this funny?

CHAPTER TEN

REVISION

In the revision stage, you strive to make your writing coherent, clear and effective. Out of chaos a fully developed story gradually emerges. Clumsy sentences become graceful; clichés become wit; muddled action becomes drama. If you wonder how to sound original, the answer is: revise and revise. Even if you think your stories don't work, you can make them work—if you revise well.

It's amazing how easy it is to lack courage as a writer. The anxiety of a concert pianist is understandable. She can't go back and improve the passages where she blundered. That you can return to your story and cut the weak parts and expand the strong ones should encourage you as you write your first draft. Therefore, don't look back until you are finished.

As you revise, don't fear changing your text radically in search of its best possible shape. And certainly don't hesitate to get rid of whatever does not work. This is how Isaac Bashevis Singer puts it: "The wastepaper basket is the writer's best friend."

On the other hand, don't rush to throw things away. Give yourself time, and if in a week you still think that something you've written doesn't work and can't be made useful, get rid of it. Sometimes, what appears weak one day may appear fine the next. This is what Conrad Aiken said about his experience: "I would find a crumpled yellow ball of paper in the wastebasket in the morning, and open it to see what the hell I'd been up to; and occasionally it was something that needed only a very slight change to be brought off, which I'd missed the day before."

So that you don't have to fumble in the garbage among banana peels and cockroaches (although cockroaches come from a noble literary lineage), save an early draft. If you cut too much, you can restore. That knowledge should help you freely look at your text. See it again. Look at what fits and what doesn't. If something is pretty but does not connect to the rest of the text, cut it. Samuel Johnson advises, "Read over your compositions and, when you meet a passage that you think is particularly fine, strike it out." He has a point—if something stands out of the text, maybe it does not belong in it.

Revision used to be painful before word processors. You had to cut out pages, glue them, white out sections, so that most often you'd simply give up on changing here and there, and you'd rewrite the whole piece. (Of course, some good came out of being forced to rewrite thoroughly.) Now, with computers, you don't need to rewrite. We could say, "The delete key is the writer's best friend." You can rearrange passages, compress—revise.

Yes, there's a difference between a revision and a complete rewrite: In revision, you rearrange passages, condense sentences, add here and there and so on, but you probably leave chunks of the text close to the original.

Before word processors, Hemingway did more than thirty drafts of a story. And we got anecdotes like this one, from Isaac Babel's friend, Konstantin Paustovsky: Babel showed Paustovsky a manuscript two hundred pages long. When Paustovsky asked him whether it was a novel, Babel answered that it was his short story "Lyubka the Cossac" in twenty-two versions.

In a rewrite, take a look at what you did in the initial draft and tackle it differently, from scratch, not even necessarily looking at the draft again.

THE FIRST REWRITE

These days when people tell you that they have rewritten something ten times, they probably mean that they have played around with the original text several times. For better or worse (certainly, for easier) hardly anybody does complete rewrites anymore. But many people arrange and rearrange their passages—tinker with the original draft. As a consequence, I think it's now easier to write clean sentences and paragraphs, but perhaps harder to get rid of the larger structural problems because it's easy to remain within the initial faulty structure of a draft.

Rather than say that with computers we have gained something and lost something, we can enjoy the best of both worlds—if we're willing to do the extra work. Write your first draft longhand or on a typewriter. (If you work solely on the computer, you can simulate the typewriter if you don't go back too much. Print out your draft and delete the original from the computer.) Now read your draft and think what you need to do differently. Rewrite it from scratch on the computer. (Or do another longhand draft, and then type it into the system). Save your rewrite and treat it as your starting point for revision.

Through this method you will make sure that you get at least one rewrite as opposed to a series of tinkerings. Not that there's anything wrong with tinkering—on the contrary, you get to play around and have fun with the story—but it should not start too early.

In the first rewrite, you want to see the story shaping out of the first draft mass of words. Cut through the words and find the story. Let it emerge. In every draft there is a story desperately trying to get out. Cut the chains and give the keys to the prisoner.

Carefully read your first draft before undertaking a rewrite. Identify your major conflict, scene, plot. Outline the plot, in a basic way.

Find the story's big moments. By knowing where they occur, you save yourself a lot of work because you will build your narration on a strong foundation. So mark your main characters and main scenes. Are there too many characters? Compress two or three characters into one. Are there too many big scenes? Can you compress them into fewer?

Once you decide on your major scenes, begin your rewrite. Expand the scenes. Let the characters act, speak, move in a setting. You don't need to accomplish everything right now, since you'll have time to revise. Complete a rough rewrite—even several of them. Don't yet worry about your spelling, diction, clichés or other minute matters.

After you finish these rough rewrites of the major moments in your story, provide the transitions and background between the big scenes. Make sense of what happens in the scenes. Put the background you cannot fit into the scenes into your narrative paragraphs, where you can simply tell us what we need to know to follow the upcoming scenes.

Read your rewrite, proofing it against the plot outline. (If you change the plot in the first rewrite, outline the new plot and proof the rewrite against it.) Whatever seems useless, cut. If something in no way contributes to your understanding of the central characters, the conflict, and the key event, cut it. Your story must make sense. Here you may spend a lot of time thinking, analyzing.

Some writers do scene-oriented story build-up intuitively, and others arrive at the basic structure after dozens of revisions. If you unfortunately don't belong in the former camp, you still might be able to avoid belonging in the latter by identifying the foundation of your story in the first rewrite stage, so that you won't need to keep restructuring. With practice, you might become so adept at this that it will appear that you work intuitively. Intuition often simply means an internalized technique so that you don't have to deliberate over what to do; a net player in tennis, who through diligence acquires good habits, can react to a passing shot without thinking about what the textbook says about footwork.

But even if you become a highly intuitive writer, you will still most likely need a lot of revision: first rough revision (macrorevision), making sure that all the parts of the story fit together; then fine revision (microrevision), making sure that each word is in its place.

When you finish your rewrite, save it. I always do. The knowledge that I can return to the second draft enables me to take a distant look at my story, without particular attachments to this or that passage, so I keep only what I need and revise freely. I often think I will return to that saved second draft but hardly ever do. And when I do, I notice that though I cut, I have lost nothing.

Be open to any change that suggests itself as important during your revising. And have fun! Most writers prefer revising to the original drafting—some write the original draft so they'll have something to play with.

MACROREVISION

There are different styles of revision, depending on how you write your initial draft. According to F. Scott Fitzgerald writers are either putter-inners or taker-outers.

Those who work from a sketchy draft must add words to give life to a story skeleton. In revision they pause where they need to add dialogue and description. (Some writers are extreme putter-inners, so when they revise even previously unedited torrents of words, they are more eager to add than to cut.)

Those who write in torrents of unedited words—hoping that the accumulation will contain a story—must eventually cut quite a bit to find the story. I don't need to quote anybody in support of the putter-inner aesthetics; Shakespeare, Dostoyevski and Balzac were putter-inners.

Elie Wiesel gives us the best description of the taker-outer aesthetics: "Writing is . . . like a sculpture where you remove, you eliminate in order to make the work visible. Even those pages you remove somehow remain. There is a difference between a book of two hundred pages from the very beginning, and a book of two hundred pages which is the result of an original eight hundred pages. The six hundred pages are there. Only you don't see them."

Many people are both putter-inners and taker-outers. If you are not, consider becoming both. You could rush through some parts, knowing that you can fill in later. And you can spend much time on other parts—adding line upon line, getting as much juice out of a scene as your imagination and free associations will give you—without fearing that you'll be boring, since you can clean up later.

As you look over your story, first check it against the "First Rewrite" questions above to find your major scenes, your story. (Whenever you have a story, you can use these guidelines. If you have one already, get it out and examine it against the checklists to follow.) Then leaf through this book, chapter by chapter. Each chapter raises questions about the elements of fiction. Check your setting, plot, POV and so on. But to give you a concentrated checklist, I will offer many questions here. If you must rethink an element of your fiction, go to the chapters that address your concerns.

Revision Checklist

All the parts of your story must work before it can fly. Make sure that each part is the best it can be, as though you were an inspector in a Boeing factory. Although a good proportion of stories could be held accountable to this list, many stories set their own rules. For example, a slice-of-life story needn't be structured around a conflict. Make sure that your "own rules" isn't merely an excuse. And if you come up with idiosyncratic rules, hold your story accountable to them.

Plot. Does enough *happen* in your story? Something must. The event need not be huge, but it must be dramatic and significant.

Is the story structured around a conflict? Can you state the conflict in a sentence or two? What is the struggle about? This is your theme. The theme should not be separate from the conflict.

Do you introduce the conflict soon enough—preferably as a crisis in the first couple of pages? Do you sustain the conflict as a tension long enough, through most of your story?

Is the conflict carried to its logical conclusion? Does the ending make sense in light of the beginning?

Can you identify the key event and its climax? This should be the turning point. You've reached the peak and now things will inevitably slide, faster and faster, to a conclusion. Hitherto, there were options; but now the protagonist's choice has become clear.

Does the story give us enough information on the causes of the main event? Although the advice remains "show, don't tell," whenever you *can't* show us enough, tell us, summarize, fill us in. After all, you are a storyteller. Whatever happens in the story must make sense.

Do you present us the right sequence of events (scenes and summaries) so that the story has the cogency of a good argument?

Do you have a stock plot? (Avoid plots too often encountered in pop novels—for example, the detective investigating a murder is the murderer.)

Is your plot easy to follow? Even if it's a mystery, what happens during the investigation should be easy to follow. John Gardner advises, "Don't play pointlessly subtle games in which storytelling is confused with puzzle-making."

Character. Who are the protagonists? Antagonists? In general, you should have at least two characters, engaged in some kind of action or tension. One character reminiscing and laughing out loud at his thoughts or smiling at ashtrays doesn't offer enough dialectical potential for a story.

Are the main characters well developed (round)? If not, give them sufficient complexity—desires, obstacles, weaknesses, strengths.

Are there flat characters? Perhaps they don't need to be round, but on the other hand, don't let them become stereotypes.

Can you find out the basic motivation—desires and fears—of the main characters?

Do the characters encounter any obstacles? Are the obstacles sufficiently tough?

Does your main character change or come to some crucial insight in the course of the story?

Setting. Is the setting appropriate? Authentic? If it's Cleveland, make sure there's no subway. If it's Venus, make sure there are no people living in forests.

Does your setting work in synergy with characters and plot? The setting could deepen your characterization and ground your plot. Realistically drawn landscapes and cityscapes increase believability, even in fantasy stories.

Have you given us the setting gradually, together with the characters and the action? Or have you dumped it all in a long chunk in the beginning or middle?

Have you used the setting for special effects (foreshadowing, mood expression, beautiful images, change of pace)?

POV. From whose POV is the story told? Could you tell it better from another character's POV?

Is the POV consistent? If it shifts, is there a good reason for it to do so?

Does your POV shift in midsentence? Midparagraph? Even in the omniscient POV, you might do better to sort out POVs by paragraphs.

In the omniscient POV, do you enter too many heads? Generally, limit yourself to the main characters. The minor ones can remain external.

Do you use interior monologues to your advantage? If there's a crisis point in which your POV carrier is alone, waiting, you might deliver an interior monologue to heighten suspense and clarify motives.

Do you use stream of consciousness where you can? If there's a crisis point in which your carrier of POV is injured or disoriented, you might switch to a stream of consciousness to reflect the crisis and to change the narrative pace.

Whom does the narrator of your story address? Is there an ostensible audience, like "Gentle reader," "Dear President," "Mimi"? Is the audience used consistently?

Who are you, as the author, addressing? An imaginary person, or a friend, or nobody? Who do you think will read your story? Children, adults, punks, U.S. Marines, Connecticut tax-evaders?

Are there authorial intrusions? Are they warranted? In the "omniscient" POV they are fair game; in other POVs, they may be distracting.

Voice, Attitude and Humor. What voices do you hear in the story? Naturally, each speaker should have a distinct voice, different from the author's in most cases, unless the narrative is a piece of overt autobiography. In the narrative part, is the voice clear enough?

Do you joke at inappropriate moments—for example, at the

peak of a tragic action? Some characters may joke under stress: it's all right to reproduce that, but make sure the authorial humor does not undermine the tension.

Are your jokes in poor taste? Offensive to women and minorities?

Do you strain too hard for sentimental effects? Any rivers of tears? Above all, especially in the third-person POV narrative, don't tell that what happened was devastatingly sad, unless you parody sentimental writing.

Timing. Does the story start at the right moment? Or does it start too early, before the main action—or too late? Identify your first crisis moment, and open with it. A swimmer jumps far into the pool rather than swim from the very edge of it. The better you write, the further into the story you'll be able to jump.

Does the story end at the right moment? Find the point when things have begun to fall into place, and cut the action; ending here implies that they will continue to do so.

Do you cover enough time in the story? Or too much? (In a short story, usually you'd cover several days; generally you shouldn't cover more than a couple of years; in a novel, you can.)

Is the chronology—and the grammar that indicates it—clear? If you frequently backtrack in time, try using the present tense for your "now" action, so you can use the simple past tense, rather than past perfect, for your "then" action.

Check your tenses. Within a chapter, unless there is a flashback or a fast-forward, the tense should remain the same. The tense should not switch in a sentence.

Keep the sequence of motions chronological, from first to last. The previous sentence should not ordinarily read like this: "After he lies on a sofa, upon walking in the room, he breathes out his anxiety. . . ." Readers strain to straighten out the sequence of actions here. The same holds true of paragraphs. Keep going forward, except when you have memories and flashbacks. But even then, once you switch into the past to explain what had happened, lay it out as chronologically as possible.

If you've used flashbacks or memories, did you need to? Could you tell the story from the first event to the last without backtracking and without losing the cogency of the story as an argument? This is a difficult choice. Sometimes you must go with the shape of the argument rather than with the linearity of time. It's best if you can accomplish both.

Has the story been paced well? Don't bore the reader, yet don't run out of plot too fast. Make sure that you've done enough showing to give body to any telling you may have done.

Scene and Dialogue. Is the dialogue natural? Do people sound like real people rather than technical books?

Do the characters sound different from the general narrative and from each other? Go through the dialogue, line by line, and give signature expressions to a character, making sure that the other characters don't use the same ones, except when being sarcastic to each other.

Is your dialogue complex enough? Combine small scenes into big ones so that they portray characters, advance the plot and raise tension.

Do you have enough dialogue in proportion to the narrative? There's no set rule, but at least some parts of your story should be written in dialogue, unless you are doing Man against Nature or some other type of story in which dialogue might not appear. And despite the current fashion in favor of dialogue, your fiction should include description, summary, and other sorts of narrative—for the change of pace, transitions and quick information.

Is the story told mostly as a nonscenic narrative? If so, your story will sound like an essay. Decide where the action is, and stage it.

Are the scenes compounded ("Mondays she would pray") or are they specific ("One Monday she prayed")? Compounded scenes work well to introduce the main event, but the main event must take place as a fully developed, specific scene. Your story or novel should contain a larger proportion of specific scenes than of compounded scenes and background exposition.

Are the right scenes dramatized and the right ones summarized? Usually, your key event should be fully dramatized (though you should skip greetings and other dull exchanges, unless they can show something important). Some supporting scenes can be summarized, others dramatized. Transitions between various events are usually summarized.

Do you have too many similar scenes? Are there ten quarrels? Maybe two will do; make each unique. If you write three similar scenes to show a pattern, distill them to one, and tell us during it that the dramatic action is part of a pattern.

Are your dramatic scenes long enough? If not, expand them.

Are the dramatic scenes suspenseful enough? Though they must be fairly long, they also must be quickly paced. Achieving this balance can be difficult. Raise the tension of the conflict, and point toward the resolution, which should make sense of it all.

Description and Diction. Do you show enough? The most important story moments must be shown in scenes.

Do you describe characters in a fresh way? (No chiseled features, sky-blue eyes, pearly white teeth.)

Do you genuinely describe settings? (No ominous train stations, squalid quarters, posh offices.)

Do you have enough dynamic descriptions incorporated into the action?

Do you tell enough? You need not show absolutely everything. Sometimes it's all right to tell, for the sake of pacing the narrative. Some crucial points can be both told and shown; if you tell them, show them also.

Are there enough metaphors? Too many? Do they work? Do they create a parallel text? Is the parallel text something you want? For example, if all your metaphors concern various beasts devouring each other, are you sure you want this Hobbesian dimension in your story—and is this killing and feeding frenzy what your story is about? If you have a tame romance with such metaphors, you have a choice: Either get rid of bestial metaphors and resort to botany (although flowers have been overused in this context) or listen to your metaphors. They may suggest a major plot change. The romance might turn into a struggle and become all the more interesting. In other words, metaphors may bring out the full potential of a story. If you listen to them, your story might grow into a larger one.

Do the descriptions drag or jump?

Are the descriptions effective? Do they engage our senses? Or are some senses atrophied? Why? In most cases, if your sentences do not make us see (hear, touch, smell, taste), cross them out. Leave what you can perceive.

MICROREVISION

When you've successfully answered all of the questions above and made all the necessary changes, you are still not quite finished; you've got to polish. You must cleanse the narrative of any superfluous words. Polishing can turn out to be a lot of work. As James Baldwin put it, "Most of the rewrite is cleaning."

Polishing the manuscript may be similar for everybody—putter-inners and taker-outers alike.

Here, you want each sentence to be sharp, each word to count. Jerzy Kosinski said, "Every word is there for a reason, and if not, I cross it out. I rarely allow myself to use English in an unchecked, spontaneous way. I always have a sense of trembling—but so does a compass, after all. I cut adjectives, adverbs, and every word which is there just to make an effect."

Some clean-up is mechanical. Check your spelling. If you don't have spell-check on your computer, use a dictionary. Now and then I encounter a student who scoffs at spelling. I haven't, however, met a violinist who doesn't care whether his pitch is perfect.

Check your paragraphs. Are they fully developed? Journalistic practices aside, your paragraphs should contain more than one sentence, except in dialogue or when you're conferring special emphasis.

Punctuate conventionally. Write in complete sentences, not comma splices or sentence fragments, except now and then for special effect. Unless you're experimenting, use conventional grammar. The less attention it attracts to itself, the more attention will remain for your story.

Make sure your sentences are not monotonous. Vary sentence length and structure. Don't start every sentence with *I* or *he*. Don't, on the other hand, start each sentence with *although*, *considering*, or other dependent clause conjunctions. It's good to alternate simple and complex sentences, to establish a pleasing rhythm and avoid choppiness and monotony.

Don't let each sentence travel like a runaway train. Some people—even some famous writers—do that, but they are hard to read. In long sentences it's easy to lose track of the subject and the object. It must be clear who is doing what to whom. Who's kicking whom. Be sure that each pronoun has a clear precedent. Consider this sentence: "Above my garage the snow has fallen over a layer of ice, but the frozen sparrow has not moved, and now that the sun is out it's melting." What is melting—snow, sparrow, sun or ice?

Make sure you are clear. Sometimes you must weed out the passive voice and abstract vocabulary to achieve clarity.

Is the language weak? Too many adjectives and adverbs? Passives? Clichés? On the other hand, can you find strikingly fresh usages, *le mot juste*?

Make sure your sentences are direct. Scrutinize your use of prepositional phrases—especially "of" and "in" construction. "The paint on the table in the kitchen" could profitably become "the kitchen table's paint." You use four rather than eight words—cut the lard factor by fifty percent—and speed up the prose. Don't use double prepositions uselessly: "get off of my case" when "get off my case" would do.

Avoid official language and technical jargon unless you need it for comedy or parody. *Hereunto*, *aforementioned* and the like belong in legal documents.

Get rid of repetitions. Some repetitions are not immediately visible; they are redundant and superfluous expressions, such as "She came to a complete stop." *Complete* is superfluous. If the stop is incomplete, it's not a stop. Or, "He lived his life." *Life* is redundant since it's entailed in *lived*. "He blinked his eyes." *He blinked* will do, because the verb implies eyes.

If in a ten-line paragraph you use *love* or *response* (or any other words, other than articles and helping verbs) more than thrice, scrutinize each use, and eliminate it unless it's essential. Find synonyms. For *response*, perhaps *reaction* could do. Of course, some essential grammatical device words, like *a*, *the*, *have*, and *like*, will recur, and you shouldn't worry about them, within reasonable limits.

Delete all unnecessary modifiers in dialogue tags. For example: " 'Will you please please go home?' he said beseechingly." *Beseechingly* wastes time; it's clear from the sentence that a plea is going on. Moreover, *beseechingly* is an awkward adverb—to the verb we add the gerund (*ing*) suffix, and then we add *ly* to make an adverb. Thus, the word is twice removed from its original verb. The more removals a word undergoes from its origin, the paler it becomes. "He beseeched" might be an improvement, in that light, but since "he said" does not commit redundancy, you should prefer it.

Omit all unnecessary indications of who's speaking. On the other hand, is it always clear who is speaking? Whenever in doubt, indicate the speaker and use *said*.

Do you misspell for any kind of effect—stuttering, dialect, shouting? Keep your misspellings to a minimum. You can indicate outside the dialogue that something is said in a Southern drawl, or even better, you can rely on syntax and word choice to give us the flavor of the voice.

Don't use clichés. Cut whatever you've heard too many times (like "window of opportunity"), unless you need to show that this is how somebody talks. If you are making fun of clichés—why? To educate others? If so, do you strike a pose of being above your reader, or one in which you and your reader are both above most of humanity?

WHEN TO QUIT REVISING

Is there such a thing as too much revision? Yes. Sooner or later you must decide that the story is finished. Further revision might actually damage it. John Dos Passos described this decision: "I usually write to a point where the work is getting worse rather than better. That's the point to stop and the time to publish."

Tolstoy too described how much rewriting may damage the text. "Often in rewriting, I omit things, substitute others, not because the new idea is better, but because I get tired of the old.

Often I strike out what is vivid and replace it with something dull."

Another distinct danger in revising over and over is that you might lose a realistic perception of your story. The lines begin to sound not only familiar but inevitable. The more you listen to a piece of music, the more you may find it gratifying because you can predict the sequences. This resonance effect through too much repetition will make your work appear fabulously chiseled and meaningful. If this happens, beware. It happens to me after too much revision. What do I do then? I lay the work aside for half a year or so, forget most of it, and when I come back, I'm amazed at how rough it is. I need to revise it at least a couple of times more. The fact is that I did not revise the story too much, from the structural standpoint of the story, but I did from the psychological standpoint. Yes, after too many spins, I get crazy, filled with delusions of grand writing. Perhaps this is some kind of psychological reaction against getting stuck in the revision mode.

Avoid getting stuck in the revision mode beyond the point of diminishing returns. Find that point. Here you need good critical abilities about your work in progress, which you can develop only with a lot of practice. And don't go much beyond that point. The problem is that the story will begin to lose your individual flavor and voice with further and further refinements. If some rough edges preserve the story's sense of life, keep them in.

The Final Test

After all the revisions, there are still two useful questions:

First, what can you still cut without damaging the story? If the word is pretty but only for its own sake, and not for the sake of the story, press your best friend, the delete key.

Second, is your story easy to follow? Give it to two or three readers. If none understands what's going on, you might have to do a lot of revising yet! Straighten out whatever is confusing—if the chronology is twisted, lay it out simply from A to Z; if the motives are not clear, spell them out simply, in summary, if need be. Writing is communication—and the burden of communication is on you. Now and then I run into a student who during the class critique of his story smiles superciliously, and at the end of it, says, "None of you got it! What happens is this. . . ."

Invariably the writer constructed the story as a puzzle without revealing what happens. I am not saying that one should not write complex stories, but there's a difference between complex and complicated. Something simple can become complicated through unclear presentation. Above all, make sure that you are clear and that you show what happens in the story. The story should reveal, not obfuscate, an event.

To do this test, find somebody willing to read your work. Anybody who likes to read stories can do it; you don't need professional writers and editors for this. (In fact, sometimes they make the worst readers because many of them are jaded—everything may strike them as old simply because they have read too many manuscripts.) Of course, if your friends read your story, they'll probably tell you that they like it. Don't listen to this. Instead, ask them questions. What happens in the story? You need to know whether you've communicated it. Are the characters lifelike? Do they sound real when they talk? Does it make sense that they would do what they did in your story? (But don't ask for what the story means in a philosophical sense. You want a reading, not a scholarly interpretation.)

This is where a group workshop is immensely useful. You can see what comes across to the readers. You need some feedback. Your intentions about how the story should be read may be one thing, the story's reception another.

If you haven't communicated your story, go back and make it clear once again. Tell it. Maybe you've tried to show and imply too much? If the showing doesn't do it, leave the showing and add the telling. I know, this going back may drive you crazy. But the first several times you attempt a story, the hardest part is looking not only for the story, but for the *pattern for writing stories*. This is also the most important part.

Be patient and keep working. Perhaps on all matters of writing fiction, that is the best advice I can give you.

EXERCISES

1. Ten pages minimum. To do the following exercises, write a fresh draft of a story. Writing the draft is your exercise. You need not spend days on it. One or two will do. Consider Raymond Carver's advice: "It doesn't take that long to do the first draft of the story, that usually happens in one sitting, but it does take a while to do the various versions of the story. I've done as many as twenty or thirty drafts of a story. Never less than ten or twelve drafts." Knowing that you can return to the story and fix it should move you forward. Find an interesting conflict, give it to engaging characters, in a setting you know enough about, and keep going for at least ten pages.

Objective: To learn how to do the initial draft, relying on the follow-up revision. You don't need to polish anything here; free your imagination, don't censor yourself, follow even the strangest impulses. Surprise yourself. Say what you don't think a person like you would say.

Check: Do the rest of the exercises. I will not supply checks at the end of the exercises, because each assignment is a form of check on your story. You will constantly go back to your story and check and recheck—that's what revision is about.

2. Print your draft because you can survey the story more easily on paper than on the screen. You get a better sense of proportion, distances between events and so on if you hold the story in your hands than if you stare at it on the screen. Take out a pencil and carefully read your draft. What is your major conflict, scene, plot? Write a basic outline of the plot on a new sheet of paper.

Proofread the draft against the plot outline. Mark your main characters and main scenes. Are there too many characters? Compress them into fewer. Are there too many key scenes? Can you compress them into fewer? This is basically a thinking stage. Mark and outline your major two or three scenes.

Objective: To find the story in your draft.

3. Work from your paper draft and your plot outline rather than from your saved first draft (delete the draft!). This will force you to rewrite your story at least once rather than just add, subtract and reshuffle elements in the draft. The advantage is that you will work from your strengths in the draft rather than from weaknesses. You don't even have to delete what doesn't seem to contribute to the understanding of the main events. Simply type the parts that do and, as you type, change them. Now rewrite your big scene. Expand it. Don't worry about any background information at this stage. You can fill us in later.

Objective: To further clarify your characters and what you want them to do—or rather, what they want to do—and to let them do it. Basic scenes must be dynamic, dramatic, engaging.

4. Print what you have, sit down with this draft and with a pencil, and connect your major scenes. Do you need minor scenes to show the buildup of the conflict? To portray your major characters? Mark the places where you can do this. Where can you describe the setting? Can you do this as you introduce your characters? During dialogue pauses? In transitions between the scenes? Go to the computer and do what you need to do. Shorten your summaries, and let your minor scenes combine summary and drama. When you are finished, save your draft twice: once for backup, and once for a working copy. Probably you won't need the backup, but let it be your insurance policy.

Objective: To give the reader—and yourself—all we need to know. Most successful stories work as revelations. Reveal and show what happens—who did it, how, where, when, why?

5. From writer-teacher John Cussen: Tell your story to someone. (While it may dissipate your energies in the drafting stage to tell your story aloud, once you've done a draft and the first rewrite, retelling the story will concentrate your energies.) After you retell the story, you'll know which parts you need, which you don't. Go back to your story, and make it conform to this new understanding. Rewrite again if necessary. You want to write a story that works.

Objective: To find out if your story works as a basic story.

When you have to keep your listener's interest, you are not likely to make lengthy digressions. You'll probably find that you gear all your information toward the climax and resolution. You'll probably also find that something must happen in the story. Who will listen to a story in which nothing takes place?

6. Print out your newest version of the story. Annie Dillard uses a conference table for this purpose—she lays out dozens of pages and looks at them to see how they relate. This perspective is impossible on the screen, which works like a peephole. The peephole of course has its advantage of concentration, and this will be useful to you when you do microrevision. (If you are more comfortable working on the screen, you will need to survey much of the story in your head from short-term memory).

Now read your story all the way through again. Indicate places that don't convince you. Scrutinize them. What is missing? Details? Dialogue? Revise. Now look again. If you still aren't convinced, perhaps the problem stems from something more essential—plausible motives? Make each character's behavior sufficiently motivated (with either fear or desire). To show motivation, you might expand auxiliary scenes and narrative passages. Perhaps this leads to another big scene. Maybe you need to restructure the story. Don't be afraid to do it. Go back to Exercise 2 and change the plot outline. Hopefully, next time you come to Exercise 6, you'll be satisfied enough to move to microrevision—working with details—rather than macrorevision (plot and character).

Objective: To make the story convincing; to give verisimilitude to everything that takes place.

7. Examine the metaphors in your story. Can you group them according to a theme? Is this theme congruent with your ostensible theme? If not, try incorporating the theme into your plot. Give your story another shake-up!

Objective: To bring out your intuitive understanding of the story. Metaphors may express your deep feelings, your subconscious grasp of the story. Synergize all the levels of your understanding. If your metaphors seem in opposition to your direct understanding of the story, fine—bring the dichotomy into the main conflict. After all, the stronger the conflict, the greater its chance of becoming exciting.

8. From Mark Twain: Cross out all the adjectives and adverbs in your story. Read it and see whether you've lost anything. Restore the adjectives you absolutely need.

Objective: To become more aware of adjectives and adverbs. I suggest that you leave some restored adjectives as they are and that you flesh out others in concrete details. Select one or two to expand into miniscenes.

9. From Exercise 8, wherever you've described something in adjectives ("ominously somber cellar"), add another sentence with details that'll flesh out the intention you expressed in the adjective.

Objective: The details must appear true; the reader should see for herself that something looks the way you say it does.

10. Find words that mention feelings; flesh them out in concrete images, and for a couple of them construct minor scenes. If she felt angry, let her do something to convince us of her anger.

Objective: To help you make the characters and their motives more convincing.

11. Go through the microrevision checklist in this chapter and proofread your story against it. Then apply the two "final test" questions from the text—namely, "Could you cut something without damaging the story?" Do it. And, "Is the story easy to follow?" Let somebody read the story, and quiz him about what came across. If you haven't communicated the basic story, simplify and tell more explicitly whatever did not come across.

Objective: To keep in touch with the basics—that the story shouldn't have unnecessary parts and that it should be readable.

12. If you have the time to do this one, do it, sooner or later, at least with one of your stories. Write five to six ten-page varia-

tions of a story centered around one event. You may write it in the third person, then in the first person. Write it first as an explanation of an event, backtracking as you need to illuminate the motives; let the story work as a cogent argument. Then write it out chronologically from first event to last. Then write it backwards, from last event to first. Then take an interesting but minor character and write it from her point of view. Make her the central character. Then change the ending—let the story go in a completely different direction that you toyed with but discarded previously. Or invent a new possibility. Brainstorm for the story's other options. Unless you do each draft seriously, as though it were the final story, you will not know all the story's potential.

Run each variation through the macrorevision questions in the chapter, concentrating on the elements that are most essential to your story.

At the end, choose your most successful variant and burn the rest. Just kidding. Keep all the variants that seem successful; it's possible that more than one do.

Objective: To explore the possibilities of your story. Let it be all it can be. This should prove immensely useful to your insight as to storytelling possibilities when you write other stories. I think every writer should do complete rewrites at least with one story. This may seem to require too much time from you and to be outside of the scope of this book. Good! After all, now you are on your own, and what better way to do it than by starting with a big project! A semester-long writing workshop could be profitably based on this variation-on-a-theme exercise.

ABOUT THE AUTHOR

Josip Novakovich was born in Croatia, Yugoslavia, in 1956. His published work includes a collection of essays, *Apricots from Chernobyl*; and a short story collection, *Yolk*. His fiction and essays have appeared in dozens of periodicals—including *The Paris Review*, *Prairie Schooner*, *Ploughshares* and *Antaeus*—and have garnered, among other honors, two Pushcart Prizes and a fellowship from The National Endowment for the Arts. Novakovich teaches fiction writing at the University of Cincinnati.

INDEX